Passing the Torch

Quaker Elders
& Their
Lives Speak

Edited by
Chuck Fager

Contributors:

Barbara Berntsen
Carter Nash
David Zarembka
Marian Rhys
Douglas Gwyn
Helena Cobban
H. Larry Ingle
Chuck Fager
Diane Faison McKinzie
Jennifer Elam
Emma Lapsansky-Werner

Kimo Press
Durham North Carolina
2019

ISBN: 9781705619490

Kimo Press
P. O. Box 3811
Durham NC 27702
kimopress.com
Email: qkrtheology@gmail.com

Contents

Ecclesiastes & Penn

1:4 Generations come and generations go,
but the earth remains forever.

5 The sun rises and the sun sets,
and hurries back to where it rises.

6 The wind blows to the south
and turns to the north;
round and round it goes,
ever returning on its course.

7 All streams flow into the sea,
yet the sea is never full.
To the place the streams come from,
there they return again. . . .

11 No one remembers the former generations,
and even those yet to come
will not be remembered
by those who follow them. . . .

From *Some Fruits of Solitude in Reflections and Maxims Relating to the Conduct of Human Life*

> The author does not pretend to deliver thee an exact piece; his Business not being Ostentation but Charity...But it contains Hints, that may serve thee for Texts to Preach to thy Self upon, and which comprehend Much of the Course of Human Life: Since whether thou art Parent or Child, Prince or Subject, Master or Servant, Single or Married, Publick or Private, Mean or Honorable, Rich or Poor, Prosperous or Improsperous, in Peace or Controversy, in Business or Solitude; Whatever be thy Inclination or Aversion, Practice, or Duty, thou wilt find something not unsuitably said for thy Direction & Advantage. Accept and Improve what deserves thy Notice; The rest excuse, and place to account of good Will to Thee and the whole Creation of God.

– William Penn, 1682

Editor's Introduction

Quakers are often very interesting people.
And generations come and go.

T hese are the modest theses behind this book. In fifty-plus years among The Religious Society of Friends (our rather pompous official name), its members, attenders, hangers-on and even antagonists, I have kept bumping into and hearing about interesting people. And many *very* interesting people.

And having had what some call "a good run," my generation (beginning, as I did, in the depths of World War Two, and extending, with a stretch, to the early 1960s), is now on its way out.

"Generations come and go," is how the Preacher of the biblical book of Ecclesiastes (one of my favorites) dryly put it. And it's our turn. Then the Preacher rubs our noses in the fetid fact of evanescence: "in future generations no one will remember what we have done here."

This last, I think, many of us don't yet believe. We've been told, from many quarters, for a long time, that ours was a critical, historic vanguard. More recent voices have condemned us as the shock troops of decadence, decay and disaster, which seemed to be running amok in our culture as these pages took shape and the curtain began descending over us; but maybe that's just envy.

We're also hardly the first ones to think we can escape this descent into the abyss of the forgotten. Attempts to defy this fate are among the oldest recorded human activities. Such efforts come in several forms, prominently monuments, stories, and books or other writings.

Of these, stories are the most weightless, typically composed and carried in memory and words. Yet they are the most durable; though they too can die. The biblical Exodus saga is one of the oldest such stories, at least in the Jewish-Christian world. The retelling of key passages at annual Seders includes elements likely 3,000 years old or more. And that ritual story's role in the persistence of Jewish culture and religion is inarguable.

Have we, today's elder (mainly American) Quakers done anything to elbow our way into the species memory? Usually this query is rhetorical, a set-up for some ambitious, maybe even landmark argument, which favorable critics will be tempted to call "bold" or "ground-breaking."

This urge to grandiosity is one I am firmly resolved to resist. Here there is no carefully representative group, honed to tick all the boxes. Nor is this a manifesto or a *mea culpa*, though it reflects our feelings and opinions.

Instead, I wrote to some interesting people, a varied bunch of a certain age and (mostly) retired, who are U. S. Quakers, and invited them to tell their stories, and offer some summary counsel, what we call Advices, to those coming up. I've dropped a few hints of my own, I hope sparingly enough to be palatable.

We're a motley crew, few of us famous, but we are varied, and, in my view, all have done interesting things. In these pages you will find Friends in the thick of wars, behind bars, facing dire disease, murder, resisting war taxes, raising families, coping with loss, and — since all are Americans – facing racism and prejudice in many forms and some unexpected guises. Yet they also took time to settle in Friends worship and business, making their own diverse ways amid its highs and lows.

Our eleven lives are all now moving into the sunset. Among us are several centuries of Quaker experience and thought. It's a longstanding Quaker tradition that, whatever we say or write, it is above all our lives that speak, across the world, and beyond our generation. That's what Passing the Torch tries to get at.

What does it all add up to? I'll leave that to others with more degrees; or defer to that ancient Preacher in Ecclesiastes:

> 8:16-17: *Whenever I tried to become wise and learn what goes on in the world, I realized that you could stay awake night and day and never be able to understand what God is doing. However hard you try, you will never find out. The wise may claim to know, but they don't.*

> *And 4:12: So I realized that all we can do is be happy and do the best we can while we are still alive. [13] All of us should eat and drink and enjoy what we have worked for. It is God's gift.*

— Chuck Fager

My Generation (Rewrite)

People tried to put us down
Talkin' about that generation,
Because some said we got
around.
Talkin' about that generation.
The ones left now don't look so
bold,
Talkin' about that generation.
But — they didn't all die before
they got old . . .
Talkin' about that generation.

What generation??
My generation bay-beh.
My generation,
My generation, bay-beh!

Some of the stuff we did will
stay.
Talkin' about that generation.
Other stuff will f-fade away.
Talkin' about that generation.
But it's too late for any re-crea-
tion,
Talkin' about that generation.
So, we'll keep talking about this
generation.
Talkin' about that generation.

What generation?
My generation, bay-beh!
My generation,
My generation, bay-beh!

We started out sure it was our
hour —
Talkin' about that generation.
To stop the wars, speak truth to
power.
Talkin' about that generation.

Women & Black & Queer Liberation,
Talkin' about that generation.
Were all in reach for our generation.

What generation?
My generation!
My generation, bay-beh!
My generation!
My generation, bay-beh!

Plain & simple, Thee & Thou,
Talkin' about that generation.
We'd Quake the world — sure,
we knew how. . . .
Talkin' about that generation.
But then one day our King was
dead,
Talkin' about that generation.
And a whole lot less was done
than said.
Talkin' about that generation.

What generation?
My generation, bay-beh!
My generation!
My generation, bay-beh!

So, we followed our Light & did
our best,
Talkin' about that generation.
Tho the world is still in an awful
mess.
Talkin' about that generation.
.
Now our friends are gone & our
hair is gray,
Talkin' about that generation.

and we ache in the places where
we used to play.
Talkin' about that generation.

What generation?
My generation, bay-beh!
My generation,
My generation, bay-beh!

And they're still trying to put us
down,
Talkin' about that generation.
Even the ones who g-got around.
Talkin' about that generation.
But in the end, past the last sensa-
tion,
Talkin' about that generation.
It's lives that'll speak for this
generation. . . .
Talkin' about that generation!

What generation?
My generation, bay-beh!
What generation?
My generation, bay-beh!

[Finish by smashing instruments,
if thee can lift them. Then be sure
to tidy up & recycle.]

Barbara Berntsen: Barbara's Story

Background and Early Years

"The humble, meek, merciful, just, pious and devout souls eve-rywhere are of one religion, and when death has taken off their masks, they will know one another, though the diverse liveries they wore here made them strangers."

–William Penn

When I was a kid the original home-steaders in the area were still alive. My paternal grandfather was one of them. There is a photograph of him, still in his army uniform with a too-big overcoat cut off at the bottom, taken on his homestead the very day he came home from France at the end of WWI. They told me, when he saw me for the first

Barbara, left, with her siblings

time he said, "She's sure a little pup, ain't she".

There was good fishing on that place, but it wasn't for the faint of heart. My brother said the guys that fished up there used to carry a loaded handgun to fend off the rattlesnakes.

Having been raised by nuns in a St. Louis orphanage, grandpa Ben was pretty much cured of religion, as far as I could tell. If we kids thought life was too hard, we were firmly assured that ours were lives of luxury and ease compared to being sent by the nuns to work in a soap factory at age 12. He actually lost a couple of fingers in a soap-cutting machine. I asked Uncle Tom one time if 7 in total was the number of fingers Grandpa Ben still had at death. Tom thought and was counting bits and pieces on his own hands and said "yah, that's about right". I think grandpa only had 3 or 4 fingers that were not shortened up a knuckle or two.

The humble, meek, merciful, just, pious and devout looked exactly like ordinary folks, and if you sat very quietly under the table and listened carefully to the grown-ups you could get an earful of reality, far beyond your years.

When I was eight months old my parents sold all their furniture and bought an eight-by-ten camping trailer. I don't think they thought they'd live in trailers for the next twenty years. In 1953 not many people lived with a baby in a camping trailer with no running water and no bathroom.

My father got sent to the Korean war, and Mom and I tried to live by ourselves in that trailer, across the alley from newly widowed grandpa Ben and the not yet grown uncles. Nobody told her she could shop at the base PX or go to the doctor at the nearest military base, even if that was forty miles away. It wasn't like she could legally drive or anything like that, of course.

My first memories are of moving out of that trailer into a bigger one after my father came home from Korea in August of 1955, when I was almost three. Until that khaki-dressed stranger that smelled like cinnamon bears turned up, I had ruled the roost. I could hold my breath until I fainted and Mom, Grandpa and the uncles all fell in line. My father was not impressed and told Mom she had a brat. The next time I held my breath I got whacked good. When I recovered my dignity, I told him to go back to Korea.

My mother's people were of the religious sort, having come to Puritan America in 1632. The Puritan streak — or at least the tendency to go for the extreme — seemed to have survived right up to my Grandmother's generation. From my observation post under the kitchen table I would hear stories of how Grandma's Christian Science sisters — who wouldn't take medicines — had died horrible screaming deaths, firmly believing their faith would eventually alleviate the pains and heal them.

I was pretty sure that kind of faith had died with them, but in 2013 I learned from the then grown grandchildren themselves that there had been several children in the extended family that were denied antibiotics when they had rheumatic fever, due to the religious convictions of their mothers.

In the 1950s Mom was of a mind to find a suitable church to attend, so the little family went church-shopping. It didn't go well at the Lutheran Sunday school when I cussed like my father always did and got sent to the naughty corner. I did much better at the Baptist Sunday school, and we were settling in nicely, when one Sunday the Baptist preacher yelled out loud, "Pray for segregation!"

I was napping nicely on the floor under Mom's chair when she just got up, told me to get out from under that chair right now and then with baby David in her arms, grabbed my little sister Nancy by the hand and walked out right in the middle of services. Strange as it may seem, little kids in Montana might never have actually seen a Black person in those days. Grandpa Ben had a TV but that was only for watching 'Fight of the Week' on Friday night. I knew very well what Indians and Hutterites were, but wondered to myself 'What is this segregation?'

When we got home the shit hit the fan. Something really serious was obviously happening. Mom called Dad a hillbilly, and she didn't mean it nice. They both grew up in Montana, but in different worlds. After the mines stopped paying their workers during the great depression, Mom's family had to survive as best they could, and Grandpa took work with The Bureau of Indian Affairs. So, Mom had actually sat in the back seat of her Dad's car with an Elder with braids and stuff that had calmly reassured her by saying, 'Little girl, don't be afraid. I am not going to hurt you. We don't scalp people anymore.'

She had visited many homes out on "the Res," and she had eaten puppy stew, so I figured Mom was the one to trust on these issues. She had incredible stories to tell, little-girl sized beaded brooches given as gifts, and she had photographs of the terrible relatives from Minnesota collecting Indian skulls and burial blankets from the bodies as souvenirs back in the 1920s and 1930s.

If that wasn't enough, after the mines closed, she had lived in the neighbourhood where the Black porters on the railroad lived with their families. My Mom said we weren't praying for segregation because when she was little and there was a dinner at the AME Church, those ladies fed all the little children in the neighbourhood dinner, ice cream included, no matter what color they were.

We were going to the Episcopal Church, which was a pretty place with nice people, Uncle Jimmy's mother playing the organ, stained glass windows and a baby Jesus dolly in a manger with real hay at Christmas time. But one day, two young men in white shirts, ties and black suits came knocking on our trailer door. They knew Dad needed some serious digging done, and they just took off their jackets and helped him dig a ditch so we could hook up to the city sewer.

I remember they had a flannel-o-graph with Jesus and angels on it. I'm not sure Dad at that time cared one bit what their particular version of Jesus and the angels was. What he cared for was that they recognized a need and just met it. So, after some drama and fussing, the folks decided we were going to join the church that sent those two young men.

This was the first time I had an opinion about which church we went to, but I'm not sure I dared to voice it. I really wanted to stay at the Episcopal Church with the pretty windows and the nice people, not forgetting the baby Jesus.

During the rest of my growing-up years I felt completely free to visit other communities of faith in a way I don't think I ever experienced another child doing. The non-denominational Community Bible Church had the very best summer camps. The Methodists had the nicest children's choir, and I really appreciated the songs they were singing both places. Especially meaningful for a kid from Montana was, 'He owns the cattle on a thousand hills, the wealth in every mine. He owns the rivers and the rocks and rills, the sun and moon that shine.'

The Roman Catholic Church had a special sense of drama and majestic silence and peace. When I was in distress, which was pretty regularly, I would walk over there during school lunch hour and sit quietly. I wasn't alone doing that. Often women came in and prayed silently while I was there. I recall cleaning the Catholic Church when we were young, along with the ASCS Office to have a little extra money to buy food. Oh, I see that is mentioned below

Death, Insanity and Shame

One day when I was in about the third grade, the phone rang. The man said he was from the Montana State Hospital and could he please talk to Mrs. Robert Bach. I told him she was at work and could I take a message. I don't think he knew he was speaking to a nine or ten-year-old, by what the message turned out to be.

He was looking for someone willing to claim the body of my Great Grandfather. He had been dead for some weeks already, and one of his children, my Grandfather had refused to have anything to do with this, so they wondered if we were interested.

My mother had never dared tell my father about her schizophrenic grandfather that had been committed to the State Hospital 40 years earlier, but now it was decided we were the decent people that would drive across the state in the middle of winter and take our immigrant ancestor to a grave in the Potter's Field, where mental patients were buried and the State of Montana would pay the bill.

My Dad said, that's what decent people do. This time around I was sure it was Dad that knew the difference between right and wrong and it was Mom that needed to be set right. So, we loaded up enough food that we wouldn't have to buy any, at higher prices, for the whole trip, and set out.

We even got to see the old man in his casket, and I recognized my own facial bone structure, and I studied his face and hands carefully. Five decades later, having pieced together his life story, his great grand-children managed to locate and place a headstone on that unmarked grave.

What we learned from his life and death is that life isn't fair and can break people to pieces and destroy families over generations, and that even in poverty, dignity requires that you do the right thing. Many years later, when we buried my father, my mother quietly commented, "It's easy to be dignified when you have kids with money".

One summer I cleaned the Catholic Church while the regular cleaning lady was on vacation and witnessed a bride crying and begging not to have to go through with the wedding that was going to take place that weekend. The guy was a drunk and a goof off, she cried. Her mother and the priest told her straight and in no uncertain terms that she should have thought of that before she got herself pregnant.

Having witnessed this confirmed the decisions I had already made about what it would take for me to escape the life I had been born to. A trailer on a muddy alley, sending your oldest child to the nuns at the hospital to deliver a check for $1 every month, because you cannot pay the bill for the last baby's birth in full, was not going to be my life, if I could help it.

LDS (Mormons)

What made each church special was the people I met there. They were the humble, meek, merciful, just, pious and devout. They were — each in their own way — the hands of God if they took a mind to be. But in each church, I was only a guest, and I saw them at their best and compared them to the every-day rough-and-tumble of my own life.

In my own church, a tiny LDS branch, there were a number of good men that liked to sit and discuss doctrine while the women were busy being the actual Christians. A few of these women were truly saints, in the deepest sense.

My mother was brutally honest when she told me I was not nice enough that a good LDS man would ever marry me. I'm sure she didn't mean "not humble, meek, merciful, just, pious and devout," but rather "not obedient, compliant and quiet".

Not being able or willing to pay tithing to their Church left our family forever on the edges of our faith community, always outsiders, looked down on as soon as we left our own little down-at-the-heel branch of the LDS Church.

God and Me

My first experience of an overwhelming presence of God was while sitting on a rug in a big cardboard box out in the rain in the yard on a summer evening. Once — when I had run away from home and was walking along down the middle of the train tracks — I heard a voice commanding me to go straight home.

Other times I just knew someone, or something wasn't right and I was told to run either to or from — or hide. And sometimes that voice just said, "Be still and wait!" I called that voice God.

I don't know how I would have survived if I hadn't had faith that somehow, something or someone was with me and had my back. God's first language may well be silence, but exceptions are obviously made.

Getting Out

Figuring out what would get me out — out of poverty, out of our small town, out of life as an unmarried woman in ~~LSD~~ LDS *(good one Barb ha ha* society — was not rocket science.) It meant working hard at school, reading a lot, but not taking subjects I couldn't get at least a B in, for fear of my grade point average. It meant learning to sew really well, in order to be well dressed. And it meant no boyfriends, to avoid wasting time and getting attached to the place.

The LDS Church teaches that "the glory of God is intelligence," and those people put their money where their mouth was. The greatest gift the LDS Church gave me, was a highly subsidized education at Brigham Young University. For that I am truly grateful.

But when, after the first semester, one of my old high school teachers asked me to marry him, saying yes seemed like a good idea at the time, too. So, I got married, just barely 19 years old and still young enough that my mother gave me a whupping if she thought that was what I needed, even during the planning of the wedding. I knew very well that she wouldn't beat me ever again if I was a married woman, with my own kitchen and my own allotment check from the US Army — that's how it works.

Finding Quakerism

With this background I first met Quakerism, as it manifested itself at Quaker House in Fayetteville, North Carolina, in 1972. Fayetteville — and the nearby Fort Bragg army base — were impressively rough, even by Montana standards. If the nice Quakers that ran the place found it difficult to live there, and if Quaker House was not universally supported by the varieties of Quakers in North Carolina, they all kept their problems to themselves and were able to give help — even protection — when needed. For that I and many others have ample reason to be grateful.

Those North Carolina and Georgia Quakers were a revelation. They practiced what they preached about equality and that of God in every one of us, even White Trash which I knew only too well that I was. I met young folks with 12-string guitars, which I didn't know existed, and with degrees from Rutgers, and I could visit with real professors from the local colleges!

I even saw and met with homosexual men for the first time in my life, and to my great surprise they looked like ordinary people and were nice to me. And I remember one woman who had a law degree and was really dignified, telling me about the latest guy she had taken home with her for the night, like it was no big deal.

One couple that I felt more comfortable with, turned out to have been raised conservative Amish and old-order Mennonite and thus came from more ordinary backgrounds, so I felt safe around them and even baby-sat their children.

The biggest shock of all was meeting lesbians, which — like 12-string guitars — I never knew existed, and then finding out they had the same lives and life problems as everybody else.

A bunch of years later, in 2008, I sent an email across the Atlantic as Quaker House approached its 40th anniversary. The Director then happens to be the editor of this book, and he kept the email. The subject line was: *"Quaker House Alumni Checking In"*:

Subject: Quaker House alumni checking in

I was only 18 years old when I married a young GI stationed at Fort Bragg and we spent a lot of time at Quaker House back in the day! Quaker House changed the course of both of our lives. My then husband . . . has been an active Quaker for over thirty years and lives in [a western state].

I have a Quaker House story of my own to tell. In about May of 1972 we were living at Quaker House. I think Kenn and Ellen [Arning], a young Quaker couple from New Jersey, were running the place then. I was about as sick as I ever have been in my life with genuine influensa, in bed in the back bedroom.

In the middle of the night, there were literally rifle butts thumping at the front door. My husband answered the door and there

15

were armed, masked men there, asking questions about me. I
had heard about the bodies [of dead U.S. soldiers] being
stuffed with heroin [before being shipped back to Bragg] from
a GI and had said so right in the middle of my on-base Psy-
chology Class at Bragg only days before. The masked men told
my husband to get control over his wife's mouth.

(NOTE: Although disputed and unproven, the heroin-smuggled-in-dead-solders' bodies story has had a long life around Fayetteville, and even figured in the plot of the 2007 feature film, *American Gangster*, starring Denzel Washington. What is beyond doubt is that the illicit drug trade thrived in those years and has not disappeared since.)

I am now 55 years old, with streaks of white in my hair and my
three kids are all grownups. I have lived in Norway for more
than 30 years. I am a historian at The National Archives of Nor-
way and have taught archival science at the University of Oslo .

I was in Palestine during the 2006 war, and returned from Cairo
10 days ago, where people are being murdered in bread lines
and most of the candidates and their lawyers were in jail for the
recent elections.

No doubt about it, Quaker House alumni most definitely had the
course of their lives changed! If the garage is still there, you will
find my PX ID tucked under one of the shingles. My name back
then was Barbara Black. Bet I look a LOT younger on the pic-
ture!

(NOTE alas, no such ID has turned up.)

I had never been inside homes like those Quakers lived in. Bookcases full, grandfather clocks, four-post beds, inherited furniture, hardwood floors and Chinese rugs seemed like out of this world — desirable, but unattainable, unless there was some secret to it. I decided I ought to look into that.

Low Points of My Life

I had the bright idea that if I made the right choices, my life would just fall neatly into a nice place. If I had been told upfront what some of my "right choices" would lead to, I would have refused to believe it. I took life seriously and expected to outsmart it.

The lowest points in my life were not part of the plan or even imaginable when I was seventeen years old. Fifty years, a post-partum depression, two divorces and three weddings later, I have concluded that the critical choices are hard to identify and hard to make, and what seems like a disaster when it's happening may turn out to be the starting-point of something I will be grateful for some years later. Unfortunately, suffering has been my best teacher.

That first divorce taught me I was capable of doing whatever it takes to survive, and that community and family are the only people that will take you in when you have no place to go. The California Quaker meeting I belonged to at the time actually took me in and put me up in their homes when I desperately needed it.

It was in that dire situation, when I was just scraping by as a student having to support myself as best I could, that I stumbled onto my second husband. He was a post-doctoral research fellow in physical chemistry, on the tenure track, who could take me to lunch at the faculty club. How could this possibly be a bad idea?

The fact that he was half a generation older, hailing from another continent and seemingly hailing from another century in his ways and views, seemed insignificant at the time. Less than a year later, my Grandma gave me enough money to buy a dress from the Salvation Army and we married in Oslo, Norway.

A few years later, a post-partum depression caught me unaware and almost killed me. I didn't know how much trouble I was in, and I was too afraid and embarrassed to tell anybody, even in my Quaker meeting.

When I finally reached out for help, two American wives from the expat community immediately showed up at my door and took me firmly in hand. They saved my life and took me into their 12-step group in the Catholic Church. For that and other reasons my children were raised Catholic. It was a good run, actually.

Many years later it was the Zen Buddhist community that sat me down and followed me through the collapse of that second marriage of more than 25 years, and then into a new life and a new marriage.

I would not have been willing or able to make that journey alone. I was too tired. The only way I know to show gratitude to the communities and people that have been the hands of God in my life, is by paying it forward.

Moralist and judgmental as I am, I often have to keep my own company and acknowledge that there are reasons why I am best suited to cleaning up other people's messes while I take their moral inventory and cuss.

I took a test, and it's a fact: If a hundred people were lined up in a row, only eight of them would be less polite than me.

High Points

The peak moments in my life often came as a surprise. On second thought, they all seem to have come after I gave up and bought a one-way ticket back to the New Mexico Zen monastery. My bags were packed, and my house was in perfect order, when into my workplace walked a stranger. He had a couple questions that pertained to my line of business, and he was nice to talk to, so we parted with a promise to stay in contact. I went to the monastery, but we kept the promise.

Several months later, by mutual agreement, he came to the monastery and asked to be allowed to speak to the Roshi, and he asked the Roshi if he could take me on a long road trip and later marry me. Roshi — always one for fixing people up — gave his consent.

But for me it was a daunting proposition. One of the women in the monastery slipped me a roll of bills and said if I didn't like him, I could get on a bus and come home, no questions asked. That was one of the kindest things anybody ever did for me. For the first time in my life I had an out, if things turned bad.

By now I knew that the guy was two times divorced and a cancer patient in the middle of post-surgery chemotherapy, with a "two out of three" survival prognosis. On the other hand, he was a fun guy to be around and seemed to be kind, and I sincerely believed I had nothing left to lose, so what the hell.

Like the song says, having nothing left to lose gives a certain kind of freedom. Also, the Roshi told us, there is no hope, so there's no need to worry about things, either, just do the right thing, one choice at a time. And like so many times before, this seemed like the right thing to do. What could possibly go wrong?

The trip turned out fine. Both being two-time losers and without too much hope, we seemed to be able to treat each other with compassion and respect, one problem at a time, or as he prefers to call it, "details, baby". Four weeks went by, and he took me back to Norway to live with him. The rest is history.

Seventeen years has passed now, and it's been quite a ride. It hasn't been without its fair share of "details," some of them even life-threatening, but in hindsight it has been wonderful and meaningful — Jordan Peterson-style — all the way. Finally, at age 50, I was able to take full advantage of my university education and make a career at the National Archive amongst highly educated colleagues, some of them turned out to be very good friends.

After a few years I came back to the Quakers, and since then my husband and I have invested much effort into that community. After we moved to be with the grandchildren, we have become the prime "movers and Quakers" of a very small monthly meeting with a 205 year history, where we take care of a wonderful, too large meetinghouse, a burial ground and a lot of outreach and inter-faith activities.

It wouldn't have occurred to me to be taken in an aerobatic glider — a stunt plane, actually — but my third, high-risk husband was determined to make it happen, at age 55. It was an extreme opposite to my own domestic, home-making life so far — well beyond anything Six Flags can offer — but still doable. Finding myself able to handle that, even laughing for joy, made an indelible impression on my sense of self.

In the same vein was keeping a very fast car for a number of years, taking it to track meets and famous racetracks. I would always ride along, and with our in-helmet intercom I could easily let it be known if pee-stops or cooling-down breaks were in order. I even have to my name fifteen fast laps on the Nürburgring Nordschleife, the world's most famous racetrack, mostly famous for being difficult and dangerous!

Living and practicing in a Zen monastery, under a genuine Japanese Roshi (master) of ill repute, for months on end, repeatedly, is the closest I have ever been to "Heaven" and "God," even if it was uncomfortable and really hard work.

I have been privileged to visit Egypt, with the pyramids of Giza and the museums of Cairo, and Palestine, including Jerusalem, and Ephesus, Smyrna, Marathon, Athens, Corinth, Delphi, Rome and Florence. I have managed to get ten minutes completely alone, in silence, with my husband, in the Sistine Chapel.

And seeing Michelangelo's statue of David, in the street outside the Uffizi in Florence, brought me to tears, for two reasons. First, it brought back those childhood moments poring over a photograph of that statue, most likely in The National Geographic. Then to my amazement I discovered that David's serene poise is make-believe, he's instantly ready to shoot his deadly sling, which is already "cocked and loaded," but hidden on his back. Having recently seen the barbaric colonization of the Holy Land up close, the symbolism was just overwhelming.

But, in the end, nothing compares to looking two little grandchildren in the eye. Being in retirement, we were able to move across the country and settle within walking distance of our recently arrived grandchildren, and not far from their uncles. Now we have endless time with those kids, day and night, unlike the parents who need to work all day and then some, just like we used to have to.

Twelve Rules for Quaker Life: An Antidote to Chaos

I would like to present something that has become really important and valuable for my Quaker life. Recently a voice of sanity has sounded out of Alberta, across the Great Plains and around the world. Friends — particularly of the middle-class orthodox academic kind — could do worse than listen to Jordan Peterson's "12 Rules for Life: An Antidote to Chaos" and apply it to what's still standing of our Quaker tradition. It's not conceived as Quakerism, but the medicine fits the malady perfectly if we have any ambition the be God's hands in this world. Here's my Friendly adaptation of Peterson's general message:

1. Stand up straight with your shoulders back.

   Sit properly during Meeting for Worship, and don't think for one minute that it's OK to sleep. If you sleep in meeting, go to bed earlier. Have some respect for yourself, your community and the Quaker tradition.

2. Treat yourself like someone you are responsible for helping.

   Go to the doctor, take care of your teeth, exercise properly, vaccinate yourself and your children, and eat right.

3. Make friends with people who want the best for you.

   You may well discover that some are toxic Friends. Not all Friends should be your friends. Don't go along to get along. Learn to stand alone.

4. Compare yourself to who you were yesterday, not to who somebody else is today.

   Be careful what you consume of Quaker history. There is way too much simple-minded glorification of the past. Quakers, like others, have a tendency to kill their prophets, now as then.

5. Do not let your children do anything that makes you dislike them.

   Be bothered to actually put time and resources in your children, and teach them to work, not just consume and be treated to the Friendly version of helicopter parenting far into middle age. Give them both responsibility and authority and leave them to it. Friends' burial grounds are full of indispensable people like yourself.

6. Set your house in order before you criticize the world.

    The first Zen master I studied under — whenever coming to teach at a Zen center away from his home zendo — would always go directly to the kitchen, open cupboards and drawers and check under the sink and in the back of the fridge, in order to assess the total state of the community.

    There is a direct correlation between the state of the meetinghouse, the library, the archives, the kitchen and the burial grounds and the state of the community — monthly or yearly meeting — that own them. If your meeting cannot be bothered to keep the premises clean and in good repair or attend to the young and very old amongst you, it has no business pretending to care for the world.

    Getting on board yet another airplane flying to yet another faraway talk-shop on climate change or on keeping alive dwindling Quaker communities may just be a case of severe cognitive dissonance.

7. Pursue what is meaningful, not what is expedient.

    The Friends and other people that control the resources or have the money, can and often do set the agenda. Forget this at your peril, individually or collectively.

8. Tell the truth — or at least don't lie.

    We like to think we are especially adept at speaking truth to power, but we are often barely capable of speaking truth to each other. When we are pushed into a corner, we try to wiggle out by adding "Speak the truth with love," conveniently forgetting that love has a duty to set limits, say "no" and prevent stupidity from getting the upper hand.

9. Assume that the person you are listening to may know something you don't.

    Take yourself and our Quaker tradition seriously and hold to the tenant that there is that of God in everyone, so you will lis-

21

ten — even to inconvenient or troubling voices. Respect competence in others and your own shortcomings. Arrogant incompetence exists, abundantly.

10. Be precise in your speech.

"Quakerese" is a barrier and a tool of exclusion. Spoken and written well, it can become an advanced form of lying, so subtle that the perpetrator believes the lie to be particularly skillful and compassionate truth telling.

Speaking in archaic language is anything but "plain," and indulging in "highly educated language" does nothing to alleviate our affliction of being strictly middle-class in a predominantly working-class world. How can we be God's hands if we cannot even visit with God's regular people?

Let your no be a no and your yes be a yes. Don't hoard positions and responsibilities you will not fulfil. Just say no.

11. Do not bother children when they are skateboarding.

Don't fool yourself into defining what Quakerism is or how it will look for our spiritual children. You and your generation don't own the tradition.

Don't think you know who will pick up the torch and carry the flame into the future, however much you think you have the gift of prophesy. You run the risk of snuffing out the very spark that is the future.

12. Pet a cat when you encounter one on the street.

Take the time to be aware of what is right in front of you. Clinging to the past, fearing the future is no way to live our individual or collective lives.

The real world matters. Impractical people — who cannot clean up their own mess or take out the garbage — are unsuited for leadership and should not be put in positions of responsibility, no matter what they think.

Carter Nash: A Sketch About Myself

How to start a sketch about myself?

Carter Nash

I have been asked by several people to write something about myself. Some have even said I should write a book. I'm a 65-year-old gay man of African descent. I was born in Huntington, West Virginia at a time when Jim Crow laws were still in effect. The hospital I was born in was segregated and my mother being very fair skinned was placed in the white maternity ward. When I was born, mom was moved to the colored ward.

Three days later we were at home at 2748 Carter Avenue; Ashland, Kentucky the home of my grandmother and great-grandmother. My father was in the Navy and mom and dad had had a disagreement and mom had gone home to her mother. They would reconcile, have 3 more children (for a total of 5, I had an older sister) and remain together until my father's death in 1986.

I wasn't born into a Quaker family (officially) but into an African Methodist Episcopal one. I was christened at St James A.M.E. in Ashland.

My father being in the Navy we moved around quite a bit. Neither of my parents were big church going people. I believe it was Dr. King that said 11:00 Sunday morning is the most segregated hour in America. Often when we lived off base, we would go to the church closest to our house.

For me religion wasn't really important until my father retired from the Navy and we moved to North Philadelphia (1740 N 3rd St). At the end of the block was St Jacobus Evangelical Lutheran Church. Sitting outside every day was a elderly man of color and my parents decided to give that church a try. As it turned out the old man was the sexton. However, this church happened to have the first Black Lutheran Pastor in Philadelphia (William Barrett). Pastor Barrett was a former Baptist minister. After hearing him preach mom said she could tell he was holding back.

The next time mom went to services there the processional hymn was "Publish Glad Tidings" a song that mom was used to being very up tempo. The organist played it like a dirge. For my mom church was supposed to be an upbeat joyous place. (Dad wasn't involved in our going to church.) At this time many of the Lutheran Churches in Philadelphia did not welcome people of color to worship with them.

When I visited my grandmother and her mother in Ashland, Kentucky I would go to church with my grandmother (my great grandmother was a Baptist but not a church goer). I also loved spending time with my great grandmother. We would take the bus to the next town over, the county seat, Catlettsburg, KY to go to the meat market. I would help in their garden. I would sit and string beans and snap them as well shuck corn. She and I would brush each other's hair, she had very long straight salt and pepper hair.

One of the saddest things I've ever had to deal with was that my grandmother died before my great grandmother. The house they lived in was my grandmother's. My grandmother had told her mother she had a home there for the rest of her life. Neighbors and I were willing to do whatever was needed for great grandmother to stay in the house, but my mom and her brothers disagreed because they wanted to sell the house. My great grandmother was moved into a nursing home and was never happy there. Fortunately, the deed to the land my great grandmother had, was written in such a way it couldn't be simply sold out of the family.

I became an altar boy at St Jacobus and my older sister Roi became the church secretary. Even when we moved to the Germantown section of Philadelphia. Roi and I remained with St Jacobus. Other than my mom

I met one of the people who were important in my spiritual journey, Fred Schott at St Jacobus. Fred was doing his internship at St Jacobus. Both Fred and my mom were key in my feeling free to be a seeker without guilt. A third person who was key in my being able to be a seeker was a history teacher at Theodore Roosevelt Jr High School, Thomas A. Brady. The school wasn't a very good one. Mr. Brady could have been at a better school but wanted to be where he could make a difference. He felt it was more important to teach us how to find what we needed to know than to be able to spit back dates and names to him. He started the school year by going over what a book is, he taught the parts of the book. He cared about his students as did most of the other teachers who were working under deplorable conditions. Mr. Brady was a person who helped instill the desire to think for myself in me.

As a seeker I visited different places of worship, many not Christian. After a while I felt that I wasn't finding what I needed. Also, I still fully believed in the American two-party political system. I was at the time a rarity, a black Republican in Philadelphia. I had joined the GOP because while they only had two at large seats on city council, those two council members were greatly under-appreciated in what they could do. They were still on city council and they could deliver services.

I was quickly asked to be the Republican committeeman for my district. This allowed me to call either of the two GOP city council members and say who was to get things done.

For instance, I was working at a public school and there was an abandoned car on the sidewalk outside the school yard. The principal tried calling for a couple of weeks to have it removed with no luck. I finally told him I would take care of it. I made a call in front of him that morning and it was gone that afternoon.

The school was a special school that was almost completely federally funded. At the end of the year I received a letter letting me know not to return the following year as a result of system-wide layoffs. I had been bumped out of my job. I made a couple of calls (including to a US Senator's office) trying to get my job restored. I was told that I shouldn't worry, all would be alright, and it was. An additional position was created at the school for me.

I volunteered on the campaign for governor of Richard Thornburgh. There were two reasons I supported Thornburgh: there were things I knew about his opponent, the former Philadelphia District Attorney, and Thornburgh had the support of Elsie Hillman, the Republican National Committeewoman from Pennsylvania.

While working on the campaign my grandmother died. I was crushed. I was living in Philadelphia; she was in Kentucky and I didn't have the money to get myself and my mom (who was in a wheelchair because of MS) there. At about midnight I was in tears and called Elsie Hillman at her house in Pittsburgh and somehow when I left my house that morning to go to work, I found $1000 in my door. The Republican Party of those days no longer seems to be. There was a time when the Republicans were really caring and respectable. My great grandmother was a Republican.

We were always taught as children that nobody was better than us. We were instilled with the knowledge that we were at the least equal to others if not better than others. We're of mixed backgrounds and sometimes were reminded that the wider the gene pool the fewer defects were likely.

My father did his 20 years in the Navy and was extremely skilled at avoiding combat. I was coming of draft age as the war in Vietnam was winding down and my father came to me to tell me that he was going to take me to Canada if they tried to draft me. (In those days we were able to avoid the draft by going to Canada). But my father and I were never friends. He was an alcoholic and was abusive to both his wife and children. It was only when I was with my family in Kentucky that I knew what love was. I wouldn't know that again until I was among Friends.

I had been bored and unchallenged in high school and so dropped out (perhaps had I stayed I'd have learned to write). In order to have more than a substitute position with the School District of Philadelphia I had to have my GED and took the test which I easily passed (I to this day don't know how I passed the writing portion). While in high school I had taken some college classes in as part of an interdisciplinary program that included a few high school students, mostly college students and a few people the community who were viewed as non-traditional students. There were a few Gay activist groups that I was involved with including helping to start called Gays in Germantown.

Later I moved to York, Pennsylvania and operated an "escort service". This was for the most part a gay prostitution ring. This was before HIV/AIDS. It was also at a time when many gay men were afraid of being outed even more than they are now. I got into this business because a friend said he needed someone to answer his phone when he out on calls (yes it was long before cell phones), I wasn't working, and it sounded interesting to say the least. He had ads in some gay papers and magazines to find clients. After a while a couple of his friends were involved in going out on calls. We took Master Card, VISA and American Express. There was one older man who worked for us who was married and had two sons in high school, he had a good professional career and his wife knew he liked men. He found this a good way to hook up. He used the company car to go on calls and he refused to keep his portion of the fees (he'd give it to me). One of the best stories is about the time a priest called in with a bad credit card, that was the only bad card anyone ever tried using.

I can say that one of the best things that happened was when some jealousy arose between a couple of guys causing the police to get involved and shut us down. This was good because HIV/AIDS was just starting, and I was looking for a good way to get out of the business. It could have been a good deal more financially rewarding but that wasn't the purpose.

When the police came, I took all the responsibility and charges as I couldn't see others having their lives ruined. The police couldn't get my records as they were kept on in digital form on a cassette tape (in those days people didn't have home computers for the most part, the one I had required a tv, a cassette player and the unit that connected the two). The district justice I appeared before the evening of my arrest was interesting in that he gave me instructions on how to operate the business within the law!!! I ended up getting 30 days and a $500 fine. While I was waiting for the final disposition of my case, I committed credit card fraud to survive, I did a year in state prison for that.

When it was time to be paroled from state prison, I needed to put in my parole plan (papers saying where I was going to live and work). Mine said that I was going to stay at a roach hotel in Carlisle along with a letter from the state unemployment office saying they would help me locate work. When the plan came back approved the state parole officer in the prison said he had never seen such a weak plan be approved. I still knew people on Governor Thornburgh's staff, and we'd stayed in contact while I locked up, I don't know if that helped or not.

I had a bit of trouble getting a job when I arrived in Carlisle, until one day I went to put in an application and started off by saying to the boss, named Bob, If my having just gotten out of state prison is going to keep you from hiring me tell me now and I'll just go away. But Bob told me to sit down. About a week later I got a call saying when I was to start. It was almost a year later when I learned my being so up front was what got me the job. Bob was one of the best bosses/people I have ever known. It was little things that made him great. I was working in a restaurant that he had just opened (he made his real money at his body shop). I was the only African American working there. Almost all the customers were white. Once a dance floor was put in for use on the weekends more African Americans came. When Bob overheard a waitress comment "the place is getting dark" she was let go on the spot. Bob and his wife didn't care that I was black or gay, they were just good people. The only time I've been drunk in the last 44 years was the night I learned Bob had died.

In Carlisle I stayed in the Molly Pitcher Hotel, which once was elegant but was now rundown, then eventually moved out into a house

27

with three reporters for the local newspaper. The next year was very dull; slowly the others moved out of town and I was left with the house to myself.

I soon ran into a couple I knew when I lived in the Molly Pitcher, she was "with child." They were still at the Molly Pitcher on the 5th floor and the elevator still wasn't working. I offered to have them move into the house. Once little Eddie was born neither Linda nor Ed were very good at caring for him. I was the one who changed his diapers in the middle of the night, I mixed formula for him. Linda got upset when Eddie reached the point that he could climb out of his crib because he did and came to my room, not his parents'. He would also be waiting by the door when I got home from work. Ed and Linda reported that Eddie would want to check my room when I wasn't home to make sure I wasn't there.

Linda and Ed were terrible at picking up after themselves and I eventually asked them to move out. I explained that Eddie was getting an attachment to me that should be for them and I thought it would be better if it was just the three of them living together. Turned out they were sharing a room but were no longer a couple and Ed wanted to stay with me because Linda was a slob. I told them they had to think about Eddie. I said that I might have a prison record, but I would still try for custody if they didn't get their act together. I said what will the court think when they see me in the courtroom and Eddie wanting to be with me? Why does this little white boy want to go to the big darkie and not his parents? They came to an agreement that I knew wasn't going to work.

I eventually had to walk away from the situation. I let those who needed to know what poor parents they were knew. It helped that I knew Linda's new landlord. I made sure that the landlord was aware of the maggots in the dirty diapers in the kitchen above his law office.

While working for Bob I developed repetitive use syndrome in my right wrist and had to have surgery. This was under workers comp and the insurance company fought it until I went back to work. After a few months, though, the problem returned, and my doctor said it was the same thing and not a new issue. I was told I couldn't work. Because I had never been asked to sign a final release, the insurance company was stuck with the liability. Now the restaurant had been sold and the new owner had a different insurance carrier but the old one was stuck with liability paying my medical bills and sending me a check every two weeks (even when I was in jail for two months). I was told by my doctor that I might want to think about going back to school and getting a into a profession that would be better for my wrist.

After a while I contacted the insurance adjuster and told her I wanted to settle out. I was still going to be able to collect from them for several years if I wanted. We came to terms with them cutting me a large check to cover the cost of classes I wanted to take, plus a car so I could get to the classes and cut the amount of time I would continue to collect workers comp. Unfortunately, the school I was going to take the classes at dropped them.

I moved back to Philadelphia to put some distance between Ed, Linda, Eddie and me. It broke my heart, but I wanted to give them a chance to get to be a better family. I worked driving a cab briefly in Philadelphia as well as being a cook at a fraternity house at the University of Pennsylvania. I decided to return to Central Pennsylvania and landed in Harrisburg.

Now I was homeless at 42 and staying at Bethesda Mission in Harrisburg, Pennsylvania. This was in 1996. Bethesda is about 3 to 4 blocks from the local Quaker Meetinghouse. To stay at Bethesda more than 10 days one had to be in either their Bible study program or their drug and alcohol program. Not having an addiction problem, I went into the Bible study program. Having been one who had done some independent study of various Christian theologies I was prepared to ask questions of the people who led the study. Not being a drinker, I asked why they teach drinking is a sin when the Bible says drunkenness is and that Christ made water into wine. The response was that the people they were talking to couldn't control their drinking so for them it is a sin. I said but according to the Bible what they were saying was a lie.

They taught to trust in the Lord and He will provide and protect you. One of the chaplains was working two jobs so his family could live in a "safe neighborhood." I said to him don't you trust the Lord to take care of your family no matter where you live? If you do, you'd work less and have more time with your family.

At that time, I was in the mission's "Christian Discipleship" program. One week we were given an assignment to go to a local church service and were given a form to critique the service. There were questions like, was the sermon biblical? What translation of the Bible did they use? We were to bring back a copy of the bulletin. I have never approved of critiquing a church service so knowing the Quaker meeting was just about three blocks from the mission and knowing enough about Friends meeting to know I couldn't fill out the form I went to Harrisburg Monthly Meeting for the first time.

I will be forever grateful for the assignment from the mission. That First Day I had finally been led to a place I felt at home. It would be several years until I would become involved with the wider Quaker community.

I felt so at home and welcomed there that I continued attending the meeting. Reading about early Friends and getting to know the members of Harrisburg Monthly Meeting (HMM) was eye-opening. While there were few people of color at the meeting, those who were there were involved in the meeting more than just by attending on First Day.

After I moved out of the mission, I got a job and a room. Soon thereafter at meeting a member who had been friendly to me handed me an envelope and told me not to open it until after she and her family had left. When I opened it there was a key with a note saying I was welcome to move into their home whenever I felt so led. When I did eventually move in, I was made to feel like part of the family. Like all families there were great times and not so great times.

After a while I felt it was time for me to request membership which I did, and I was accepted. When I joined, I had no idea what that would really eventually mean.

I came to believe/accept that being a Quaker is a lifestyle not just First Day go to Meeting. This affected how I worked on a couple of jobs. One was when I took a job selling meat door to door. When I started, I asked about the form that people doing in home sales are to give out explaining the customers right to void the sale within three days and they said they didn't do that (it's federally required!).

The meat was of a lesser quality than purported in the literature. I read all the material about the products and looked over the food and realized it was a fraudulent operation. I tried reporting this to the proper authorities and was rebuffed. I wanted to find a way to get it into a record someplace. Bad choice time (and not my only one). I decided to go to the local public housing project, where people couldn't afford it, and give away all the food on the truck.

I returned the empty truck knowing I would likely face some kind of trouble, and I ended up getting charged with theft. I was given 90 days in prison with work release and sent to work at a local printer.

During the 90 days I was on work release, only during the first two weeks did I have days without visitors from meeting. Unexpectedly a member of meeting showed up before I had let anyone know what had happened. Other inmates were as surprised as I was. She happened to work with the Pennsylvania Prison Society and to this day I, over 20 years later, I don't know how she knew so quickly.

Because we don't have paid clergy the meeting sent a letter with a list of three people who were to be given the privileges of clergy, which meant they could disregard prison visiting hours. They were also able to [work] in a more relaxed atmosphere. One person was there almost every day and 2 others were there twice a week each. Other inmates were confounded by the support I had. Twice meeting for Worship was held in the prison by several people from meeting with me.

The other inmates regularly asked me how it was I had so many visitors and found it hard to believe they were from my "church". One person was referred to as Moses because of long beard. One person was there every day — even a day when there was a bad ice storm and I had called and said not to come.

The timing of my release was interesting in that there was a guest speaker at meeting that First Day. His opening remark was that he understood that there was someone who had just been released from prison there and to remember that in the early days of Friends anybody who was anybody had been in prison. At times there have been Friends in the local state halfway house who have worshipped with us and who have been able to do their community service at the meetinghouse.

My supervisor at the printing company and I got into interesting conversations on religion and faith. Often, he'd take me out to lunch (against work release policy). When Thanksgiving came, I was asked if I was willing to work and I said yes. It turned out that it was against prison policy for anyone to leave to work on thanksgiving. My supervisor told the prison that if I couldn't work when he wanted me the program would be discontinued and nobody from the prison would work there at all. I was the only person who left to go to work on Thanksgiving Day and Christmas Day that year.

When I did real work there it was in quality control. After I was released, I continued working for the printing company. When my supervisor was on vacation I was assigned to a military project, printing a weapons manual. I told the person that made the assignment that for faith related reasons I couldn't do that job. I was told it was a very slow time and most of the people from work release had already been laid off. I was told I could be on the DOD project or be let go. I said I couldn't do anything to support the war machine and that was my final night.

I was living with the family from meeting that had given me a key to home at this time. When I told them what happened they were supportive and agreed with my decision. The head of the work release program's daughter it turned out had baby sat for the children of that family. Six degrees of separation.

I worked at the airport cleaning at night for a brief time (until my car broke down). Life has a way of taking odd turns. I learned there was an opening for a weekend cook at Bethesda Mission and applied for the position. As a Quaker I couldn't say that I agreed with the fundamentalist theology of mission and being Gay was definitely not in line with their teachings.

I got the job. The reason I was hired? I was the only person who said their work hours had to permit me to get to worship. Eventually I was promoted to food service director. This was a good job and I was extremely busy in this position. After a while I moved out on my own. I kept in close contact with the people I had been living with. Many people from meeting helped to furnish my new apartment. All was going well. The folks I had lived with gave me $10,000 for things I didn't have for the apartment. I was still on parole but wasn't bothering to report in.

But I found myself under a lot of stress. And I went home from work one day and decided I was just going to go away. I got into my car with a friend and three days later arrived on the west coast.

Once I calmed down, I contacted the mission and told them to wire me the money I had coming. They never did wire it but did eventually express mail it. When I went to Western Union to pick up the money, I was told there was money for me but not from the mission. I had to figure out who would have sent me money not knowing where I was or that I was in need. It was, of course the family I had lived with. They had called the mission because they hadn't heard from me for a couple of days and were informed about my call to them. This was after they had contacted my mother and were told they needn't worry about me because G*D was with me and always made sure I survived.

Over the next few years my mother would be proven right. Not everything I did was just by the standards of current social norms, but I caused no physical harm to anyone. Some good to a few.

I backtracked across the country a bit and stayed at various missions in midsized to small towns. At nearly each one I was asked why I was there and told I didn't belong there (it seems that drug or alcohol abuse is the standard for being homeless these days). At all I was soon put in a position of responsibility even though it was known I didn't agree with their basic theological bent. At one mission I remarked that all of Paul's writings could be tossed out for all I cared. I said Paul tended to teach law when Christ taught a love written on the heart.

Shortly thereafter the father of the director of the mission died. The director called me into his office and told me his dad had died and he was tired of people telling him his dad was in a better place, that he's with God/Jesus now. I told him that there's nothing anyone could say to make his loss any less difficult or more acceptable. I asked him what he told people that lost a loved one. His response was that it was going to change. I said that G*D walks with us because He is always in us. That if he believed his father was with G*D his father is with him because G*D is. I told him that I can only make it from day to day by talking with my grandmother and great grandmother daily both of whom had "died" and few years earlier.

He said he wondered about how a person with as little as I have could be at peace and joyful without "self-medicating" (drinking or doing drugs) or being obsessed with gaining power or material goods. I explained that I had wanted the material things of this world until I came to see the social gospel was the true one far more in line with Christ's teachings.

This was in a town that had no Quaker meeting. I had been put in a position that gave me keys to all of the mission building. I would daily go to the chapel alone to have a period of meditation and contemplation. I was there for that day which the world calls Christmas and on that day as I left the building a pickup truck pulled over to me and the driver asked if I was staying at the mission I replied yes. He told me he had gone to visit his son at the juvenile detention center next door and his son had refused to see him! He said he had an envelope he had intended to give his son but wanted to give to me instead. In it was $100 cash. The hotel around the corner was having a holiday buffet for $12.50 per person. I took the first seven other guys from the mission to the buffet. There are times in life that I have done some things that were less than smart.

In some ways I believe that my parents helped raise me to be a Quaker. Neither of them were real church goers. As Vietnam was winding down the draft was still in place and my father told me that if they were to try to draft me, he'd drive me to Canada himself. While my mom was "a good Christian woman," she never forced her beliefs on us. Mom knew I was a seeker and one day we were looking into the backyard from the kitchen when she said, "You've got to believe in something, I don't care if it's the leaf on the tree, but you have to believe in something."

When I first went to Harrisburg Monthly Meeting (mid 1990s) I was warmly welcomed by everyone I encountered. It didn't matter to them that I was staying at the mission or that I am Black. I was invited to stay for hospitality and encouraged to return. Unlike some people I wasn't in the least bit uncomfortable with the gathering in expectant waiting, in fact I found it enveloping me in a kind of comfort I'd never known before. I noticed there was a mixed-race family by marriage at Worship. It was also clear that being gay wasn't an issue to these Friends. Later I'd learn that one family had adopted both their daughters from China, another had adopted children of more than one ethnicity. As I sat in worship that First Day, I felt that I was there because it was where I was meant to be.

I failed to mention that another guy staying at the mission went with me and he never went back. After I started attending, I was impressed that almost everyone was either involved in things that would make a positive difference or helping support the work of others doing so. There were (and are) members of meeting who are former US Marines. There were at least two families that could trace their lines in America to before the revolution (while not all had Quaker lines that back that far) one family pre-dated William Penn's arrival.

The meetinghouse was built only about 52 years ago. One reason they chose that location was so that they would be able to be of service to the community. This meant to me that the meeting wasn't made up of "limousine liberals". As I learned more and more about the people in the meeting and the work they were doing it became a matter of who wouldn't want to be a part of this community of people that wanted to make the world a better place? Over the years being part of Harrisburg Monthly Meeting (HMM) and Philadelphia Yearly Meeting (PhYM) has greatly changed me for the better. Being part of these spiritual communities is what has given me the strength and support to keep active in trying to make a positive difference even while facing my own mortality.

In October of 2014 I made two visits to the Emergency Room two nights apart. On the second trip I saw the same doctor I had seen two nights before. After running a second set of tests Dr. Geeting sat and told me he believed I had cancer. From the way he was behaving I was ready to hear bad news. After talking with my primary care physician and having more tests as well as visiting specialists it was confirmed that I have stage 4 prostate cancer.

I have since been in a clinical trial, had radiation therapy, lots of tests on an ongoing basis. I'm up at 2am to take medications. I deal with the symptoms that women do during menopause (hot flashes, night sweats, mood swings) – if you're male and you know someone going through this, be nice and try to be understanding, it might be you one day. Sex drive is gone, and the equipment had stopped working anyway. I have days that I tire very easily. The cancer having spread to my spine and hips I'm in a great deal of pain all the time. (Opioids are really needed by some of us). I truly believe that if weren't for the Love I receive from Friends and being allowed to maintain a meaningful life through service to Friends I would not be doing as well as I am.

I'm still serving on PhYM committees as well as committees at HMM. I'm able, on a limited basis, to help some people who are living in the streets. I keep going and doing what I can for others because I'm lucky enough to be still able to because of the love I receive from Friends. Everything I distribute is donated by a few nonprofits. I've had times when I've been slowed down because my car needed repairs and Friends helped cover the costs. When there have been people I've been working with who've needed help to either get a place to live or to prevent their eviction, Harrisburg Monthly Meeting and individual Friends have stepped forward to help (they have also helped with medication, utilities and bus tickets etc.). When I'm hospitalized, I'm fortunate to have a wonderful group of Friends who visit me.

When I first became a Friend, I never dreamt that I would ever need the various kinds of love and support that I have and even more importantly I never thought that it would be there for me to anywhere near the extent it has. It's important that people remember that I'm not a writer. In an earlier section I mentioned that being gay wouldn't be an issue at Harrisburg Monthly. I could tell this because Lambda, a LGBTQ 12-step program, met at the meetinghouse twice a week (they now meet once a week) and the local Metropolitan Community Church also met there weekly (after many years they were able to get their own building). Even before I became disabled people in the meeting knew I didn't make much money. I was working at a soup kitchen. There was a member, who happened to be a doctor, that almost every time we spoke, he'd ask me a question that for a long time I wasn't sure what he meant. Finally, I asked him what the question meant. He told me he knew I didn't make much money and he wanted to know if I was in need of anything!

After being a member of HMM for several years I met Al, the person who is now my partner. Al isn't a Quaker but is well accepted by the meeting. He worked in construction until I became disabled and he has taken on the task of being my caregiver. There went much more of our income. Harrisburg Meeting has helped by having Al do jobs around the meetinghouse and some members have him do work for them. They understand that there are sometimes delays because of his focus on me. When I [have] meetings to attend away from Harrisburg Al is the one who drives me (unless someone else happens to be going to the same meeting and offers to take me). Most of the time he just hangs out at the car.

While I was waiting for my Social Security Disability to be approved, I was told of a Quaker fund that could help me (I learned about it while attending a PhYM Standing Committee meeting). HMM applied for a grant for me and it was given. (The grant was more than I get on Social Security). This grant was from neither my meeting nor my Yearly Meeting. As time has passed, I have needed increased help because of things not covered by insurance and I have been fortunate enough to qualify for other Quaker aid. (On none of the applications has there ever been a question about race or sexual orientation. One asked for initials and not the applicant's name). There are some things that if I didn't have help with, my functionality would be greatly reduced, and I'd feel my life was far less meaningful. I have learned that many church bodies don't provide their members the practical help that I've received from the RSoF.

On another concern, Harrisburg Monthly Meeting is not new to the fight against mass incarceration. Neither are they new at having a heart for people who have made bad choices. Years ago, the meeting was involved in a bail program for those who couldn't make bail. Unfortunately, the program was taken over by the county and is no longer what it was intended to be. The meeting still has members who are actively involved in the fight against mass incarceration.

****

I started writing this with a focus and began to ramble. For me, part of what is wonderful about being part of my faith community is we can disagree with each other and still love each other. We are willing to try, with G*D's help, to work through our differing perspectives. I can feel differently about something than another Friend and still go to dinner and a movie. We respect that of G*D in each other and that we are each walking in G*D's Light to learn G*D's truth. Knowing that we aren't all at the same place we are willing to listen to one another in love so that we can gain more of that truth.

Sometimes when we believe we know what the best way forward is, after listening to others we can understand that another way may serve us even better. Is seeking revenge ever truly the best way forward? We can't change the past, but we can learn from it. Both of those are things that I have learned over the years from Friends. I have learned that when I forgive someone, I'm doing it as much for myself as for them. When I forgive, I try to also educate the person/people who offended me as to how they can do better in the future.

I can't speak here for all Black people, LGBTQ folks or people with cancer, I can only speak for myself. Again, things I have learned from Friends. Unfortunately, one of the ways I have learned some of these things has been when people have said they were speaking for a group I belong to and I disagreed with them.

I'm a bit tired of hearing more about what's wrong with my faith community, rather than about all the wonderful things I have known it to be. I'm going to write about my experiences with the RSoF and how it has been key in sustaining me in the years I have been part of it. I know that many people came to Quakerism as a result of seeking after being wounded at another denomination. I became a seeker early in my life. I've always been a biblical person, even knowing how it's been used to inflict harm on many people, and knowing of the contradictions it contains, I still believe the Bible is a wonderful guide for my faith relationship with God. My seeking has been guided by the Jewish and Christian texts both within accepted canon and outside it. I never felt wounded by any church but often didn't feel at home in them either.

In my life I have been physically attacked for being gay as well as for being Black. I wasn't able to hate the people who attacked me. While I never got to know the people who did those things, rather than hating them I felt sorry for them, sorry that they had such hatred in their hearts. I still have a scar on my nose from the racist attack over 35 years ago.

Some attacks took place before I became a Friend and I was even at that time following Friends principles. Did I fight back? Just to the extent needed to keep damage to me to a minimum without inflicting much harm on the attacker(s). (Our Peace Testimony is one that speaks against war). I couldn't find it within myself to hate. As I reflect back on this, I understand more why I felt at home when I first came to Meeting. I do not understand how any Friend (regardless of race) can be in favor of imposing a judgment of guilt and the imposition of punishment on someone without thoroughly checking out the accusations. Too many people have suffered because of this very kind of behavior. We are members of a faith community that has been referred to as seekers of the truth. If we do not work to see the truth in each situation what have, we become? Will we be any better than a lynch mob?

In Philadephia Yearly Meeting there has in recent years been a lot of controversy over racism and how to deal with it. I happen to also be a multiple minority member here. I'm a person of color who is gay, "elderly" and disabled, not to mention in the lower socioeconomic class. I have been in prison, I'm a former Republican (to some my worst cross to bear). So, I'm a person who has a personal perspective that isn't often expressed.

If I wanted to, I could look at things that happen that I disagree with and pull out one or more cards to play in order to claim discrimination. I don't think that way, I look deeper to see what other things might be at play. You see I do believe that intent matters greatly. Intent matters because it determines if or how we can make something into a teachable moment. If there was no intent to do harm, making it into a teachable moment is a real possibility, (as is forgiveness). If the intent was to inflict pain the chance of making it into a teachable moment is far less (making forgiveness more difficult but not impossible). While the pain might be the same no matter the intent, the options we have for dealing with the pain change with the intent. I think that too often when we are offended instead of taking the time to explain why and how we have been hurt to those who have hurt us and have no idea what they have done so we complain to others and rip apart the person who offended us. Instead of making it into a teachable moment it's made into a time to exacerbate anger and pain.

There are people who encourage this behavior. Instead of wanting to hear both sides of what happened they fully and completely agree with the person who has been offended/hurt without trying to get to the root. I hope that Friends know when "eldering" a person who has done something offensive, that saying what was said or done was wrong isn't enough. We have to be willing to try and find out what led to it being said or done and try to explain what was wrong with such thinking/belief.

37

It needs to be done in a gentle, loving, caring way so the person being eldered knows we care about them as much as the person who has been offended.

In my life I have been physically attacked for the color of my skin and at another time for whom I cared to love. I didn't let those incidents embitter me about whole groups of people, I instead struggled with why people would do such things. I found myself praying for them.

I still have a scar from when I was attacked by a drug addicted homeless man, I prayed for him also (he's now in prison for second degree murder in New Mexico). I believe that if I believe in That of G*D in everyone I must treat all with love and work as hard as I can to forgive others. When I fail to forgive others, I am failing to forgive G*D.

There are all too many people who are willing to instead of seeking ways to forgive and work with the offender so that it doesn't happen again, would rather find reasons and ways for revenge. Too often people are more willing to hold onto a painful past than to forgive and work for a hopeful, joyous and healthy present and future. Some people want to avenge what took place in earlier generations (often they refuse to acknowledge all the positive things that happened in earlier generations).

We need to understand that different things are offensive to different people. It's interesting that people are so willing to hold the bad things have done in the past but want to take away all credit for good they have done. Yes, some early Friends were involved in slavery, but they were also very early leaders in the abolishment movement. There have been many more positive actions by Quakers when it comes to racism than negative ones. We're not always the most unified as we find our way into G*D's will (some Yearly Meetings are still splitting over the LGBTQ issue.) When we spend so much of our time tearing ourselves (the Yearly Meeting) apart, I wonder if we are really just distracting ourselves from other problems in the world we should be addressing?

I'm afraid that we have reached a point of over-sensitivity. In the musical play, "Avenue Q" there's a song "Everyone's a Little Bit Racist." If not racist, there's going to be another form of bigotry you most likely have. Expecting perfection from people is foolish and if you think you're perfect you're fooling yourself.

One group that I have had to learn to forgive and try to ignore is the white saviors. I'm tired of their being offended for me (if you think I might have been offended ask me before you go complaining, I might be fine with you thinking I should have been offended by something, and if I was I can ask for help dealing with it, if I need any).

I'm tired of hearing them saying what acts are racist. I'm tired of them telling everyone else they have the solution to either racism generally or a problem they perceive. I am tired of hearing from them how people of color should deal with racism (which we do every day). In many ways I find the actions of white saviors to be saying people of color don't have the ability, the agency to work for their own improvement, to demand their own equality to strategically plan to achieve their goals.

I realize how difficult it is for concerned whites to do but please stay in the background. It's not always easy for members of the oppressed group to agree on what is discrimination or how to respond when they do agree. So how can a non-member make either determination?

Pay attention to if the non-group member is the first to complain about something. When you get into savior mode you have gone into white supremacy status. One of the most racist things I can think of is when People of African Descent are lumped together as if we're all the same. "Black People have been waiting for......" Black People need....." These are often over-generalizations. (Notice that Rev. Barber has a Poor People's Campaign).

I have the feeling that if they didn't have people of color to lead to the promised land, they would find someone else to take care of. There are times when people create things to complain about. Rather than saying that it's not right that the appointed leadership is older, cis, white men, work at getting people of color, women and LGBTQ people qualified and willing to serve in leadership. I question setting up affinity rooms based on race, they feel like returning to segregation to me under the guise of making people comfortable. Who are they really trying to make comfortable? People of color or white people? I find affinity spaces based on race and not common interest or goals more likely to perpetuate the separation of people.

I believe that a failure to be welcoming, accepting and loving of one group is the same as doing it to all groups. To look at one group and not others at the same time is a mistake. What I find to be truly sad is that when a group becomes accepted, they might look down on others not yet as accepted. This is another reason we have to learn to accept all equally.

Personally, I can't think of a time when I felt that I wasn't seen as an equal among Friends (with the exception of the economic part and I cannot blame that on the Friends). Because I don't have the wherewithal to participate in something isn't the fault of my meeting or yearly meeting. They have both made funds available so that I can fully participate to the point of insuring that if needed my caregiver can accompany me. Both organizations rely greatly on volunteers to function and both have welcomed my willingness to do so.

To say that I haven't been disappointed in some decisions would be disingenuous but I, as part of our community, accept them. I believe that if they are truly G*D's will, all will be as it should, if not our community will be led to find a way to correct itself.

I honestly am uncomfortable with the term "anti-racist." I'm more comfortable with saying I'm pro-inclusion. Perhaps it's because I know I can hear that a place welcomes people of color and get there and find out I'm not welcome because I happen to be Gay, or it's very difficult if not impossible to get into the building because I am handicapped or there are no handicapped facilities. What happens if I am a conservative either politically or theologically? A person who shows up should be made to feel welcome and appreciated and they should feel as if we to include them in the life of our meetings.

Here is part of my view of "anti-racism" work. One size doesn't fit all. We are all different people at different places. What might work with one group or person most likely isn't going to work with others. If you want to "improve the situation" giving them options is far better than trying to give them "must dos". Also consider that they may not feel their situation needs to change.

Philadelphia Yearly Meeting has a long history and has survived some intense internal trauma during that time. We're currently dealing with the matter of racism. Are we or aren't we a racist organization? (I personally don't believe we are). If we are what can/should be done to change that? I have full faith in the ability of PhYM to overcome this issue and move forward to the place it should be in the showing the way of love in to mending the world.

When I look at the generations coming up behind us, I see people who seem to have a greater understanding of what matters to make the world a better place for all with fairness understanding without knowing it what G*D is calling them to do. They are doing a better job of following the Light than we have done. I'm secure in my faith for the future because of the Young Friends and Young Adult Friends I see in action.

David Zarembka:
Passing the Torch

I find the world an extremely interesting place and I participate in as many aspects of it that I can. Conversely, I don't find myself very interesting at all and therefore don't often write much about my life's 76-year journey. This article therefore is a major exception.

In order to understand where I ended up, I have to explain where I came from. Although it might seem that my life has been unconventional, it really hasn't been when one considers where I came from and how I grew up.

My paternal great-grandfather, Mathias Zarembka, came from then

David Zarembka

Russian-occupied Poland to the United States to work. Those were the good, ole days in the late 19th century when people could just come and go. He stayed in the US for seven years and then went back. He had seven children, six of whom immigrated to the US, while only one remained in Poland. My grandfather, Frank Zarembka, immigrated to the US in March/April 1914. If he had waited a few months longer, the guns of August which started World War I would have begun, and he probably would have been drafted into the Russian army where the ill-equipped and untrained Polish soldiers were mowed down by the Germans. He left behind my grandmother, Lotti Wilant (notice the German name although she knew of no connection to Germany), and my one-year old father, Richard Zarembka. They were not able to immigrate to the US until 1921 when the family reunification act was passed in the United States. They lived in St. Louis in the Polish section of town. My grandfather worked for St. Louis Coal and Ice and pulled ice from the ground to be cut up in blocks to be put in iceboxes. Even when I knew him as a child, he was physically very strong.

My maternal grandfather was Ernest Elmer Colvin. He was a newspaper man. My Mom, Helen Jane Colvin Zarembka, was a great family storyteller so I have lots of old stories. My grandmother was so worried about my grandfather when the Associated Press in St. Louis assigned him to cover the 1919 so-called "race riots" in East St. Louis – it was actually just a massacre of what were then called Negroes. When he retired around 1954, he was copy editor for the *St. Louis Post-Dispatch*. My maternal grandmother, Flora Scott Colvin, died even before my parents were married. She had grown up in Kansas City where my grandparents met. She and her sister, Fanny, started the first kindergarten in Kansas City. Each morning they would hitch up the horse and pick up the kids for school – something that women were not supposed in those old days. So, my roots run deep.

My grandfather Colvin had an unmarried younger sister, Joy Ester Colvin, who worked for the YWCA which was then quite a radical group as it tried to improve the conditions of all the new immigrants. Auntie Joy, as we called her, was our favorite as she would visit us for a week once every year or two from New Bedford, MA, where she was the head of the local YMCA branch. She was a pacifist (she signed the non-violence pledge for the Fellowship of Reconciliation), a suffragette, probably a lesbian, and greatly concerned with social issues. When she was dying in 1972, I told her that my wife, Rodah, and I had agreed to name our expected child, if a girl, after her (a very African custom). So my daughter is Joy Mutanu (meaning "joy" in my wife's Kamba language) Zarembka. Our son, Thomas Mutinda Zarembka was born a year and a half later.

Even my running off to foreign lands is just a replay. My Mom's uncle, Don Colvin, had gone to the University of Kansas for two years and then decided to go to Mexico for adventure. He soon became involved in building railroads there for the American capitalists. He stayed through the 1912 Mexican Revolution and then continued on building railroads for the newly nationalized Mexican railroads. Shortly thereafter he was sleeping in a rail car for the night and a flash flood swept the car away and he drowned.

My parents, Richard Zarembka and Helen Jane Colvin Zarembka, were married in 1940. At that time this was considered a "mixed marriage" because my Dad was of Catholic background and my Mom of Protestant background. My mother graduated in math and astronomy from the University of Missouri in Columbia. She commented to me that she was frequently the only female in her science/math classes. My father only took a few college courses. They met while playing violin at the St. Louis Philharmonic Orchestra. Dad was first violinist and Mom was third violinist. The conductor noticed that sparks were flying so he asked the second violinist if he would change places with my Mom so that my Mom and Dad could share the same music stand. Fortunately for my existence, he agreed.

I suspect that I was conceived as a war exemption. My Dad's attitude to being a soldier was somewhat on the line that "it was foolish to join the army and be killed." At the beginning of WWII, only unmarried men were drafted. He was married. When married men were drafted if they did not have children, my brother, Paul, was born in 1942. When married men with one child were drafted, I was born just a year after my brother in 1943. My speculation is that our closeness in age is why I was a result of resistance to fighting in war. During the war my father worked at the Chrysler factory making ammunition. At night he began taking pictures of the soldiers off to the wars and their girlfriends or wives.

This began his photography business that was his occupation for the rest of his life. It was a one-person occupation except during the busy time right before Christmas when my Mom would go to help out. In those days, when taking a picture was still difficult, his specialty was taking pictures of children. He never failed to get a smiling picture of the child – I remember one picture where the child was smiling with tears coming from his eyes. Later when cameras became much easier to use and began snapping shots of their kids, he began taking wedding pictures which he didn't enjoy nearly as much as taking the pictures of kids. I estimate that he took pictures at 700 weddings.

It always concerns me that, if one is white, one is assumed to come from a prejudiced background. This was certainly not my case. Most Americans are not aware that in 1901 when President Theodore Roosevelt invited Booker T. Washington to have lunch at the White House, there was such a negative reaction that no president did it again for 38 years. This was in 1939 when Eleanor Roosevelt invited Marian Anderson to lunch following her outdoor concert after the Daughters of the American Revolution refused to rent the hall for her concert. It seems ridiculous now, but before the Second World War, around 90 percent of the white population would not sit down and eat with a Negro. (What were those 1950s sit-ins all about?) Even in those early days before

WWI, my Mom told me, her parents would eat lunch together with the Negro help.

Once when Mom was in high school, she sat on the streetcar next to a Negro girl. One of her white friends chastised her for this. Mom says she dropped that white girl as a friend. Note: My present wife, Gladys Kamonya, lived in Pakistan for three years and she told me that in all those years not one Pakistani, male or even female, would sit next to her on the bus. In her usual good humor, her comment was that she always had the seat to herself.

Until I was in the sixth grade, I went to segregated schools. The summer camp that the Clayton School District ran was not segregated so I knew all the colored kids. I was well aware of this inconsistency. When Brown vs the Board of Education ended segregation, my Mom was totally supportive of the case and glad my school would be integrated which it did the next September. When I was first married to an African – only two years after state laws against interracial marriages where outlawed by the Supreme Court – and my parents were at a function where someone sitting at the table complained about interracial marriage, my Mom replied, "My son has done that and I don't see anything wrong with it." She then got up and left the table in a huff.

I have one brother, Paul, a year older than me; a sister, Elaine, who is two and a half years younger than me; and a second sister, Arlene, who is four and a half years younger. I am right in the mainstream of my siblings. Paul Zarembka is a Marxian economics professor at the University of Buffalo. If you want to succeed as an economist in the United States, don't be a Marxist. Be a disciple of Milton Friedman's school of neo-liberalism. He is also the editor of a book called, *The Hidden History of 9/11,* which challenges the official government explanation of that event. This also is hardly mainstream America. When he was appointed chair of the economics department at the University of Buffalo, the local paper headlined this with something like "Communist takes over the University of Buffalo."

My sister, Elaine Belmaker, went to Radcliffe/Harvard College, married an American of Jewish descent, and studied medicine at Duke University. In 1976 the couple moved to Israel where she still lives. She became the head of medical services in the Negev, the desert southern part of Israel. One of her major endeavors was to develop medical services for Bedouin who prior to that had almost no medical services. She first had to just train Bedouin translators, then developed programs to train Bedouin nurses, and after winning their confidence worked on projects to assess the numerous genetic issues among the Bedouin because they only marry within their own small clan.

Lastly my sister, Arlene Zarembka, who attended Swarthmore College and St. Louis University Law School, is a lesbian lawyer in St. Louis. In 1986 she had a ceremony of commitment with Zuleyma Tang-Martinez, a biologist at University of Missouri, St Louis. All our family attended, and my parents had absolutely no problem with this relationship. My Dad's attitude for this and most everything else us eclectic kids did was, "If that is what makes you happy, then fine." Arlene and Zuleyma are real political activists.

Then I need to mention that in 1962 when my brother and I were at college and our bedroom was open, for a year my parents hosted a female Japanese foreign exchange student, Michiko Shimizu, who attended our local high school. This was quite bold so soon after World War II. One of my uncles refused to meet her because he had fought the Japanese during WWII. Our families have remained close ever since. This led my parents to host Mrs. Abe, one of the Japanese atomic bomb survivors under a program arranged by Quaker Barbara Reynolds from the Wilmington College's Peace Resource Center.

As you can see, I am not outside the mainstream of my family background. Therefore, from my vantage point, nothing I have done is particularly unusual.

*****

Let me now turn to myself. I was born in St. Louis, MO, in 1943, but my family moved to the suburb, Clayton, in 1946. They chose to move there because the Clayton Public Schools were considered the best public-school system in Missouri. I attended the Clayton Public Schools from pre-kindergarten through high school. Its reputation was well deserved.

When I was in third grade, 9 years old, I asked my teacher, "If 2 minus 1 is equal 1, then 1 minus 2 is equal minus 1." My teacher hesitated, looked at me, and replied, "No, no, no. When you do subtraction, you have to put the bigger number on the top." From her hesitation, I realized that she was lying. I learned early to "question authority". One should not underestimate a child.

Sometime while in high school, I realized that, if I didn't spend money, I didn't have to earn it. If I didn't have to earn a lot of money for an expensive lifestyle, then I could be myself and do what I wanted. I would not need to join the "rat race." As part of this I never smoked (as over 50% of the males did at this time), drank, did drugs, gambled, or any other wasteful, self-indulgent activity.

When I was in 9th grade, I took Latin. Near the end of the year, we took a national Latin examination. Our teacher prepped us for about a week before the exam. I clearly remember her telling the class to have a look at pages XYZ concerning gerunds because we hadn't yet covered that in class. (If you don't know what a gerund is, don't worry; it's unimportant.) I looked up the section on gerunds and found that it was easy to make one in Latin. When the test came, the last question was on making a gerund. I easily figured that one out. When the results came in later, I and two of my classmates received a mark of 96 or more. I got 98, meaning I missed only one regular question. A student who got over 96 points received a certificate of merit. Since the last gerund question was worth five points, I had to have answered this correctly in order to earn the certificate.

Since three of us had received the high marks, the school was awarded a trophy. At a school assembly the three of us were paraded in front of all the other students and teachers and lauded for our results to the pride of our school. The trophy was displayed in a glass case in the hall near the front door with all the other athletic trophies the school had earned. This award solidified my reputation as a bright, outstanding student in the school. As a result, in the future teachers had great expectations from me and I responded according, never receiving anything below an A and graduating second or third in my class rankings.

This was a fraud. A few years after taking the exam when I was still in high school, I was talking with that Latin teacher. She told me that she had opened the exam before we took it, realized the gerund question was important, and therefore coached us. Perhaps she had coached us on other questions she knew were going to be asked. She said she did this because Latin was then going out of fashion being replaced by French and Spanish, so she needed to "prove" that Latin was important. I was horrified. I helped win that trophy for the school because she cheated. I didn't earn it, as I had thought, on my own merits. Yes, I understand that it was the teacher who cheated and not me, but then I had been manipulated in the teacher's interest. It's over 60 years later and I am still ashamed that I received inappropriate credit for something I did not do fair and square.

This great, partly unearned, reputation got me into Harvard College. In the early 1960s, Harvard College had decided to diversify from the mostly New England/New York City private school students that were the vast majority of the students at that time. There were only twelve out of 1200 students in my freshman class from the state of Missouri. I was an affirmative action student. I was from the Midwest, went to a public school, and had a non-English last name. I received a scholarship of $1000, my parents put in $1000, and I had to earn $1000 per year for a total of $3,000. It now costs $78,200 per year to attend Harvard College. I graduated from college with no debt to pay off, so I was then free to do whatever fancied me the most.

My classmates at Harvard included a 17th generation of Lowells who had attended Harvard, Theodore Roosevelt, IV, and many others with "proper" backgrounds. There were a few African American students and some foreigners including a few Africans. During my first weeks at Harvard – I went 10 days early to help clean dormitory rooms in order to help pay my share – I must have been told fifty times that now I had entered the elite world of Harvard students that were superior to other people (including people from Yale) and were destined to rule the United States and the world.

I didn't believe a word of this superiority complex. I realized that my fellow students were not much different from the students I had attended high school with, some who did not end up going to college at all and many who went to local public colleges. As you can surmise, I didn't feel that I fit in.

I had no difficulty with the academics – some of those private school graduates, including one of my roommates my freshman year, were as lazy as they could be without flunking out. I hardly ever missed a class because I calculated how much each class cost of that $3000 and didn't want to miss what I was paying for. My Mom was disapproving when I told her that I had gone to Goodwill and spent $15 to buy a second-hand coat because at Harvard we had to wear a coat for all meals and it would spoil the nice blue suit my parents had bought me when I went off to college.

My expectation of not becoming one of America's ruling elite was due to something that happened just before I graduated from high school. I was born on May 6 and during my senior year in high school, just before I graduated but after I knew I was accepted to Harvard, I had to sign up for the draft. One spring sunny summer day as I walked across Shaw Park from my high school to register for the draft, I realized that I couldn't kill anyone and, although I didn't know anything about it, I signed up to be a conscientious objector (CO).

At least I didn't remember that I knew anything about conscientious objection. My Mom's second cousin, Dan Suits, had been a CO during WWII. (He later became a Quaker, an economist, and a member of Ann Arbor Meeting). Since he and his five brothers grew up in St. Louis, I may have met him when I was a child. If so, I don't remember him. I do remember that his parents, Hollis and Dorothy Suite, and our family often had dinner together either at our house or their house. My Mom had told me about Dan, stating that she respected his decision to be a CO, but that she did not agree with it because the United States had to defeat fascism. My parents did not express any reservations to me about being a CO.

The 1950s and early 1960s when I grew up were the height of hysterical anti-communism. The minister of the Episcopal Church I attended would sometimes preach on how we should kill the godless communists, which wasn't what I was reading in the New Testament. If I were a conscientious objector, I realized that I would never be a part of the establishment, but a non-conformist outside the mainstream of American life. This was fine with me, even at 18 years old. Looking back, I am satisfied that I realized this at 18 rather than much later when much of the "damage" would have been done.

In 1961, which was well before the Vietnam War interest in conscientious objection, the only people who were given that status were Quakers, Amish, Mennonite, and Church of the Brethren members. My Episcopal Church was hardly a recommendation for CO status. In those days, to become a CO, one had to fill out a detailed questionnaire to "prove" that you were sincere and not just a "chicken" afraid to die for your beloved country.

I realized that I needed to study up. Somehow lost in the mist of my memory, I went to the Book Nook bookstore in town and found Leo Tolstoy's *The Kingdom of God is Within You*. The first chapter includes a discussion of the pacifism of the British Quakers. Since I am now better informed, I recently re-read this chapter and I see that it is not particularly accurate. Yet it was good enough for me to decide to attend the Friends Meeting at Cambridge. I was hooked from the first time I went. No problems with the pacifism, simplicity, equality, and so on. I had already determined these values on my own.

I joined a Quaker meeting for a very bad reason. In 1971 I moved to Pittsburgh and with my then wife, Rodah, began attending Pittsburgh Meeting. When she became pregnant, I remembered that, if the child were a birth-right Quaker, it would be easier for him (if the child were a boy) to become a CO. We applied to become members and were accepted. I have been a member/attendee of Pittsburgh, Rockland, Yellow Springs, Bethesda, St. Louis, and Lumakanda Friends Meetings.

In the end, my Clayton draft board did accept me as a conscientious objector. In 1968 I was in Kenya, starting the Mua Hills Harambee Secondary School. The military sent me a notice to attend a medical induction in Italy so that I could be assigned to alternative service. Wow, what should I do? By this time my sister, Arlene, who was a student at Swarthmore College, was a draft counselor. She advised me to wait until the day of the appointment and then send a letter saying that I would be unable to attend. By the time they would respond I would be 26 years old and no longer subject to military alternative service.

I never heard from them again.

*****

48

[Note: Excerpt from American Friends Service Committee, *Acting in Faith,* April 12, 2016.]

And Jesus said to them, "Render to Caesar the things that are Caesar's, and to God the things that are God's."

— Mark 12:17

While most people have interpreted this verse from the New Testament to indicate that they are required to pay taxes to the government, I have a different interpretation. In 1961 when I turned eighteen, I applied to become a conscientious objector to military service. I did not feel that I should participate in killing other human beings. Shortly thereafter I realized that it would be hypocritical, if I was unwilling to do it myself, to pay others to kill on my behalf. This passage says to me: I must first give to God that which belongs to God. The New Testament clearly states that we ought to love our enemies. When Caesar demands that I should participate in activities contrary to God's will, then it is my duty to put God first and resist Caesar.

When Jesus was walking and preaching in Galilee and up to Jerusalem, people believed in many gods. There were family gods, town/village gods, and other local gods. But the greatest god was Caesar himself who was a god with temples, statues, and obligations to Roman imperial power – much like our reverence for the United States where we pledge allegiance and support with our taxes. In those days some Jews and early Christian got into trouble because they would not participate in the worship of that Caesar god.

With about fifty years of war tax resistance (WTR) activities, during which my life situation and the tax code has changed, I have had many experiences and I AM STILL ALIVE. When I talk to people about WTR, I find that many of them fear Caesar (the IRS) like an all-knowing, all-seeing god. The reality is that the IRS is a mess and the first rule in dealing with them is to make a copy of all documents you sent to them and take them with you when you visit their office since they probably can't find a good number of them. Let me review some of my experiences.

During the Vietnam War, there was a 3% telephone tax to support that military aggression. At that point this was the main war tax I was required to pay – I resisted it. I did not feel that I should voluntarily pay for this war making and it was important for me to resist even if interest and penalties were added. After a few years, the Internal Revenue Service (IRS) placed a levy on my wages for $39 for resisted taxes, interest, and penalties.

It is clear that it cost the IRS more than $39 to collect this tax so in a sense I took some additional funds from the war-making machine. I also kept exact records of my resisted telephone tax each month and my calculations were that at that point I owed them $84 in resisted telephone tax. In other words that almighty Caesar failed to collect about $50 that I owed. As my war tax resistance continued, I found that frequently they did not collect the amounts that they were legally entitled to. This meant that to some extent my resistance was financially successful in keeping the government from getting what they demanded from me.

I always gave away my resisted war taxes to life-enhancing organizations which, naturally, included many Quaker ones — these organizations benefited from my resistance. One year, due to a quirk of life and the tax code, I resisted over $6,000 and gave it all to worthy organizations – usually it was more like $300 (in my early years) to $1500.

At times I had a regular salaried job and I resisted the war-related part of the taxes which in the 1970's was about 33% for current and past wars as calculated by the War Resister League each year — now it is closer to 50% as the American Empire has expanded at the expense of domestic needs.

For three years in a row, I was called in by the IRS for a tax audit. Since my income and tax returns were simple – I didn't make that much money – this was no problem. I was told that this was a randomly generated audit, but then the only other tax resister I knew at that time in Pittsburgh, Marian Hahn, was always called in for an audit at the same time. The second year the agent I met with wanted to disallow one of my deductions which I was clearly entitled to. I filed for a hearing on the issue. The hearing lasted about 30 seconds since the IRS agent at the hearing immediately realized that I was correct. Then after the IRS audited me two years in a row with no change and wanted to audit me for the third year, I showed them the IRS regulation that they couldn't audit me for the third year. I walked out of the office without being audited. I realized that the IRS did not have godlike qualities.

One year when I was audited, I went in and the IRS agent was clearly quite tense. As soon as I told her that I was a war tax resister, she relaxed. Since my letter on why I was resisting war taxes was not in my file, I had to give her my copy for her to duplicate for my IRS file. After she read it, she asked to be excused and went out of the room for about five minutes. She then came in and asked me if I would be willing to write a check to the Department of Health, Education, and Welfare in lieu of one to the IRS.

I had ten seconds to think and made one of the greatest mistakes of my peacemaking career. I said, "No." While this is illegal, I should have said "yes" to see what would have happened with my check and if it would have been credited to my tax liability. If this had worked, there never would have been the need for the National Campaign for a Peace

50

Tax Fund for us war tax conscientious objectors. I think there are sufficient court cases that determine that this cannot be legally done.

About 1983 I was assessed a $500 frivolous fine for not paying the amount I owed and sending in a letter of explanation. When I told my ten-year-old son, Tommy, about this, his reaction was "You are going to lose." I asked why and he replied, "The government pays the judges." My case was taken up by the Pittsburgh ACLU, consolidated with similar cases in Philadelphia, went to court, and we all lost as Tommy predicted.

About this time, I attended the organizing meeting for the National War Tax Resistance Coordinating Committee (NWTRCC) and was its treasurer for a number of years. It is a great organization for those resisting or considering resisting war taxes.

Later I realized that even if I paid some taxes to the IRS, they would still take 33% to 50% of what I paid for war-making. I sometimes lived below the taxable income, stopped filing, and worked as an independent contractor. My contact with the IRS then diminished considerably, although I would sometimes get letters from them in Spanish because I lived in a neighborhood outside of DC with many Latino neighbors.

I always paid my state taxes and gave away my resisted war taxes so that I received no private financial benefit from my resistance.

Now I live in Kenya and I am so below the taxable income that it is embarrassing. The taxable income for someone living overseas is in excess of $70,000, a fortune for my modest income and living standard. The IRS did attach a savings account for some back taxes they say I owed. Since the savings interest rate was .05%, this amounted to about 25 cents per year (again costing them more to collect than they did collect). Nonetheless I closed the savings account. The IRS has also attached 15% of my social security benefits for a past tax liability – I do not know why. I have asked the IRS for an explanation, but they have never responded.

My resistance has not curtailed the expansion of the US military-industrial complex, but that is not why I am a war tax resister. I resist because I don't want to participate in killing people, directly or indirectly. I have lived the life as I wanted to live without letting the IRS god determine my choices. Quaker simplicity has surely helped out a lot in my resistance.

Let me end with a joke, sort of. I was once at a NWTRCC meeting and a young couple of war tax resisters announced that they were getting married but would have no children because they didn't want their children to have to "suffer" from their war tax resistance. Wow, I didn't realize that my kids might be suffering from my resistance. Fortunately for my children, they had already been born and I couldn't put them back in the womb.

I don't think my children, or even I myself, have suffered a bit because of my war tax resistance. In fact, it has made me a more caring, compassionate person since I realized that I shouldn't aspire to making a large income. It also keeps me aware that I was an outsider to the so-called "American Dream" as a non-participant in America's war making that sustains American affluence. Moreover, there is no doubt that my involvement in peacemaking in East Africa is the flip side to my war tax resistance — I not only need to oppose militarism but work to restore peace and reconciliation to places that have been beset by violence and war.

****

I didn't want to be cloistered in the Harvard College bubble. Phillips Brooks House was a student-run social service agency founded in 1900. I quickly signed up as a volunteer and was assigned once a week in the afternoon to tutor high school students at a settlement house in Cambridge, the hometown of Harvard College. I continued this for my first three years at Harvard. In my third year I also volunteered for a project at a Roxbury public school that gave away free paperback books to elementary school students.

Two of my fellow volunteers in this project were Alison Liebhafsky Des Forges (later to become the major researcher for Human Rights Watch on the 1994 Rwandan genocide) and Karen Weisskopf Worth. As participants in a Phillips Brooks House program called Volunteer Teachers for Africa, they had spent the previous summer teaching Rwandan refugees in northwestern Tanzania. They encouraged me to apply which I did.

The placement was for a year so I would need to take a year off from college. I was accepted but, since I was then only twenty years old and the age of maturity was then twenty-one years, I had to get the permission of my parents. My Mom sent me a most encouraging response of approval.

I was so grateful for this warm approval. It is only later when I was organizing work camps for the African Great Lakes Initiative that I realized that even in the Twentieth-First century many parents will not agree to have their child go off to Africa. My Dad was accepting with the proviso that I come back after the year off and finish my last year at Harvard. I agreed to this, although I have to admit that this last year at college after my year of adventures in Tanzania was the most difficult year of my life.

I was assigned for the year to teach Rwandan refugees at Muyenzi Refugee Camp in northwestern Tanzania and was paired with Randy Kehler, who later became noted for being a war resister (he sent two years in jail for protesting the Vietnam War), the founding director of the Nuclear Freeze Campaign, and then led a large resistance after his house was seized by the IRS for resisting war taxes.

I considered this a great opportunity to see another part of the world. I wanted to see how people in a remote part of the world lived – that is, remote from the worlds of Clayton and Cambridge. How were they the same? How were they different?

Yet there were deeper questions I wanted to consider. What values did I have that were important, core ones that I could not give up without giving up myself? What values were just superficial characteristics I had picked up while growing up and were not essential to my personhood? I have to admit that after my so safe cultural upbringing, there was a sense of adventure, a sense of wanting to see the unknown, and to discover those places difficult for me to imagine.

****

As I expected, the fourteen months I spent teaching Rwandan refugees in Muzenzi Refugee Camp in northwest Tanzania were adventurous. Halfway through the year, the UN High Commission for Refugees cut off the rations to the refugees. This led to a famine in the camp and half of my students migrated elsewhere. I have written an un-published book on this called *The Unnecessary Famine,* but I don't think I can insert it into this article. While I sent it out to a number of publishers, I didn't receive even a nibble. I think that this was because, unlike so many books I have read about personal experiences in Africa, my book did not come with the tone of the White knight coming to rescue the primitive Africans from their precarious existence.

After I finished college, I decided to return to the Tanzania by joining the US Peace Corps. I was accepted into a settlement scheme program and was trained for 13 weeks at Syracuse University. Here I learned Swahili.

At that time in order to be in the Peace Corps one had to sign a loyalty oath. I had already decided that I would refuse to sign and see what the consequences would be. We were told that we would be given the oath on our plane ride over to Tanzania. This never happened to I don't know what would have been the result of this refusal.

At the Rwamkoma Settlement Scheme where I was posted, the camp director was stealing money in every possible way. When the assistant director and I went to the local chief to report on what was happening, the Peace Corps (quite correctly, I think) pulled me out of that placement. I have to admit that I was happy to leave such a negative situation.

This was in 1968 and by this time, relations between the US government and the Tanzanian government were nose-diving. The reason for this is hard to believe these days. The country of Tanganyika had recognized West Germany and the then independent island of Zanzibar had recognized East Germany. When the two countries united to become Tanzania, President Nyerere decided to recognize both East and West Germany. This was verboten to the US government and the relations deteriorated. Among other things, no new Peace Corps volunteers were assigned to Tanzania. As a result, the Peace Corps moved me to Kenya.

In Kenya I finished up my last eight months teaching math at a secondary school. In the meantime, I had run into one of the teachers from my Peace Corps training, Kivuto Ndeti, who asked me to start a *harambee* (self-help) high school in his home in the Mua Hills. This I did starting in September 1968 with school opening in January 1969. I was headmaster of that school for the next two years. After I left, the school became the Mua Hills Girls Secondary School. It is classified as a national school in the highest category of secondary schools in Kenya.

In May 1969, I married Rodah Wayua Malinda, a local woman from the Mua Hills. By this time, it was difficult for a white foreigner to be principal of a school, so I resigned and became a trainer for a Peace Corps group. Rodah wanted to go to the United States and I knew it would be difficult for me to find adequate employment in Kenya. We moved to the US in December 1970.

After returning to the United States, I got a job at the University of Pittsburgh designing a computer assisted math primary school program. As a side benefit, this allowed me at minimal cost to get a master's degree in International Development and Education.

Beginning in 1972, one interesting endeavor I participated in was the Pittsburgh Quaker Community where I was the founding treasurer for the first six years. We borrowed funds from the older, established members of Pittsburgh Friends Meeting, for a down payment on a large, old Victorian house in a transitional area of Pittsburgh. We then rented out the rooms to six people connected with the meeting.

After a year or two the Pittsburgh Quaker Community bought a second house across the street from the first. This one had a room on the first floor which we turned into a bedroom for elderly members of the meeting so that this became an intergenerational house. Three members/attenders of the meeting also bought houses nearby – our house was about a mile away. Addition a few more people rented apartments nearby. When we bought the houses, we had numerous work parties to clean up and paint them. There was a weekly potluck.

Within five years we had paid off the members of the meeting. At the time this housing project was significant and helpful. As Alida Harris, one of the elderly residents, said, "I don't want to go into a retirement home because I want to be around young people." A couple of marriages resulted from this project. I was no longer in Pittsburgh when the Pittsburgh Quaker Community was laid down. The houses were sold and netted the meeting about $50,000 in profit – a lot for those days. I understand its interest is still being used to sponsor Pittsburgh Quakers to attend Quaker meetings and conferences.

With the East End Cooperative Ministries, I was Principal of the Penn Circle Community High School for two years. It was an alternative high school in those chaotic but exciting times. Since it depended upon VISTA volunteers for its teaching staff, it was always precarious and lasted about fifteen years. Likewise, I helped found a group home for six teenage girls. It was later bought by a larger organization with many group homes and they changed it to a group home for boys.

In 1977, after Black activist Steve Biko died from injuries suffered while in a South African prison, I became involved with the anti-apartheid movement. I worked through Pittsburgh Meetings' Peace Center.

From 1980 to 1984 I was treasurer of Lake Erie Yearly Meeting (LEYM) which had its account at Pittsburgh National Bank (then PNC). In 1982, I think, South Africa's economy was going bankrupt and a consortium of American banks including PNC bailed out South Africa with massive loans. I wrote a letter to PNC objecting to their participation in this bailout and said that LEYM would remove the yearly meeting account to another bank. I circulated copies of the letter as widely as I could. It was well received by the membership of LEYM, but the clerk of the yearly meeting gave me a dressing down by not following "proper Quaker procedure." I took the "heat" but knew that some things were more important than "proper Quaker procedure."

In 1985 I was arrested protesting apartheid in front of the South Africa embassy in DC. Shortly thereafter I arranged a US speaking tour for Jackie Williams, a colored South African associated with Archbishop Desmond Tutu. This was a prelude to the many speaking tours that beginning in 2002 I, as Coordinator for the African Great Lakes Initiative, arranged for East African activists to publicize their peace work in the US and Canada.'

I was also very involved with my children, Joy and Tommy. I coached their baseball and soccer (both outdoor and indoor) teams for years. When Tommy entered second grade at the local racially mixed elementary school, there were four reading classes based on ability. They were named after birds. Although Tommy was then reading the comics and sports pages of the newspaper, the teacher put him in the lowest group. This group consisted of only African American boys. It was called the "Blackbirds".

To me the racism was blatant. I went in and complained to the teacher. She "promoted" him to the second from bottom group. I was not satisfied so I complained to the principal and Tommy was placed in the second from the top group.

I separated from my wife, Rodah, in 1985. In order to create QFT, "quality family time," as Joy called it, in the summer of 1986, Joy, Tommy, and I drove across the country from New York to California and back, taking six weeks. I had an old Dodge Ram van and we put mattresses to sleep on and agreed to eat at McDonalds no more than once every two days. We mostly ate peanut butter and jelly sandwiches and fruits.

Each day I would get up as the sun rose during the long summer days, drive to the next site under Tommy's assessment from the maps, spend the day sightseeing, and then drove some more in the evening before dark and slept in rest stops which you were then allowed to do in the west in those days. It was a great, memorable adventure.

As the kids grew older and went to college, they would work with me in my home repair business during the summers. Joy became great as a painter and Tommy did a better job of cleaning up than I would usually do myself.

In 1985 I left Pittsburgh to become the Business Manager of the Fellowship of Reconciliation in Nyack, New York. I visited Nyack for interviews, and in the final interview, I said the organization was sexist and racist. I thought this ended my chances of being hired, but they hired me anyway. I assumed they wanted me to work on correcting these inequalities. Two Quakers who had previously worked for the Fellowship of Reconciliation (FOR) told me that, since it was a mainstream, paternalistic Protestant organization, it was difficult for Quakers to survive in its environment.

They were correct. I lasted less than two years. While the organization gave lip-service to sexual and racial equality, when I implemented programs to rectify this, I lost the hierarchy's support and was dismissed.

One of my responsibilities at the FOR was to take care of the massive 44-room mansion where it was housed. I soon realized that the people I hired to repair the building were making much more money than I was. Moreover, their time was much more flexible.

When I left the FOR, I needed to earn income and started working with the group I had formerly hired. This turned into my main income source for the next twenty years: repairing houses. Whenever I moved to a new place, I would stand up in Quaker meeting and announce, "Does anyone need their house repaired?"

I never ran out of work. I started charging $10 per hour and, when I ended this and moved to Kenya, I was charging $50 per hour. As my son, Tommy, complained to me, I was undercharging since this kind of work usually cost $100 per hour. Once my Mom commented that I was doing this repair work "between jobs." I corrected her saying, "No, this was my job." Clearly my Harvard education was not a prerequisite for this work.

While I easily earned enough to live on in my simple style, the great advantage for me in the home repair business was the flexibility. After I left the FOR in Nyack, NY, a friend told me that Yellow Springs, OH, was as near as possible to the Garden of Eden in the US. So, I moved there for a little over two years. One interesting activity I did was to teach the introduction to writing and English literature at Lebanon Prison as part of Wilmington College, Ohio, a Quaker college sponsored by Wilmington Yearly Meeting.

In 1988, I moved to Montgomery County, Maryland, and moved my membership to Bethesda Friends Meeting.

In 1989, Joy and Tommy suggested we do another QFT (quality family time) adventure. At this point my old friend from my Harvard African experience, Randy Kehler, and his wife, Betsy Corner, were having their house seized for failure to pay federal income taxes as they opposed warmaking. There was a constant vigil to keep their house from being repossessed.

I suggested to Joy and Tommy that we could go there for a week and be part of an affinity group from the Washington, DC, area. To my surprise, they agreed. I think it was because they knew Randy and liked him very much. It was a nice week.

One of the adventures I had in 1996 was to spend a month in Boligee, Alabama, helping to rebuild three of the 145 Black churches that had been destroyed by arsonists. The following summer Tommy and I went to South Carolina for a week to help rebuild another burnt Black church.

In 1993 I met Quaker singer Susan Stark whom I had known from Lake Erie Yearly Meeting. I then began distributing her musical tapes for her. Bethesda Meeting also nominated me to the support committee for Patricia Loring's release from Bethesda Meeting to write her two books called *Listening Spirituality*. In 1995 I connected with Annette Breiling who wanted to start a Quaker school. I joined her as Chair of the Board of Friends Meeting School. We found an ideal 55-acre lot in Ijamville, Maryland, in next door Frederick County and began classes in 1997. I resigned in 2000 when I moved to St. Louis. The school now goes from kindergarten through high school.

I met Gladys Kamonya, my present wife, at Bethesda Meeting in the summer of 1995. She was taking care of the two children of a doctor couple. The wife was of Indian descent from Kenya and her mother had recruited Gladys to take care of the children. They were attending Sidwell Friends School summer camp and she saw the sign, Bethesda Friends Meeting (Quakers) which met on the Sidwell School campus.

Since she was raised as a Kenyan Quaker, she decided to attend the meeting. When Sunday came, she got all dressed up in the usual Kenyan Sunday best and arrived at meeting at 7:00 AM — as they do in Kenya.

No one was there. Fortunately, it was a nice day, so she sat there alone for about two more hours, then went home.

Gladys went again the next Sunday at the correct time. I was not there that day. Mary Holmes, a member of the meeting, whose husband had served in the 1960s in the US embassy in Kenya, talked with her.

She asked Gladys if she had any family in the DC area. Gladys said, "No." She asked if she had any relatives in the United States and Gladys again responded, "No." Mary, who has told me this story numerous times, then commiserated with Gladys with not having any family around. Gladys response was, "But you (Quakers) are my family." Mary thought that was so cute.

This actually indicates a profound difference between Kenyans and Americans. When I once gave a talk at Baltimore Yearly Meeting and related this story, I then asked, "Could you go to Kenya and meet the Quakers there and consider them your family?" I was told by someone in attendance that this was not well received.

Gladys and I married in November 1999 under the care of Sandy Spring Meeting. At that time, I was clerk of the Seneca Valley Worship Group under the care of Sandy Spring Meeting. It was a traditional silent Quaker marriage with somewhat over 100 people attending. Lowell Christy made sure that we had goat (the favorite meat of Kenyans) for the potluck after the wedding.

My Dad had died in St. Louis in January 1999 when I was in Rwanda. My Mom who has Alzheimer's was put in a nursing home, but she needed attention and care. So, in May 2000 Gladys and I moved to St. Louis to help out. As usual I stood up in meeting there and asked if anyone needed their house fixed. I also renovated the third floor of the World Community Center, the office of most of the peace/justice organizations in St. Louis. And I bought three run-down houses and renovated them.

[Note: By 2007, Dave's mother had died, and the couple gathered their resources and soon built a house in Lukamanda in western Kenya. Dave has lived and pursued his ministry of peace work there ever since. He notes that in the U.S., their house and its comforts would be considered modest, barely middle class; in Kenya he and Gladys are "rich." This is one of many sharp contrasts that have been driven home for him in his U.S. — Kenyan odyssey. Others, as shown below, have to do with the Quakerism both countries have, at least superficially, "in common."]

****

[Abridged From October 2019 issue of *Friends Journal,* "Life at Lumakanda Friends Church]

My wife, Gladys Kamonya, a Kenyan, and I, an American, are members of both Bethesda Meeting of Baltimore Yearly Meeting and Lumakanda Friends Church of Lugari Yearly Meeting. When you look at the Friends World Committee for Consultation's (FWCC) total of Friends worldwide, be sure to subtract two from their total since we are counted twice.

I must admit that I prefer the silent, unprogrammed worship of Bethesda Meeting. On the other hand, as a child, my parents sent me to an Episcopal Church. The programmed worship of that church with singing, prayers, preaching, offering, announcements, marriages, and funerals, was similar to Lumakanda Friends Church. Both sing the same songs: "Stand Up, Stand Up for Jesus;" "Onward Christian Soldiers;" "Rock of Ages" (for funerals); and all the same Christmas carols. The difference is that most of the songs here are sung in Swahili.

The differences between the Quaker church and other churches, though, are important. One major difference is that there are many female Quaker preachers in Kenya, contrary to the other churches in the area. During the 2008 post-election violence, 32 pastors – all male – asked Friends Church Peace Teams (Kenya) to conduct a peace seminar at the local internally displaced people's camp. Three of its four presenters were women. This astounded those pastors who commented, "We didn't know women could preach so well." Women preach at Lumakanda one, two, or even three times per month. Gladys's sister, Josephine Kemoli, is the pastor at Pendo Village Meeting, one of Lumakanda Friends Church's village meetings.

Long ago, I learned that theology is quite fluid and changeable while church structure is usually not. Consequently, the Quaker structure is similar everywhere and has not changed much since the original Quaker missionaries came in 1902. There are yearly meetings, quarterly meetings, and monthly meetings. In Kenya, there are village meetings under the monthly meetings because a church needs to be within walking distance of the parishioners. Lumakanda's monthly meeting is composed of four village meetings. We attend the local Lumakanda Village Meeting which is about three blocks from our house.

Much of the teeth-gnashing about membership decline that happens among American Quakers sounds strange in Kenya. Lumakanda Village Meeting has over 600 members or official attendees including over 200 children. The Sunday school, where we send our six grandgeneration children, has 60 to 80 younger children attend every Sunday.

There is another class for the older primary school students. High school students mostly attend the service.

To join the Quaker church each person has to join a study class called "Book One" and "Book Two," which lasts about an hour with instruction after service each Sunday for a year. When a person moves through these two years of study, he or she becomes a member. Every year there are about six to ten people in each class.

In contrast to the United States and Britain, the Quaker Church in Kenya is growing. Likewise, as the church is filled with younger people, there is no worry about the church being attended only by old people.

About 100 people attend the morning village meeting service every Sunday. There are three rows of benches facing the podium; there is no altar as in other Christian churches. The women mostly sit on the left side and the men mostly on the right side. The younger people tend to sit in the middle. Gladys and I are unusual in that we sit together in the middle row. After twelve years in the church, I know many of the people, but because husbands and wives sit on opposite sides, even when I know both, I may not realize that they are married.

In addition to Sunday school, the church is divided up into three groups: (1) Young Friends — which includes people from 18 to 35 years of age, the age range American Friends would call "young adult Friends," (2) United Society of Friends Women (USFW), and (3) Quakermen. Each group has its own officers, as do the village meeting and monthly. Elections are every two years, and when the new officers are introduced, the front of the church is overflowing with them. They are then approved by the congregation, welcomed, and blessed with a prayer.

Fundraising for the church and its activities is multifold. There is an offering each Sunday that does not produce much, usually about $20 to $25. Then there is the monthly ten percent tithing that raises significantly more. There are also specific fundraisers called *harambee*, meaning "let us pull together." This is used for many purposes for example to fill the allocation due to Lugari Yearly Meeting; to make some improvements to the church (this year they are tiling the floor which will cost over $2000); special fundraisers for people in need such as a student from a poorer family that needs school fees; medical expenses; to build or repair a house of a member, and so on.

A few years ago, a well-liked pastor, Edward Muluya, wanted to get a master's degree in theology. He needed $900 for the tuition. The church conducted a *harambee* for him and in one day they received $1120. They gave him the extra for books and travel.

Another interesting fundraising method is that when the bean harvest and later the maize (corn) harvest come in, farmers are encouraged to make an in-kind donation. Members give up to a 200-pound bag of maize so that the whole front of the church is filled. The harvest is then sold to support the church. Another time the church collected clothes for those parents and grandparents of limited means who were raising children or grandchildren.

Like meetings and churches in the United States, Lumakanda Friends Church rents out its space; since it is one of the largest halls in Lumakanda, this happens often. Another income-generating activity the church began some years ago was purchasing 100 plastic chairs (rented out at ten U.S. cents per day) and a tent to hold 100 people (rented out at $20 per day) to anyone who needs these for weddings, funerals, or other celebrations. Last year, after raising the capital through a *harambee*, the church put up three metal kiosks at the end of their property and now rents them out for $20 per month each. They are now planning to buy a fourth kiosk.

A major activity of the church is to arrange for weddings and funerals. When this happens, the church appoints a committee which makes the arrangements for the event. Part of their charge is to raise about $2000. Of course, the families involved contribute their share, but everyone in the church donates what they can. For a funeral, the amount needed includes the medical expenses that the deceased incurred before dying. The largest expense I have seen is $20,000 for a prominent Quaker woman who had to be air-evacuated to Nairobi before she died. In the United States, almost half the population cannot afford a $400 emergency expense. Here at Lumakanda Friends Church, everyone can "afford" a $400 expense because the church membership will raise the funds. Since Gladys knows the situation better than I, she is the one who decides and makes the contributions for both of us. We want to pay our fair share, but don't want the church to become dependent on us. So far this has worked out well.

Lumakanda Quakers never discuss or worry about community, but the church is clearly a community. Since everyone lives near the town, there are frequently out-of-church interactions. We hire church members when we need some service: three members, for example, are veterinarians; another does Gladys's hair; the clerk of the meeting cares for our bushes and trees; another has a team of oxen we hire when we need to carry sand, stone, or firewood.

As can be surmised from the description above, Lumakanda Quakers are firmly middle class. Many own plots of land. Since this is in a settlement scheme area, people were allocated about 20 acres of land which now sells at $7500 per acre. When we built our house, we bought a very large tree for $250 from the then-clerk of USFW. This was sufficient to make all the rafters we needed for our house. Many church members are teachers, nurses, police, small business owners, and town property rental owners. Others are retired Friends who worked in places like Nairobi and have now returned to their plots near Lumakanda.

What do I not like? Every five years there are elections in Kenya. Then politicians come to the church and to funerals, where up to 1000 people can be gathered, and, for a small donation, are allowed to make a campaign speech.

I am not the only one who is appalled by this activity. Moreover, in some cases this politicking divides the church into opposing sides: there have been yearly meeting splits in Kenya over politics.

Another issue is that almost everyone in the church is of one tribe called the Luhya. Tribalism is the racism of Kenya and people can be intolerant. One wedding included a large contingent of relatives and friends from a different tribe, but the pastor spoke in the Luhya language for over fifteen minutes, erroneously conveying that Quakers are only Luhya. While Lumakanda Friends Church is fairly well gender-balanced, this is not true of Kenyan society as a whole nor of the Quakers at the yearly meeting level, which is almost exclusively male-dominated.

Although there are three Asian Indians who work at a local quarry, I am the only *mzungu* (stranger, white person) in town. So, if you come to visit, in order to find our house, all you have to do is ask, "Where does the *mzungu* live?" I have been here for over twelve years, so at the church I am just part of the scenery. If I am treated in any special way, it is not because I am a *mzungu* but because I am elderly.

As Americans who come to Kenya comment, Kenyans are always friendly and welcoming. In Swahili, the word *mgeni* means both "stranger" and "guest." As is traditional for grandparents at this time, we are taking care of three grandchildren (ages 3, 6, and 6), a grandniece (5), and two grandnephews (both 11). One of our daughters-in-law, the mother of two of these children, lives with us also.

Half the world's Quakers live in East Africa. I find that the division of Friends World Committee for Consultation into continents means that American unprogrammed Friends know little about Quakerism in Africa and do not visit at nearly the rate of FUM and Evangelical American Friends. FWCC Section of the Americas has a great inter-visitation program for the Americans but this excludes Africa. I think this oversight should be addressed. Kenyan Friends will welcome visitors with their usual warm hospitality. Unprogrammed American Friends would greatly benefit from such an interaction.

[End of *Friends Journal* article.]

When Gladys and I first came to live in Kenya in 2007, I thought of Lumakanda Friends Church as a "tired" church as it was led mostly by the elderly. This has changed in the last twelve years as there has been a concerted effort to have a younger leadership in the church. This means a movement from people in their 60s, 70s, and even 80s to those in their 40s and 50s. This has led to a much more lively church with increased activity, more energy, and a yearly improvement to the church property. The Young Friends Association for people 18 to 35 years old are still mostly excluded from the leadership in the church and there seems to be little interest or effort to include them. This, though, is a reflection of the larger Kenyan society at this time.

****

I have had decades of experience with Quakers in Africa. According to the Friends World Committee for Consultation–World, in 2017 Kenya, at 119,285 **adult** members and increasing, had the largest number of Quakers in the world. Burundi had 47,600, Rwanda 6,000, Uganda 1,040, Tanzania 3,100, and Democratic Republic of the Congo 4,220. Altogether Africa had 49.45 percent of the world's Quakers. The yearly meetings in Kenya, Tanzania, and Uganda are affiliated with Friends United Meeting, while those in Burundi, Rwanda and eastern Congo are affiliated with Evangelical Friends Alliance. Once at a Quaker conference in Burundi, I was asked to give a twenty-minute presentation on the four major varieties of Friends in the United States. The first comment I received from my presentation was, "I really don't understand the differences you are talking about, but can you American Quakers keep your disagreements in America and not bring them to Africa?" (This is not an exact quote but the gist of the comment as I remember it.)

Some Snippets:

Once I attended the three-hour long service at Kagarama Friends Church in Kigali, the "mother church" in Rwanda. It was not boring at all. Two thirds of it was entertainment with a little kids 'choir, an older children's choir, another for teenagers, a young adults' choir, the normal adult choir, a visiting choir, a praise and worship group, and a traditional young women's dance group. The church was packed with people, most of whom were children or young people. There were not even enough adults to be the parents of all the children. I was one of the few elderly people in attendance.

Another time I was at Kamenge Friends Church in Bujumbura, the largest church in Burundi. It was packed with 700 people for the service. Children were crowding in all the windows and doors to get a peek at the service. Since this church was above capacity, they have built a new church including a balcony around the old church and then removed the old inside church. I estimate it can hold 2000 people. It may be the biggest Quaker church/meeting house in the world.

In the old days it was American and British missionaries who brought Quakerism to East Africa. Today it is particularly the Kenyan Quakers who are expanding Quakerism in the region.

Due to the fact that the Quaker missionaries stressed education even before Kenyan independence, there are about 750 Quaker-sponsored primary school and 250 secondary schools, including some of the best secondary schools in Kenya. During the 1950s and 1960s there were about 200 Quaker missionaries, many retired British teachers who staffed the burgeoning Quaker educational establishment. The result is that many Kenyan Quakers have employment in substantial occupations.

Do not think that Kenyan Quakers are poor. For example, the new Donholm Friends Church in a not particularly well-off section of Nairobi is costing $175,000 and most of the funding is being raised by the local Quakers. The United Society of Friends Women (USFW) is developing a massive center near Kakamega, collecting the funds annually from that very strong Quaker women's organization. While most Kenyan Quakers are solidly middle class, this is not quite as true in Rwanda, Burundi, Uganda, Tanzania and eastern Congo. Note, though, that one Quaker businessman in Bujumbura, Burundi (one of the poorest countries in the world), gave a donation of $50,000 to build Rohero Friends Church which cost over $100,000.

This is not to say that everything is perfect. The leadership at the yearly meeting level is almost exclusively male and elderly. This is partly due to the reverence given by paternalistic Kenyan culture to the elderly, particularly males. To be called an *mzee,* old man in Swahili, is a term of endearment, not abuse. The first female yearly meeting presiding clerk in all those Kenyan yearly meetings was just appointed a few years ago. It has only been recently that yearly meeting officers retired at the end of their two or three three-year terms to be replaced by someone new. Previously they had stayed on and on until they became too old or died or were ousted after bitter in-fighting, or worse, after yearly meeting splits.

****

As I mentioned above, the Quaker church is the leader in Kenya for female pastors. Like Quakers throughout the world, East African Quakers are also acknowledged as the leader in peacemaking. Much of this has to do with the terrible violence in the region – the genocide in Rwanda, the civil wars in Burundi, the fighting in eastern Congo, Joseph

Kony's Lord's Resistance Army in Uganda, and post-election violence in Kenya.

In 1998 when I was one of Baltimore Yearly Meeting's representatives to Friends Peace Teams, I suggested that we ought to visit the Quakers in East Africa to see what peacemaking activities they were doing in this region of much violence. This was approved and in January 1999 a delegation of seven people visited the Quakers in Kenya, Uganda, Rwanda, Burundi, and North and South Kivu in the Congo. The delegation found that the Quakers were much involved in peacemaking work, particularly in Rwanda, Burundi, and eastern Congo.

To the shame of all varieties of American and English Quakers, we also learned that they were not getting mentoring or support for this peace work from American/British Quakers. This mentoring and support were being provided by the Mennonite Central Committee. We asked the African Quakers if they would like to partner with Friends Peace Teams and this led to the development of the African Great Lakes Initiative (AGLI).

The first joint endeavor was to introduce Alternatives to Violence Project (AVP) in the region. AVP continues to be quite successful in the area.

Quaker peace leaders in Rwanda and Burundi told me that both these countries needed individual and societal trauma healing from their conflicts. In 2003, with the support of the American Friends Service Committee, a one-month seminar and training on trauma healing and reconciliation was conducted in Kigali, Rwanda. This led to the development of the Healing and Rebuilding Our Communities (HROC) program.

While the experiential methodology was similar to AVP, the content was quite different. Twenty-five HROC experimental workshops were conducted in Rwanda and the program was launched. Beginning in 2007, the African Quaker-developed HROC program was introduced in North Kivu and Kenya. As interest in HROC expanded, beginning in 2011, a three-week training of HROC facilitators has continued with usually two trainings per year.

(If interested, contact me at davidzarembka@gmail.com for details on the next HROC International Training.)

I consider my involvement in organizing the development of HROC as probably the most important activity I have done in my life. By now thousands of three-day HROC workshops have been conducted for tens of thousands of participants. I still coordinate the HROC-International program. As time went on, we also introduced transformative mediation, listening sessions, community dialogues, and Turning the

Tide/Nonviolent Campaigns for Social Change program (from Quakers in England).

****

This is all an introduction to the theme of this book, mentoring younger Friends. I felt that I needed to describe in detail the situation of Quakers in East Africa since it is so different from that of Quakers in the United States and England. In my peacemaking work in East Africa, I found that my main task was not to implement peacemaking, but this was rather a means to a larger end, to mentor young East African Quakers in peacemaking work.

In December 2011, I addressed the annual Lugari Yearly Meeting's Quakermen conference. There must have been about 200 older Quaker men present. In my presentation I outlined a system Friends Church Peace Teams (Kenya) (FCPT) wanted to use for the following year's Kenyan election, namely, the development of citizen reporters and a Call-in Center.

The idea, which I outlined to those present, was to develop an early warning system for violence before, during, and after the scheduled December 2012 election. This was to respond to the any potential or actual violence as had occurred extensively, with many deaths, after the 2007 election. We would train the citizen reporters for a day or two on how to observe and report unrest and pending violence. Those who completed the training were then given the number of our Call-in Center where they could send a text message concerning any potential or actual unrest to alert the FCPT staff who then could respond appropriately.

After my presentation, the first question was, "How much are the citizen reporters going to be paid for this work?" Non-government organizations, the United Nations, and the Kenyan government have a policy to give "sitting allowances"/stipends to people involved in all activities. This has destroyed the concept of civic responsibility. The answer I gave that people would not be paid for this was not well received. As I went home, I was discouraged. I vowed that even if we had only 50 people who were willing to be citizen reporters without any compensation, well, we would go for that.

In the end we trained 1200 citizen reporters. These were not the old men who had come to my Quakermen presentation, but young people mostly in their 20s and 30s who had adopted the cell phone as a life's necessity. [The next Kenyan national election, rescheduled to 2013, saw less violence than 2017.]

As the various peacemaking programs were introduced in the region, I quickly realized that the audience was mostly young people, many in their early twenties. The oldest was a Quaker pastor in Rwanda who was about 35 at that time. These young people had seen the violence in their countries, were victims of that violence, and were determined to develop a new, better, non-violent world from what was then happening.

I therefore realized that my real job – and I was 55 years old in 1998 when this all started – was not the stated one of developing the various peacemaking programs and introducing them into the East Africa countries, but to develop good, experienced, innovative, dedicated peace makers. As Florence Ntakarutimana from Burundi has said, "People have to have the heart for this work." My task was to find these dedicated youth and develop their peacemaking knowledge and ability.

There isn't space here for the story, but a wide range of peace work has since become active. Much of it just developed organically out of the previous work without any major planning or even awareness.

There are many concrete, formal activities that enhanced the peacemakers' knowledge and experience, academic and otherwise. Just as important, I thought, was the informal mentoring of these young people.

As with all guidance and mentoring, this was tricky, particularly due to the fact that, while I had lots of experience in East Africa, I was still a foreigner. I also had to be careful not to impose my views as an elder, telling the young people what they should do, as is commonplace in the cultures in the region. The youngsters had to develop their own abilities which in turn would give them the confidence needed for this emotionally difficult work.

Another means of increasing the Africans' abilities was to assign experienced American experienced volunteers to help promote the peacemaking activities. When AVP was introduced in all these countries, at first, we needed to bring experienced AVP facilitators from the United States. We would pair them with African AVP facilitators in order to introduce the program This was quite a challenge for all those who were involved.

Peace work after a genocide, election violence, civil war, and/or armed groups is extremely taxing. The security of the society has been destroyed, a new round of violence could occur unexpectedly at any time, individual and societal trauma was rampant. I found that most of those young peacemakers, like many people in their country, were affected by the violence. Support and self-care of facilitators was an important and necessary condition for people to continue.

This mentoring is also culturally tricky. The cultures in the region vary drastically. The differences between Rwanda/Burundi and Kenya, for example, is much greater than the differences between the US and England. When a person is dealing with such a sensitive issue as trauma and reconciliation, it is essential that the facilitators respect the local culture. This is not something I could do myself or advise others on the details. In other words, these young people had to negotiate the intricacies of their culture.

On the other hand, I couldn't leave all my own values behind. One of the major ones that was in conflict with traditional society was gender inequality. If I left matters to flow with the culture, workshops would be all or mostly male. Few women would be "allowed" to attend and if a few did, they were supposed to be mostly silent.

I imposed a requirement that workshops would be half male and half female. While this helped some, it still resulted in only one-fourth to one-half women. I needed to make a stronger rule: There would be ten positions for men and ten positions for women in a workshop. If ten women could not be found, then the positions would be lost. If I limited a workshop to only ten men, then ten positions for women were usually also filled. With half women, the women themselves were must more likely to actively participate and speak up. Nonetheless I realized that I was forcing my own value system on the workshops. Was it valid for me to do this? The women sure appreciated this including those who then had the opportunity to become facilitators in the various workshops.

There was another issue, though, that disturbed facilitators from the United States. In the East African countries, each day of a workshop was started with a half-hour worship service. In this case I sided with the Africans. I didn't think that this was a custom that should be changed since it was mostly an American hang-up and it made the participants more comfortable at the beginning of the workshop to do what was familiar to them.

I can't emphasize enough how impressed I have been with the "guts" that these young Africans have. For example, in the HROC workshops in Rwanda, the participants would be half victims of the genocide and the other half perpetrators of the genocide. Before the workshop, the victims would sit together, and the perpetrators would sit together. Although they came from the same community and knew each other, they did not greet each other. The tension in the room was immense. The facilitators had to enter that workshop confidently knowing that in three days they would be able to turn this around so that the two groups would reconnect and restore normal relationships as they had been before the genocide. The workshop is so well organized that this invariably happens

After twenty years in East Africa doing this mentoring, the result has been most gratifying. There are now many experienced East African peacemakers, with frankly more experience and knowledge than I have. Those who were once young are now mature leaders in their home communities. Now I don't even know or only slightly know of some of the up-and-coming new peacemakers because those who I have mentored are now mentoring many more others. The peace network in all these East African countries continues to expand. Excellent.

****

My strategy in life has always been to jump right in. This includes Quakerism, Africa, peacemaking, war tax resistance, home repair, or any of the other activities I have done. At my age now I can't jump as high as I used to, but I still jump as much as I can. My latest venture is to write articles on Clean Energy Africa.

Matthew 7:12 states, "So in everything, do to others what you would have them do to you, for this sums up the Law and the Prophets." I learned, when I was in my 20s, probably the hard way, that this does not work for me. I have not lived the "ways of the world" and have learned that I cannot follow this. If I treat others according to my own value system that those others do not subscribe to, I get into deep trouble. Fortunately, I have never tried to be "popular," but more worried about being true to myself. Sure, I have had disasters, mistakes, and situations that didn't work out, but so what? I think my Dad was right with his attitude that people need to take the road that satisfies them the most. I appreciate my Mom's enthusiastic support for anything that I did. Whatever happens is always interesting.

I write a weekly blog called "Reports from Kenya." I now also write another one called Clean Energy Africa. If you are interested in subscribing (you will get both since there is only one listserve), send me an email at davidzarembka@gmail.com.

Marian Rhys: Life, the Great Balancing Act

Y
ou shall love the lord your god with all your heart, with all your soul, and with all your might." This commandment is to me the essence of spirituality. I interpret it as meaning "Immerse yourself in reality, as much as humanly possible."

Marian Rhys

We can't, of course, completely immerse ourselves in the infinite, as we are limited, in both time and space. We are, after all, animals. We need to maintain our separate individual existences, with food, water, warmth, and physical safety. We are social animals, and we need to cultivate and maintain relationships with our fellow humans and other living entities on this planet we inhabit.

But the function of spirituality in human society is, I believe, to lift us up out of our natural narcissism, if only partially and intermittently. To remind us that there are other people who may need our help sometimes, that we are part of a community, and that there are things that we do not understand or control.

I was fortunate not to have been bludgeoned with any brand of fundamentalism in my childhood, and therefore have been able to approach spirituality without the negative emotional baggage that many people have been burdened with. I was brought up primarily Unitarian, at least from the age of six on. My mother, who had grown up Methodist, and originally sent us to Methodist Sunday School, discovered the Unitarians when the local minister was going door to door in the small New Hampshire town where we lived, recruiting new members.

My father — whose mother had converted to Christian Science when he was a child and had subsequently, in her fervor, neglected her children — had turned against all religion and never participated in church, except to attend Christmas and Easter services with the Unitarians, as I recall. But my mother became fairly active in the church. We children attended Sunday School regularly, and later, when we were old enough, services. My mother often played the organ on Sundays.

So, I did get the message that belonging to a spiritual community was an important part of life. And although I eventually left the Unitarian church and turned to other religions, I spent my childhood and youth there. The friends I met through the Unitarian youth group, Liberal Religious Youth (LRY), and the corresponding group for college students, Student Religious Liberals (SRL), became my social crowd for the two years that I attended the University of Colorado in Boulder, my only college education. (I dropped out midway through my junior year and moved to southern California to become a computer programmer.) Although only one of these people became a long-term friend, this was the first group where I really felt accepted, where I found kindred spirits.

My family moved frequently during my childhood, as my father signed up for another four years in the U.S. Army in 1956, having first served during World War II. We moved from New Hampshire to Pennsylvania, to the Monterey Bay Area of California, to Texas, and finally to Colorado, where I graduated from high school. But whenever we arrived in a new town, our first two actions were to seek out the local Unitarian church (if there was one) and the library. Spirituality and education: these were the two most important aspects of life outside the home and family.

Yet, despite our involvement with the Unitarian church, the main message I got about religion, growing up, was that, aside from enlightened people like the Unitarians, most followers were ignorant and superstitious. Catholics were the worst, with all their rituals and rites of passage. My Catholic friends had to go to catechism classes, which sounded perfectly awful. I was afraid of the nuns, too, with their long flowing habits and tight-fitting hoods, making them seem larger than life. I would often encounter them, walking the streets. (People did a lot of walking in those days — the early 1950s — running errands, traveling to work or to school, visiting one another, etc. It was the primary way one got around then, especially in small towns.) They reminded me of the descriptions I had read of witches, and I was sure they had some kind of malignant magical powers.

I was vaguely aware of the Jews, but more as an ethnic group than a spiritual one. My mother, having grown up in New Jersey and worked in New York City (regions with large Jewish populations), had socialized with Jews, and from her talk about them, I got the impression that they were some sort of strange subculture, like the Gypsies. It wasn't until I was in high school that I realized Judaism this was actually a religion.

It was also in high school, as I attended a class entitled "Humanities," where we studied the Bible as literature, that I realized that religion dealt with allegory and symbolism, that religious tracts were not to be taken literally. By that time, I was mentally mature enough to understand abstract thinking, and to have come to the realization that reality was indeed beyond the grasp of the rational mind, that there is something greater than ourselves. (I'm still not sure why my mother never seemed to get this, or at least never voiced it to me; we never discussed it, even in my adulthood.) These Bible studies also introduced me to what was essentially a Jewish concept: that God was undefinable: "I am what I am" or "I am becoming what I am becoming": the rough translation of the word 'Yahweh'.

As for Friends, I first became aware of their existence in 1959, when my elder sister, as a high-school student, got involved in the civil rights movement (we were living in Austin, Texas at that time). Most of that effort was being led by the local AFSC office. Actions consisted of mixed groups of blacks and whites trying to access services: college students went to lunch counters and high-school students to movie theaters. When the blacks were turned away, the whole group left. Afterward, many of the places were picketed, to publicize their discriminatory practices.

My sister also volunteered at the AFSC office and attended several of the youth work camps they used to sponsor. She eventually became a convinced Friend, in the late 1960s, in southern California, when her own children were old enough to attend First Day School.

When I myself was in high school, I also participated in several AFSC weekend work camps in Denver, where we were living at the time. We painted apartment walls in some of the housing projects. I remember one painful incident in one of those apartments, where a single mother was living with several children, and a strange man showed up while we were there. The teenaged daughter clearly felt very intimidated and harassed by him; he appeared to be trying to get her to either come away with him or go into a room alone with him. She was crying, and the mother was trying to intervene on her behalf. I can't remember exactly how the situation was resolved, but he was somehow removed from the apartment. Looking back on this incident later, I realized that the man was trying to sexually assault the girl, but at the time all I knew was that something very painful was going on for her, and I empathized with her but felt helpless in the situation, as I was indeed, being only a teenaged girl myself. I was relieved that she seemed to be rescued for the moment, but wondered what happened later, when we were gone.

Despite this service-work connection with Friends, it was not until my early twenties that I became engaged with them on any regular basis. By that time, I had begun to feel the need for some spirituality in my life, and started attending Westwood Monthly Meeting in Los Angeles, where I had moved in 1968. I joined the meeting after about two years, eventually serving as treasurer and on Ministry and Oversight Committee.

But it was attending Pacific Yearly Meeting that really drew me to Friends. I experienced Yearly Meeting as a wonderful gathering of highly energized, dedicated and spiritually centered people. Worship sharing sessions seemed infused with truly meaningful discussions about important issues: what are our values? what does it mean to lead an ethical life? how do we address the suffering in the world?

I was particularly impressed with the older Friends I met, the World War II generation (and even older): in California, Lloyd and Eula McCracken, Ed and Molly Morgenroth, Russ and Mary Jorgensen, Red and Madelaine Stephenson, Bob and Marie Schutz, Earl Reynolds; and in the Midwest, Louis and Nancy Neuman, and Raymond and Sarah Braddock. Howard and Anna Brinton were speakers at the first yearly meeting I attended, in 1971; Howard's book, *Friends for 300 Years*, had just recently been published, and I bought a copy at the gathering and read it avidly.

The men in this generation had been conscientious objectors in World War II, and many couples had met while doing service work for the AFSC in Europe, after the war. These people were still vibrant and politically radical, even in their old age, taking part in civil rights and anti-war marches. Some of them were war tax resisters or were living deliberately 'simple 'lives rather than — like most people in their generation — trying to acquire as many material goods as they could afford. And most of them had worked in lower-paying careers in social service work.

Earl Reynolds has remained one of my heroes. He, along with his wife Barbara, had sailed his small ship, The Phoenix, into the atomic-weapons testing site in the South Pacific. When asked whether he was worried about the military detonating a weapon while he was in that area, he replied, "That's their problem, not mine." People like this were great role models for me, in my mid-twenties.

The most memorable event of my Pacific Yearly Meeting attendance, though, was the Meeting for Business in 1971, when the Peace and Social Concerns Committee, clerked by Earl, brought a minute endorsing amnesty for men who had evaded the draft by moving to Canada, but also (for balance, in a good Quaker way) for soldiers like Lieutenant Calley who had committed war crimes.

There were about 400 attenders at that Meeting for Business, and considerable discussion followed, much of it contentious. Many Friends were strongly opposed to granting amnesty for war crimes, while others argued for compassion and understanding for those (mostly young) soldiers who had, under the duress of war, committed acts that they normally would not have. Although Post Traumatic Stress Disorder had not yet been identified or named, some Friends clearly grasped the concept.

Eventually, the committee was tasked with doing more research on the amnesty question and bringing back a modified minute on the following day. In those pre-internet days, research meant going to the library and poring over books. The committee, and Earl in particular, spent many hours at the library, returning to the next meeting with some interesting information: the president does not have the power to grant amnesty, Congress does, and amnesty cannot be granted for what are called "common crimes" such as murder, although persons who are convicted of such crimes can be granted pardons by the executive branch.

At this subsequent meeting, a modified minute was brought forward, urging amnesty for the draft evaders and pardons for the soldiers committing war crimes. The minute was approved with little discussion this time, and there was a tangible sense of spiritual unity in the meeting such as I have rarely experienced. This incident introduced me to the idea that perpetrators of evil suffer just as do victims, albeit it in a different way.

Yet I had my struggles with Friends, even in those early years. I went through a crisis of faith in 1972 when I read about the tortures being perpetrated in the South Vietnamese prisons — tortures funded by U.S. taxpayers. Although we did not have photographs of these atrocities, as we did thirty years later from Iraq, I had a good enough imagination to visualize them, and they made me sick.

I was never able, though, to get Friends, as a group, to address the issue of human evil. Although I did meet a few individuals here and there, who had experienced some struggles with the issue of evil, I did not find anyone who seemed to have been as deeply affected by it as I had, who could not get it out of their mind. When I brought up my struggles over the torture issue in a discussion group at PYM in 1972 or 1973, another Friend told about her social work with a family headed by a single mother, whose new boyfriend refused to let her daughter from her previous marriage sleep in the house at night; the child had to sleep outdoors, under the porch.

I was horrified at this tale, as were several other Friends. Yet no one seemed to really be willing to address the issue of the evil that this incident represented. One Friend proposed that we all go and rescue this child. "Sure," I thought, "that's really likely to happen. And even if it did, what about all the other abused and neglected children, of which there are no doubt millions, all over the world?" Other Friends simply responded by saying that we all need to perform social justice work, and eventually situations like this would get fixed.

But clearly, there was way too much evil in the world to fix. People were suffering, horribly, in many ways. Millions of people, every day, day in, day out, year after year. I was overwhelmed by it all; I thought about it constantly, for years. Yet virtually no one was willing to talk about it; I did not maintain ongoing relationships with the few people I encountered who at least admitted that it was an issue, and Friends as a whole simply refused to discuss it, most offering only useless platitudes like those put forth in that discussion group where I had first brought up the issue.

So, I stopped trying to talk with Friends about evil, and tried to find other individuals here and there in my life, who were willing to acknowledge the existence of evil, and talk about it.

My first successful step in this direction was in 1983, when I started attending self-help groups. There I met people who had suffered and survived abuse and even torture, including many who had learned to cope with the wounds. Invariably, it was spirituality, of one kind or another, that had helped them through this process.

In fact, it was in these groups that I met a woman who became my best friend for a number of years, who had suffered horrible torture as a child, within her family. Surprisingly (to myself), I was one of the few people able to listen to her narratives of these tortures. I discovered out that it was helpful to her, to be able to talk to someone about them, to deal with the memories. Hence, I came to understand that just listening and accepting the reality of evil was helpful. It was service work, something I could do in response to evil.

Finally, I had learned to come to terms with the existence of evil, to keep from being overwhelmed by it myself, and to support its victims. And ever since then, not a day goes by — indeed, not an hour — that I do not think about evil. It is a constant awareness in my life, and sometimes the most mundane things will make me think of it: a taxi will drive by and I remember that my friend was driven in a taxi for the first time in her life at the age of four, to be taken to a party where her father had sold her for sexual services. Or I pass a high-rise apartment building and remember that her father used to hold her by the wrists over the porch railing of their apartment on the thirteenth floor, threatening to let go of-her. Or excessive heat from a hair dryer will remind me of a boy who was severely burned, and whose Christian Science mother refused to let him have any medical care, berating him for keeping the family awake at night with his screams.

These remembrances are still painful, but they are no longer paralyzing. I have come to accept that human beings are capable of great evil, even while we are also capable of great good. As George Fox said, there is both an ocean of darkness and an ocean of light. What he did not say specifically, although he perhaps implied it, is that you can't have one without the other. It is who we are, as a species.

And, as some spiritually enlightened people have observed, we all have the capability of evil within ourselves. I came to realize this also. There is a part of me that is capable of perpetrating evil, although hopefully not in its most extreme forms.

And what, really, is evil? I finally came to believe that it is, essentially, total self-absorption: being so preoccupied with one's own needs that one becomes incapable of seeing others as fully human, worthy of understanding, respect and compassion. Other people are simply objects for us to use for our own gratification. In this sense, it is an ongoing, daily struggle, to remember that others are just as vulnerable, frightened and confused, sometimes, as we ourselves are. This is the Golden Rule, that all major religions speak of.

Helpful as it was, for my own peace of mind, to come to some resolution about the issue of evil, it was also gratifying to realize that I could use my hard-won insights to be of service to others, in many situations. In 1986, a few years after my experience with my torture-victim friend, I started volunteering on a telephone crisis hotline, and a few months after that, took up part-time paid work as a phone sex operator. In both of these jobs, I heard many stories of abuse and suffering, and learned both to listen and to use my voice to express empathy and understanding. While I gave up the crisis line work after eight years, I continued the phone sex work for twenty-eight years, finally retiring from it at age sixty-eight.

This telephone work has been the most spiritually meaningful work of my life. As a phone-sex operator, especially, I was able to develop long-term relationships with some of the callers, and most of these men were survivors of sexual abuse from female perpetrators. The calls would consist of my playing the perpetrator role, giving me a whole new perspective on the abuse relationship. While it was painful to me to hear their stories — after all, I came to care a great deal about these men — it was clear that my performance, my acceptance of their feelings, gave them some relief. And sometimes it was therapeutic for them, leading them to some healing, although only one of my callers actually gave me details about his abuse, and eventually began seeking help from professional sources — an avenue I had been encouraging him to follow for several years. (Those who are interested in hearing more detail about my phone-sex work can read my article in the March 2013 Friends Journal, "Loving the Difficult People".)

Admittedly, I do not feel free to talk about my phone-sex work, in either of my spiritual communities. Very few people, even in the most left-wing circles, are willing to hear anything positive about sex work. Perhaps the best thing I can say about this situation is that it has given me insight into what it's like to be in the closet, for any reason. And I will say that it is a sad place to be, not being able to bring all of myself into my interactions with people.

Another important source of enlightenment for me has been — strangely enough — walking city streets. It was during my early adult years, as a college student, that I first experienced verbal sexual harassment on the street, as every woman does. This experience of being objectified invariably sent me into a murderous rage. Nothing in my life had prepared me for this experience, and I had no idea of how to handle it. Yet I often had to walk the streets, just to get to places where I needed or wanted to go. Obviously, I had to find a way to deal with these situations; otherwise, I felt I was eventually going to kill somebody. (I certainly had fantasies about this.)

Finally, in 1970, at the age of 22, I decided that at least I was not going to take this treatment passively. I could be defiant, stand up for myself. So one day, on a sidewalk in Los Angeles, as I heard a car approaching from behind me — a car that, I could tell from the sound of the engine, was populated with the kind of young men who verbally harass women — I turned to face it, rather than simply cringing and hoping that the encounter would be brief.

To my utter amazement, the car (which was indeed occupied by four or five young men) sped off, with hardly a glance at me, and no verbal communication whatsoever from its occupants. I stood there on the sidewalk, stunned, staring after the car and wondering if there was something wrong with them. Had this really happened?

I tried this technique again, the next time I heard one of these cars approaching. By the third time, I realized I had made a discovery. And ever since, I have used this technique — facing the people who may be about to harass me. Not timidly, not seductively, not arrogantly, but simply clearly and assertively. I've never had a moment's trouble since, in these fifty years. The few times (maybe five at most) that someone has made a brief verbal comment, I simply smile and laugh; that invariably defuses the situation. In fact, many years later I was at a social gathering where one of the people present, who worked in a prison, was asked how he protected himself in that atmosphere. "With a sense of humor," he replied.

Ever since my 1970 discovery, I have loved walking city streets and riding public transit. In these fifty-plus years, I have refined my technique, which essentially consists of treating people like human beings rather than threats. I have wonderful experiences in this environment. I meet interesting people and encounter challenging situations. On the street, human beings behave like the animals we actually are. Almost all the communication is non-verbal, and in the small amount of communication that is verbal, the tone of voice is more important than the words. When I say hello to someone on the street, I instinctively use my 'phone-sex 'voice: soft and mellifluous. The effect this has on people is palpable; I feel it instantly. It calms them down.

I have also become very good at "reading" people, and all my work with abuse victims has helped me develop real compassion and respect for the people who live on the streets, the outcasts. Almost all of those who seem annoying are merely that; virtually none are dangerous.

(Of course, I'm very privileged to be able to behave this way. I'm an older white woman, and no one sees me as a threat. Now that I am old, I am no longer even a sexual threat to straight men. This gives me a tremendous amount of freedom: I can go wherever I want, at any time of day or night. It also gives me the ability to de-escalate potentially dangerous situations, and I consider this one of my social responsibilities.)

The city-street environment feels like a very spiritual place, as it brings me face to face with my fellow human beings, in a way that is primal and genuine. We are all equal out there, standing on our own two feet (if we are able-bodied enough to do that), without any of the accoutrements of social class to back us up. That is how we come into and go out of this world, and it is really how we spend all the time in between, if we are honest about it.

So it was that I found various ways of practicing spirituality in my daily life. Yet I still sought an organized religious community where I could speak freely of my pain over evil, and the insights I had gained in my struggles with it. In this search, I have been only partially successful. And it was my inability to find all of what I was looking for among Friends that led me to continue searching.

It was in 1986, about a year before I took up phone sex, that I finally started actively exploring Judaism. In some sense, it had been a part of my life since 1974, when I married a Jewish man. And our son, born in 1976, had a Jewish education and a bar mitzvah. Yet, although I was intrigued with this religion, I did not really engage with it until later; it was not my Jewish husband who drew me into it, but the realization that my life was going by and I had not satisfied my curiosity about it.

I decided to start attending a gay Jewish congregation in San Francisco, where I had recently relocated, not because I was gay but because I thought they would be progressive and welcoming to a non-Jew. I was correct about the first assumption but not about the second. Most progressive Jews, of the Boomer generation like myself, were struggling with their Judaism, not feeling that it spoke to their spiritual needs, yet not wanting to abandon it either. They could not understand why anyone would be drawn to Judaism and voluntarily seek it out; why couldn't I appreciate how lucky I was not to have to deal with this problem?

Still, it was in this congregation that I learned the basics of Judaism: the services, the holidays (there are many!), the customs, the culture. I fell in love with the Jewish people, as I still am, although so far, I have not converted.

Meantime, in the early 1990s, I had another contentious time with my monthly meeting, in California, over the issue of child sexual abuse, which at that time was just beginning to surface as an issue that could be talked about publicly. The specific problem in my meeting was that one of the elderly male Friends shared, in a Meeting retreat, that two of his daughters had accused him of sexually abusing them as children. Yet, rather than investigating this allegation, the Meeting almost unanimously (two other women Friends were exceptions) took the side of the accused Friend, assuming that he was innocent. Not surprisingly, this was a Friend who was held in high esteem, one of that World War II generation who had devoted much of his life to social service work, including volunteer work with UNESCO. My suggestion that this Friend might not be appropriate to be alone with First Day School children was ignored, and I was castigated for even suggesting it. I was treated as though I were the problem, not him.

I was eventually able to contact one of the daughters (neither belonged to any Meeting or was active in any other Friends organization), who told me an entirely different story: it was the older Friend himself who initiated the topic of sexual attraction between him and the daughter (an attraction that he seemed to think was mutual, but was not).

After this incident, I withdrew from the Meeting for a while, although I retained my membership, hoping to find another meeting where I could be comfortable. During this time, I also attended several progressive Jewish congregations, but did not feel deeply connected with any of them. My Jewish connection did lead me, however, to a bout of reading holocaust survivor literature. This effort lasted about a year and gave me many more stories of evil to grapple with.

In 2003, I moved from California to Portland, Oregon, and quickly became very active in Multnomah Meeting, serving on committees and as recording clerk, treasurer, and personnel clerk. I played a major role in the fundraising effort for expanding the building, in 2006-2007.

It was after that expansion, though, that I began to feel that the Meeting was drifting, losing its sense of direction and purpose. The quality of vocal ministry deteriorated; speakers often related personal problems with no spiritual context, went on political or emotional rants, or even promoted their personal businesses. I also felt that there was a lot of 'phoniness': faking spiritual passion. One Friend in particular spoke almost every First Day and seemed to mistake voice volume for passion — the louder, the holier. He spoke about his emotional "insights," yet the tension in his voice was so palpable that it belied his words; he was clearly full of fear and anxiety. That other Friends did not seem to be able to perceive this disparity astounded me.

Another Friend would often break into tearful entreaties in Meeting for Business, whenever any opposition to her opinions arose. Her performance invariably swayed the Meeting to her side, usually with comments about how insightful and caring she was and how lucky we were to have someone so spiritual in our midst. Another long-time much lauded member often waxed eloquent about how much she learned simply by sitting with people and listening to them: behavior that I never actually saw her engage in. She talked incessantly; she was one of the worst listeners I have ever met.

Friends often expressed adulation for other people who to me were clearly egotistical and manipulative. There was a traveling Friend, for example, who spoke about the economic struggles many people were having. He invited several people (not affiliated with Meeting in any way) who were particularly suffering, to come and speak about their struggles. Yet he proposed nothing to actually help these people; they appeared to be there as "Exhibit A" — objects rather than human beings. I was appalled at his callousness, his willingness to exploit people in order to promote himself as a spiritual leader, rather than to reach out and actually help them, or encourage others to do so. Yet many Friends raved about this man, how wonderful and spiritual he was. Again, I kept my observations to myself. It seemed futile to speak out.

The most egregious problem within Multnomah Meeting, though, was their tolerance of an ongoing adult discussion group that met early on First Day mornings, before the main Meeting for Worship. The group had originally been formed as a support group for a meeting member (someone who was actually one of the most dedicated and knowledgeable members, for whom I still have a lot of respect) who had recently suffered a family tragedy. Over a period of about two years, though, the group morphed into a general-purpose discussion group, with no real focus. Nor was this group taken under the care of any Meeting committee. It was a free-for-all, given an air of legitimacy by its meeting on First Day mornings, in the Meeting house, rent-free.

The group, although open to all, came to consist of a core group of about half a dozen people, some of whom had no affiliation with either the Meeting or any other Friends organization (e.g., AFSC, FCNL, Wider Quaker Fellowship, etc.). Not only did some of these people have no knowledge of Quakerism; they were not interested in learning anything about it. They never attended Meeting for Worship, Meeting for Business, or any Meeting social gatherings; and never served on any Meeting committees or performed any other volunteer work for the Meeting. Nevertheless, they considered themselves Quakers. One of the core group — an avowed atheist — even remarked: "I'm more of a Quaker than those so-called Quakers who meet upstairs every Sunday."

I tried to get Worship and Ministry Committee to take some responsibility for this group, even researching all the other monthly meetings in the yearly meeting to see if any of them had a similar discussion group. None did; although some meetings did have discussion groups, these always had a designated leader and specific topics they discussed and were under the care of either a meeting committee or the meeting clerk. And most were only temporary, formed for a set period of time and then disbanded. Yet the only action the committee would take was to assign one of their members to attend and monitor the group; this lasted for a few months and was then forgotten.

It was only when this situation got completely out of hand that the Meeting finally took some action on it. The group met in a room close to the front door of the meeting house, and discussions sometimes got so contentious that participants were actually yelling at each other; this obviously did not create a good impression on newcomers entering the meetinghouse on First Day mornings. The Meeting's response, however, has been tepid: two Meeting liaisons were appointed, from among the regular group participants; a set of guidelines was drawn up, posted in the room where the group meets and shared with newcomers to the group; and the liaisons are required to report to the Meeting for Business periodically. It remains to be seen whether these changes will result in any significant improvement, especially since the issue of discussion group participants 'lack of commitment to Friends has not even been addressed.

In addition to these specific problems, the Meeting seemed to be losing its focus, trying to be all things to all people, not knowing who it really was as a congregation, or perhaps even as a denomination. Friends often seemed apologetic to newcomers who had their own ideas about what Quakers should be, who expressed no interest in learning about Friends 'traditions or values. Were some Friends uncomfortable with Christian terminology? Then surely, we must refrain from ever using the word 'Christ' in our vocal ministry. Were some women uncomfortable with what they perceived to be the historical patriarchal nature of Friends? Then we must embrace a new terminology derived from the Goddess religion, or, worse yet, tolerate rantings against men in general, in vocal ministry. Did transgendered people feel unaccepted? Then we must announce, at every Meeting for Business, what pronouns we prefer, as we introduced ourselves.

The Meeting even had a clerk, a few years ago, who could never seem to understand the meaning of the terms 'standing in the way' or 'standing aside' in regard to business meeting decisions. He kept asking for this to be explained to him, again and again, but the concepts seemed to be beyond his grasp.

The most recent clerk, as of this writing, is even more problematic. Although this Friend has indeed contributed much to the life of the Meeting over the years, she is totally inappropriate as a clerk, being an angry, contentious person who is easily set off when she is confronted by any information she does not want to hear. I expressed my concern about this nomination, to Nominating Committee, but was assured that the Assistant Clerk would be able to exert an ameliorating effect on the Friend. I doubted this, but decided the issue was not worth pursuing, especially considering my previous experiences in trying to make any real changes within the Meeting.

Yet my fears were well founded. This Friend's anger has started to come out in her communications and decisions, often via confrontational emails (I received one of these myself, in response to my suggested edits to the Meeting for Business minutes). And she recently shut down an ad hoc committee that was working on security issues (particularly focusing on cyber security), via an email to the committee members that was so vicious that no one even dared to respond.

While I am still not sure whether these kinds of problems are unique to Multnomah Meeting, or are indicative of a wider dysfunction within the Society of Friends as a whole (or at least the Hicksite branch of it), I received some confirmation of the latter possibility at the Friends General Conference Gathering in 2013. When I mentioned some of my concerns to a long-time Friend at the Gathering, she assured me that I was not the only one who perceived that the society lacked the spirituality it had had in earlier times. I also had a bad experience at the morning workshop I was taking at the gathering. The leader allowed one Friend with a strong personality to hijack the workshop, sitting there passively and doing nothing to intervene. I left the workshop, walking out midway through the final day. Although one of the attenders later apologized to me, that no one else had followed, or had stood up to the leader, I received no other acknowledgment of the problem, nor any apology, from anyone else.

So it was that, as Multnomah Meeting, if not the Society of Friends in general, seemed to be melting down, I began thinking about leaving, and Judaism was the logical alternative for me. I researched the local Jewish scene and found that there was a congregation that offered high holiday services for free (this is the major fund-raising event of the year for most congregations). So, in 2011 I attended (making a voluntary donation, as many people did).

I attended again in 2012, and as I was leaving, someone I spoke with in the elevator made the comment, "Yes, it's a very special group of people." "Oh, yes," I thought to myself, "they're here the rest of the year, too." So, I went to their Passover seder the following spring. I chanced to sit at a table with four or five people who, I later found out, were some of the core group: the ones who get everything done. They seemed to be wonderful people, and I decided to start attending regular Shabbat morning services.

I felt at home almost immediately. The congregation had been founded in 1978 by a group of Boomers, like myself, and, since it was part of the Reconstructionist movement — the only branch of Judaism that truly welcomes non-Jews — they allowed me to join even as a non-Jew. I have been involved ever since, serving on committees and volunteering my time and energy where I can. I have found it to be a vibrant spiritual community, full of thoughtful, dedicated, competent and articulate people. They get things done!

While it's true that they don't know about the Friends way of conducting business (the one exception there is another ex-Friend), they strive for consensus in all their decisions. When the rabbi retired a few years ago, there was a two- to three-year process to hire a new one. When it came time for the membership to vote on the selection recommended by the subcommittee, four or five people (out of a membership of several hundred) were not in unity with the decision. While they were overruled by a vote, their concerns were not brushed aside; a small group from the Steering Committee met with them to address these concerns.

My Jewish congregation is extremely participatory; many members lead services, not just the rabbi. The word 'havurah' — part of the

name of the congregation — means 'meeting' and is considered a particular form of Jewish congregation.

Judaism, as one rabbi explained it in an introductory class I took,
has three major emphases: belonging (a strong sense of tribal identity),
behaving (the rules of living, as expressed in the Torah), and believing
(theology: What is the nature of God, reality? Is there life after death?
What is the soul? etc.). Of these three (just as for Friends), the 'believing 'part is the least important. There is no creed. What matters is what
you do, not what you believe. A convert to Judaism (known officially as
a "Jew by choice") takes a loyalty oath to the Jewish people; they do not
sign on to a creed.

Judaism has a much more accepting attitude toward human fail-
ings, than does institutionalized Christianity, realizing that human beings
err, that they are not perfect. For example, one is supposed to light the
Shabbat candles eighteen minutes before sunset; that way, you can be
sure that, if you plan to do it early, you will at least get it done on time.

Since the destruction of the second temple, around 300 C.E.,
when the priesthood was dissolved and replaced with rabbis, the Torah
has been taken as an allegorical document, not a literal one. The rabbis
proclaimed this reform, realizing that not only did they need to bring
Judaism into a more modern era, but also that it was the only practical
thing to do; the sacrifices could no longer be performed, and hence it
only made sense to re-purpose the idea of sacrifice to a more abstract
concept. With that shift, it was necessary to say the same thing about
many other proclamations in the Torah.

(There are, to be sure, exceptions to both these practices. The
Kabbalists are focused on theology, particularly mysticism, and there are
fundamentalists Jews, who do take the Torah literally. These groups,
however, are in a minority, and do not represent mainstream Judaism.)

Besides the emphasis on 'behaving' rather than 'believing,' Judaism shares other values with Friends as well. There is no hierarchy,
and no official organization that represents all Jews. Jewish weddings
are also similar to Friend's, in that it is the couple who marry themselves,
not the rabbi. While the rabbi has authority from the state to 'perform'
marriages, just as the clerks of Friends meetings have the authority to
sign marriage certificates, all a rabbi does at a Jewish wedding is to make
sure everything is done correctly, according to Jewish law. Technically,
a Jewish couple could be married without a rabbi, as long as this law is
followed.

And, surprisingly, Jews, like Friends, have an unconventional
approach to oaths, or vows. Friends have a testimony against taking oaths
because doing so implies that one is otherwise not sincere; vowing to tell
the truth in a court trial, for example, indicates that without the vow, one

might be lying. But one should simply tell the truth all the time, with no need for an oath.

While Jews are not this idealistic, they do take an ambivalent attitude toward vows. According to Jewish law, a vow is not irrevocable; if one finds out new information that pertains to a vow, one is allowed to re-think it and be released from it if appropriate (although this requires another person's participation — someone with some spiritual authority; one cannot do it by themselves). In fact, part of the High Holiday service is to declare that one is released from vows — not only the ones made in the preceding year, but also the ones that will be made in the coming year. (There is some evidence that this may have been added to the Yom Kippur service during the Inquisition, in order to absolve Jews who had been forced to convert (and take vows) to Christianity.)

Where Judaism differs most from Friends, and from most other religions I am aware of, is its strong emphasis on tribal identity: the 'belonging' aspect. While many people may be put off by this, I have found a way of accepting it, partly by recognizing that it is what has held this people together over millennia of displacements and persecution, and partly by mentally translating the word 'Jew' in the liturgy to 'spiritual person.' In fact, the rabbi in my current congregation once made this substitution, when he was reading from the prayer book. To be Jewish, in this sense, means to be a seeker, someone striving to live a spiritual life.

And as for my struggle with facing evil, Jews do not, cannot, run away from evil or pretend that it doesn't exist. They have suffered too much from it, to deny its reality. They struggle with it, to be sure, but they do not deny it. It is mentioned in the commemoration of many of the holidays. (A well-known Jewish joke is that the quintessential Jewish holiday theme is: "They tried to kill us. We won. Let's eat.")

The Jewish precept that I find most inspiring is the concept that there are three major relationships in life: with oneself, with God, and with other human beings. I translate this into three actions: to be and express our own unique selves; to appreciate, indeed, to stand in awe of, the miracle of the physical world, of life, of the universe; and to be of service to others.

Correspondingly, there are, I believe, three great balancing acts of life: how much do I live for today, versus how much I plan for the future? (relationship with self); how much time and energy can I put into spiritual pursuits, versus the practical business of maintaining life? (relationship with God); and how much do I live for myself, versus being of service to others? (relationship with other people).

At this point in my life, I feel once again that I have found my true spiritual home. While I retain some long-time friendships among

Friends, and I do value, in particular, their method of conducting business, Quakerism no longer meets enough of my spiritual needs for me to continue in membership. Judaism does. Besides, the Jews always serve good food at their events, and have a wonderful sense of humor.

Douglas Gwyn: Of Torches and Generations

Douglas Gwyn

"Passing the Torch" suggests a relay of sorts. Being one of the elder Friends Chuck Fager has invited to contribute on this theme, I think of a relay between generations. The torch itself suggests some source of light. So, I have pondered what light I have received over a lifetime of experience and from years in ministry among Friends. What might be useful to pass on to next generations? The more I mused, the more perplexed I became.

My perplexity sent me back to the sociologist Karl Mannheim's essay, "The Problem of Generations."[1] I discovered it in the late 1990s when I was researching *Seekers Found.*[2] In

---

[1] Karl Mannheim, "The Problem of Generations," in Essays on the Sociology of Knowledge (London: Routledge & Kegan Paul, 1952) pp. 276-320.

[2] Douglas Gwyn, Seekers Found: Atonement in Early Quaker Experience (Wallingford, PA: Pendle Hill, 2000). That project was initially inspired by reading Wade Clark Roof's sociological study, A Generation of Seekers:

that book, I compared the seeking patterns of my own baby-boom generation with the experiences of the English Seekers of the 1640s who became Quakers in the 1650s. Now I am drawn to consider the intergenerational dynamics between the baby-boom generation and millennials.

Mannheim observes briefly that intergenerational dynamics are comparable in some ways to interclass relations. Indeed, while class relations are the dynamics of social stratification at any given time, we could view generations as a form of class through time. We start out under the tutelage of parents and teachers, move on to work for employers and bosses older than ourselves, until we work ourselves into better paying jobs and/or more responsible roles, often with supervision over younger workers, while perhaps also raising families of our own. Intergenerational resentments against parents, teachers, and bosses accompany that process, much as class resentments pervade society in general at any given time. The biological rhythm of generational succession – birth, growth, work, aging, death – is a primary aspect of our individual lives and our collective existence.

Fresh Contact

Generational cohorts are in an ongoing process of conflict and collaboration. Each generation inherits cultural and religious traditions from its predecessors, but Mannheim emphasizes that each new cohort appropriates that heritage from the perspective of a new set of social experiences. It has its own "fresh contact" with old material, assimilating and modifying or rejecting the heritage passed on to them. My own generation's coming of age in the 1960s, a time of major social conflict and change, profoundly affected the ways we engaged with our cultural heritage. Within that decade the civil rights and antiwar movements, together with the beginnings of the women's, gay rights, and environmental movements profoundly affected – and continue to affect – everyone. Some were led to progressive engagement, others to defensive reaction.[3]

The Spiritual Journeys of the Baby Boom Generation (San Francisco: Harper, 1993), which makes some use of Mannheim's work.

[3] In Getting Saved from the Sixties: Moral Meaning in Conversion and Cultural Change (Berkeley: University of California Press, 1982) Steven M. Tipton follows different trajectories of baby-boomers whose world was rocked by sixties upheavals. Tipton went on to join with Robert Bellah and others in researching and writing Habits of the Heart: Individualism and Commitment in American Life (Berkeley: University of California Press, 1985), which adds further dimension to post-sixties social trends.

But we were just as profoundly affected by the consumer technologies pervading our world: television, the youth culture of rock and soul mediated by the specialized formats of FM radio, and the intensified listening experience of stereo sound and headphones. And then there were the drugs that further intensified personal experience. Meanwhile, the medical technology of "the pill" expanded sexual freedom and experimentation. In many ways, the registers of personal experience were enlarged in ways that our parents and grandparents, formed by the deprivations of the Great Depression and sacrifices of World War II, could not grasp.

While rates of religious participation had reached all-time highs in the newly prosperous 1950s, the churches often seemed flat-footed or outright reactionary toward the progressive politics and new morality of the 1960s. Certainly, religious traditions were much less exciting than the spirituality of sex, drugs, rock and soul that filled the tumescent present of baby-boom consciousness. Boomers dropped out from church life in massive numbers during the latter 1960s and 1970s. (They parallel the generation of young Seekers in the 1640s, coming of age during the English civil war and experimenting freely with religious options that had been suppressed by the state-church before the war. The early Quaker movement of the next decade was a synthesis and advancement upon those new registers of experience and experimentation.)

Some of us returned to traditional churches, often more acutely conservative than before. Others sought alternative churches, Eastern religious traditions, or new age spiritualities. And still others left religion and spirituality behind altogether. In my own case, I grew up in a large, mildly liberal pastoral Friends meeting in Indianapolis. Amiable but tepid, it gave me little to rebel against, but not much to inspire or motivate me either. I did not attend any church or meeting during my college years. But I had a spiritual sense that gravitated toward the natural world. I might well have explored an Eastern spiritual discipline, had I not received a distinct calling to ministry in 1968, at age nineteen. I had never considered ministry before (I was a zoology major). All I knew was that my first love relationship had recently ended, and I was devastated. As they say, God meets us in our extremity. The subtle but clear call, "be a minister," came as I sat alone in my dormitory room one evening. It came as a seismic non sequitur that felt strangely hopeful.

I understood my calling to be a Christian ministry among Friends. But I was sure it needed to be something more prophetically Christian and more seriously Quaker than what I had received in my youth. I enrolled at Union Theological Seminary in New York in 1971 (though I admit it was New York that drew me most). Union's rich tradition of Niebuhr, Tillich, and Bonhoeffer, and the presence of the black

89

liberationist James Cone and other leading biblical and theological scholars, were augmented by the ferment of new feminist theologies. The professors weren't sure what to think of us baby-boom seminarians, many of whom had enrolled primarily to avoid military conscription. But we were ready to learn from them – on our own generational terms.

My prophetic Christian faith grew during my Union years, ending in 1975. But since there were no other Friends at Union, it was only afterward, during my first Friends pastorate back in Indiana, that the Quaker dimension began to develop. The most important influence for me was Lewis Benson, two generations my senior, a high school dropout who began studying George Fox and early Friends in the 1930s and soon became a critic of Rufus Jones and the liberal Quaker renewal – something very unpopular in those days. Like the neo-orthodox theologians of that day such as Reinhold Niebuhr and Karl Barth, Lewis questioned liberal optimism about social progress and reclaimed the countercultural edge of early Friends, which spoke to my experience of the sixties. I was drawn to Lewis 'outsider status and his identification of the prophetic spirituality of George Fox's message.[4] It was much more trenchant than anything I heard from the pastoral meetings I knew in the Midwest or the liberal unprogrammed meetings I attended in the East.

Outliers and Forerunners

Mannheim notes that cultural traditions evolve through the interaction of more than two generations. Often individuals from an earlier generation who had been outliers or rebels serve as forerunners and mentors to members of an emergent generation. Lewis Benson played that role most acutely for me. Also important were T. Canby Jones, Dean Freiday, Wilmer Cooper, and Sandra Cronk, all ranging between one and two generations ahead of me.

Other Friends in my acquaintance report similar experiences. In interviews, George Lakey told me that he was mentored by A.J. Muste, two generations his senior, and George Willoughby, a generation older, in the development of his nonviolent social change activism in the 1960s.

---

4 For more on Benson, see None Were So Clear: Prophetic Quaker Faith and the Ministry of Lewis Benson, T. H . S. Wallace, ed. (Camp Hill, PA: New Foundation Publications, 1996). Sadly, Lewis Benson is largely forgotten among Friends today. But I am pleased that David Hanson has completed a very good master's thesis this year at the Earlham School of Religion on Benson's life and theology. I hope it will eventually find publication in some form.

And today, at age eighty, he continues to mentor new generations of non-violent activists. In Eating Dr. King's Dinner,[5] Chuck Fager describes the formative experience of working among older African American activists in the Southern Christian Leadership Conference. In Meetings,[6] he comments on his brief but riveting encounter with Milton Mayer while a student at Friends World College later in the 1960s. Sandra Cronk had profound influence on many students seeking spiritual direction at Pendle Hill (at a cost to her personal health).[7] She was later the central figure in the founding of the School of the Spirit. And if we go back many generations to the beginnings of the Quaker movement, the first ally George Fox records in his Journal was Elizabeth Hooton, a woman twenty years his senior.

Still, what I learned from my mentors had to be appropriated by way of the "fresh contact" of my own personal and generational experience. My apocalyptic interpretation of George Fox, which was published as Apocalypse of the Word,[8] built on Lewis Benson's prophetic interpretation, but took Fox's experiential eschatology much further. My reading of Fox was informed by my calling to ministry during the apocalyptic year of 1968, and by the intensified registers of personal experience particular to my generation, as described above. Lewis was not sure what to make of my interpretation, and our paths had begun to diverge by the time of his death in 1985. But many mentorships end that way, and our friendship remained intact to the end.

Mannheim notes that the affective currents of any generational zeitgeist are not unilinear but develop dialectically. He cites the diverging progressive and reactionary responses to the French Revolution in nineteenth-century Germany. His observations about Germany are am-

---

[5] Chuck Fager, Eating Dr. King's Dinner: A Memoir of the Movement, 1963-1966 (Fayetteville, NC: 2005).

[6] Chuck Fager, Meetings: A Religious Autobiography (Durham, NC: Kimo, 2016), pp. 48-63.

[7] See A Lasting Gift: The Journal and Selected Writings of Sandra L. Cronk, Martha Paxson Grundy, ed. (Philadelphia: FGC Quaker Press and School of the Spirit, 2009).

[8] Douglas Gwyn, Apocalypse of the Word: The Life and Message of George Fox (Richmond, IN: Friends United Press, 1986, 2014).

ply confirmed by the culture wars that developed in post-sixties American society.[9] The polarization of culture, religion, and politics since the stalemated outcome of the revolutionary sixties continues to enervate American society at large and the Society of Friends in particular. My ministry unfolded as a series of sojourns crisscrossing that divide between liberal-progressive and traditional Christian camps of American Friends, sometimes as a Friends pastor, other times as a teacher at Pendle Hill (and at Woodbrooke among British Friends).

All the time, I continued to research and write about early Friends and attempt in various ways to present early Quaker witness as a more vital faith and practice than either liberal or evangelical Friends offer. In *Unmasking the Idols: A Journey among Friends*[10] I suggested that there is no future for either major branch of American Friends as long as they refuse to learn from the prophetic vision of early Friends but continue to hybridize their faith and practice with evangelical and liberal-humanist streams in the wider culture. Indeed, membership statistics since then continue to suggest that the world doesn't need "we too" Quakers.

But sojourns among the variety of Friends have also inspired my quixotic penchant for songwriting (sometimes recorded under the name The Brothers Doug). "A Process in the Wind" lampoons Quaker group decision-making. "Eighty-Weighty Friend" celebrates Quaker gerontocracy. "Yonder Stands the Quaker" views us from the outside as "an endangered species of spiritual life, practiced in the art of lost cause." "That of Odd in Everyone" explores where "oddliness and godliness intertwine." "The Blue Bonnet Inn" imagines a Quaker gentleman's club, where everything starts out sounding salacious and ends up gently repressive. It is a sign of their spiritual health that Quaker communities enjoy laughing along with these songs.

A Third Term

Mannheim also observes that the protracted stalemate in nineteenth-century German politics (a generational dialectic degenerating into sheer dualism, a binary), eventually produced a third term in the proletarian socialism of Karl Marx and others. Of course, I grew up as

---

9 The classic sociological analysis is James Davison Hunter's Culture Wars: The Struggle to Define America (New York: Basic Books, 1991).

10 Douglas Gwyn, Unmasking the Idols: A Journey Among Friends (Richmond, IN: Friends United Press, 1989); for other observations on the Quaker divide, also see Gwyn, Words in Time: Essays and Addresses (Bellefonte, PA: Kimo, 1997).

oblivious to Marxist thought as the vast majority of Americans. But during the latter 1970s, in the earliest stages of my study of Fox and early Friends, I found the work of Marxist historian Christopher Hill helpful in putting a larger socio-economic frame around early Friends and the revolutionary situation of their time. I didn't feel Hill understood early Friends very well, but his broader Marxist analysis became a vital complement to my apocalyptic theological interpretation.

I was able to take the social-revolutionary meaning of the early Quaker movement much further in my second study of early Friends, *The Covenant Crucified: Quakers and the Rise of Capitalism.*[11] There I explored the early Quaker Lamb's War as a nonviolent cultural revolution with a covenantal vision for the future of English society. I showed how it was eventually beaten down and contained as a countercultural sect by the rising powers of the new capitalist regime. The book's conclusion suggested that the early Quaker example can stimulate our religious imagination today as we confront the juggernaut of global capitalism.

By that time, I was beginning to learn from contemporary Marxist cultural theorists such as Fredric Jameson. Jameson's seminal work, *The Political Unconscious* (1981) explores the gravitational effects that socio-economic structures exert on writers and their texts. Historical theology needs the grounding materialist analyses offer. Conversely, they could really use the transcendent perspective theology brings. A powerful synthesis of the two is Norman Gottwald's landmark social study of ancient Israel, ci (1979), which provided an important model for my revolutionary reinterpretation of early Friends in The Covenant Crucified.

But the eighties and nineties were the belle epoque of neoliberal capitalist expansion and the collapse of the Soviet empire. To most white, middle-class, baby-boom American Friends, many of whom were happily riding the currents of economic prosperity, a Marxist analysis seemed ludicrous. Friends are perennially disturbed and ready to protest the various racial, economic, environmental, and militaristic symptoms of capitalism but unwilling to confront the system itself. The coordinates of white privilege and middle-class normativity are hard to miss.

Of course, I have benefitted from white privilege in more ways than I will ever know, and my upbringing was as middle-class as two public school teachers could afford. But I remained unsettled and economically precarious for a number of reasons. Early Quaker critiques of professional ministry kept me from becoming too comfortable or settled as a Friends pastor. And though I earned a PhD from Drew University in

---

[11] Douglas Gwyn, The Covenant Crucified: Quakers and the Rise of Capitalism (Wallingford, PA: Pendle Hill, 1995).

1982, Lewis Benson's independent scholarship and outsider status abetted my ambivalence toward academia. Moreover, back in 1970, after reading Paul and Anne Ehrlich's book, The Population Bomb and Garrett Hardin's article, "The Tragedy of the Commons" (both published in 1968), I had decided that I would not contribute to the accelerating growth of the world's human population. That renunciation was motivated by concerns for the earth's integrity and for the quality of life of future generations. But it also freed me to pursue an itinerant/sojourning ministry among Friends. My two marriages have been intimate friendships and mutual support in our different paths of ministry and service.

I completed a trilogy of early Quaker studies, ending with the aforementioned Seekers Found in 2000. By then, I noticed that while Apocalypse of the Word (1986) had gained significant readership and discussion across the Quaker spectrum, The Covenant Crucified (1995) aroused less interest, and Seekers Found garnered very little, despite being some of my best work. Reviews of these books were very positive, but sales kept declining. Of course, I considered that perhaps I had provided more about early Friends than anyone wanted to know. But I also realized that the internet was overwhelming the time and attention of Friends, like everyone else. In the 1980s, Friends had read and discussed books much more widely. By the turn of the century, book conversations were declining sharply, at least in my anecdotal awareness.

I decided that more books about early Friends would be more along the lines of a personal hobby than a religious concern. And feeling unhopeful about significant renewal among Friends in general, I turned my attention to Pendle Hill. That Quaker educational community had profoundly renewed my spirit during my sojourns of life and work there, and I knew it had similarly affected many others. Pendle Hill, like all twentieth-century Quaker institutions governed by external boards, is a para-Quaker invention. But it maintained an internal community life that counterbalanced — and sometimes vigorously challenged — its institutional basis.

Beginning in 2008, I began researching and writing Personality and Place: The Life and Times of Pendle Hill.[12] Giovanni Arrighi's economic history, The Long Twentieth Century (1994), was particularly helpful in framing the larger coordinates of that work. By the time the book was published in 2014, Pendle Hill had been forced to lay down its resident program, the centerpiece of its community life. The book turned out to be more an elegy for what had been than a call to continue a great

---

[12] Douglas Gwyn, Personality and Place: The Life and Times of Pendle Hill (Philadelphia: Plain Press, 2014).

Quaker experiment. But Pendle Hill continues as a unique conference center, hosting Quaker educational events and a wide variety of Quaker and non-Quaker groups. It is still a place that exerts subtle but profound effects upon personalities that meet and work together there.

The multi-generational saga of the Pendle Hill book was followed by a similar saga of the first fifty years of Friends General Conference, *A Gathering of Spirits*.[13] I drew upon the new field of affect theory to explore how cultural currents change through generations. Focusing on a particular Quaker institution's evolution gives those larger, wafty currents specificity. So, this past decade of Quaker research and writing has no doubt helped shape my thoughts for this essay. Meanwhile, all through my years of ministry, the multigenerational dynamics of Quaker communities, both local meetings and study centers, have been among the most satisfying — and challenging — aspects of my work.

So?

Millennials have been formed by social and technological changes as profound as those that formed my baby-boom generation. The global, instantaneous Now of the digital revolution has interconnected and captured the attention of younger (and many older) folks like nothing before. In addition, the related rise of finance-driven capitalism – moving at light-speed in global circuits and generating perpetual crisis – has made the vocational and economic lives of millennials increasingly precarious.[14] Not surprisingly, there is some palpable intergenerational resentment against baby-boomers, who have so broadly contributed, or otherwise acquiesced, to the environmental decline, entrenched racism and sexism, and economic insecurity that millennials inherit today.

Whatever millennials choose to learn from the Quaker tradition and from the generation or two before them will be mediated by the "fresh contact" of their own generational experience. At present, the most influential elder Friend among millennials I know is George Lakey, in his nonviolent activism and teaching (mentioned above). Lakey engages the activist interest of young Friends. That's all to the good, although I am concerned that many young Friends seem to regard the

---

[13] Douglas Gwyn, A Gathering of Spirits: The Friends General Conferences 1896 – 1950 (Philadelphia: FGC Quaker Press, 2018).

[14] Ross Hennesy has shared with me an essay, "Finding Meaning and Purpose within Late Capitalism: A Guide for Young Adults," which I hope will soon find publication. I am encouraged to see young adult Friends willing to confront the C-word: capitalism as a global system. The theme for the June 2019 Continuing Revolution gathering of young adult Friends at Pendle Hill was "Experimenting beyond Capitalism."

deeper registers of Quaker spirituality irrelevant to social witness. But without that deeper foundation, the proliferating intersectionality and rapid pace of a digitally mediated life easily leads to burnout.

As for me, I am still stuck writing books, which are so last century. But they seem to be the best way to convey the richness of Quaker history and theology. It's not just SPICES and "Quaker values." At the bookstore of the 2015 Friends General Conference Gathering I met millennial Friend Ross Hennesy, who was at that time working with Quaker Voluntary Service. He was searching for a Quaker book that the various QVS houses could use for group study in the coming year. He decided on my recent book, *A Sustainable Life: Quaker Faith and Practice in the Renewal of Creation.*[15] I was pleased, of course, that young adult Friends and other young adults in QVS would read and discuss my attempt to integrate the various aspects of Quaker faith and practice within the horizon of global sustainability. But I also understood and accepted Ross's comment that this book would not engage QVS participants very well. It just seemed the best available option. Indeed, no expressions of interest came my way from the QVS orbit the following year.

I suppose you could say I have been "carrying a torch" in the sense of tending the wound of some lost or unrequited love, some unfulfilled hope. Friends today (all generations) increasingly regard history as irrelevant to the all-consuming what's-happening-now. But some like myself, study and feel history more along lines expressed by the maverick Marxist Walter Benjamin:

Doesn't a breath of air that pervaded earlier days caress us as well? In the voices we hear, isn't there an echo of now silent ones? . . . If so, then there is a secret agreement between past generations and the present one. Then our coming was expected on earth. Then, like every generation that preceded us, we have been endowed with a weak messianic power, a power on which the past has a claim. That claim cannot be settled cheaply.[16]

Benjamin viewed present struggles for liberation as the redemption of past generations of suffering, oppression, and dashed hopes.

---

[15] Douglas Gwyn, A Sustainable Life: Quaker Faith and Practice in the Renewal of Creation (Philadelphia: FGC Quaker Press, 2014).

[16] Walter Benjamin, Theses II and XII of "Theses on the Philosophy of History (1940)," in Illuminations: Essays and Reflections, Hannah Arendt, ed. (New York: Schocken, 2007), pp. 254, 260; and Benjamin, "On the Concept of History," as quoted in Jonathan Flatley, Affective Mapping: Melancholia and the Politics of Modernism (Cambridge: Harvard University Press, 2008), p. 145. Also see Michael Löwy, Fire Alarm: Reading Walter Benjamin's 'On the Concept of History' (London: Verso, 2016), pp. 78-84.

Because Quaker faith is experiential rather than creedal, our theology is narrative in character. The Quaker penchant for journals, memoirs, and histories bears this out. Our present succession of generations takes its place within the larger "cloud of witnesses" the writer of the Letter to the Hebrews saw streaming behind him or her (Hebrews 12:1). We are poorer spiritually and bereft of evocative models of prophetic faith without the echo of their voices.

In recent years, I've been drawn to the story of Simeon and Anna in Luke's Gospel. These two old-timers hung around the Jerusalem temple, awaiting the redemption of Israel. When Mary and Joseph took the infant Jesus to the temple to be dedicated to the covenant (i.e., circumcised), Simeon and Anna recognized the first glimmer of redemption in that infant. Of course, they knew they would not live to see any such redemption unfold. But it was enough to see a glimmer of it. They lived in darkening times for their people: the violently oppressive Roman occupation, its withering taxation, the collaborationist regime of Judea's priests and aristocracy, the desperate poverty of their people, the rising level of brigandage, and the futile violence of Zealot resistance.

All that made the glimmer of a newborn life stand out all the more to the eyes of faith, like the star of Bethlehem in the night sky in Matthew's gospel. Of course, it's an irony of the gospel that the redemption Jesus offered was diametrically opposed to the aristocratic regime that ran the temple. Still, these two elderly Jews encountered him there, at opposite ends of the generational cycle. All the factors that darkened the times of Simeon and Anna would lead to the destruction of the temple seventy years later — forty years after the lynching of this infant they beheld.

We too live in darkening times: climate change, gun-madness, renewed racial violence, masculinity in crisis, and the global capitalist regime of wealth-extraction from the earth and its peoples. I feel like Simeon and Anna, an old Quaker still hanging around Friends meetings, looking for a glimmer of redemption. I'm not sure that any coming redemption would have much to do with Friends meetings. But that is where I wait and watch.

Helen Cobban: Journeying

T his is far from a complete memoir. It is more like a series of quick reflections on times in my life when I've experienced the power of "continuing revelation" to pull me up short and force me to reconsider long held shibboleths. Here goes:

Israel/Palestine: I was born into a very traditional (Church of England, Conservative-voting) family of the British upper middle class. I was 14 when the Israeli-Arab war of 1967 broke out. As I recall it, just about all the news coverage on our grainy black-and-white television and in the two newspapers my father took, the *Times* and *The Daily Telegraph*, was solidly pro-Israel. The British conservative elite was still smarting from the rise of that upstart, President Nasser, in Egypt, and was delighted to see him "taken down a notch."

Helena Cobban

Besides, the Israelis were "modern". They were "like us". They had "made the desert bloom," etc.

Three years later, in April 1970, I spent a month in Lebanon with my elder sister Mary and her husband, Martin Gostelow. They were both working at the American Community School in Beirut; and I had an eye-opening time staying in their little flat, right on the city's sparkling Mediterranean coast.

Martin was a big adventurer, and every weekend we'd cram into their powder-blue sports car to go visit someplace interesting. We went to Crusader castles. We went to many amazing places in neighboring Syria. We went to Baalbek, and Byblos, and the Cedars of Lebanon. The country was very tense. There were many roadblocks, especially around the big Palestinian refugee camps that ringed just about every Lebanese city of any size.

"Who are the refugees? Why are they there? Why are there roadblocks?" I would ask. Mary, who later wrote many excellent books about the art of embroidery, was working with a group of women who sought to provide income to women in the camps by helping them market products made with their fine, Palestinian-heritage cross-stitch. She directed me to an information office some upper-class Palestinian women she knew had set up, not far from their apartment.

I started reading the testimonies many of the refugees had written about the ethnic cleansing they had suffered at the hands of the Jewish forces that took over Palestine in 1948. I wanted to learn more.

In fall 1970, I enrolled at Oxford. In the hurly-burly of the matriculation week, I connected with some intriguing student social-justice networks. One was a feminist group. A couple were leftist/Marxist. One was the Oxford University Arab Society. I established lasting connections with people in all three types of group. One ardent Trotskyist at Oxford with whom I worked closely was Alan Adler, who had earlier attended the most elite Jewish boarding school in Britain, Carmel College — a place from which he was notoriously expelled because he had tried to establish there a cell of the Palestinian liberation movement, Fateh. (Tragically, a few years later, Alan died by suicide.) Many of the Oxford leftists at the time were Jewish, and most of the ones I knew shared the concern I was developing for the long-usurped rights of the Palestinians, including their right to return to the homes and farms from which they had been expelled in 1948.

For Palestinians themselves, it was a turbulent time — as so many other eras have been, throughout the past century. September 1970 was what Palestinians and many other Arabs called "Black September". During the 1967 war, the very well-prepared and well-armed Israeli military had trounced the armies of all its Arab-state neighbors, bringing huge additional swathes of Arab land under direct Israeli military occupation. The Arab state leaders were in disarray.

But that period after the 1967 war also saw an explosive growth of Palestinian guerrilla groups, which found a strong, supportive base in the Palestinian refugee camps ringing the area of "1948" Israel: in Gaza, the West Bank, Jordan, Syria, and Lebanon. The guerrillas prime demand was to see their right to return to their family's homes finally met. They were particularly strong in Jordan, where Palestinian refugees made up a clear majority of the country's population; and from 1968 on they sought to expand their influence and their control there as much as possible.

In Black September of 1970, Jordan's King Hussein fought back, with some help from the United States and Israel. Amid bloody fighting he pushed the guerrillas quite out of his country, though most of the country's noncombatant Palestinian refugees still remained. Most of the expelled fighters ended up in Lebanon, a country whose state was too weak to keep them out and was anyway riven with numerous sectarian and political divides.

I graduated from Oxford in 1973, not brilliantly, and after a few months' consideration I decided, yes, I really did want to become a foreign correspondent. I followed in the footsteps of many male British adventurers before me, picked up my notebook, and decamped to a foreign clime. What better place to launch my career than Beirut? My friends from the Oxford University Arab Society had contacts and relatives there; and I was on my way.

My journalistic experience? At the elite girls 'boarding-school I attended I had hand-produced (and "published" in five blurry carbon copies) three issues of a small satirical magazine; and at Oxford I was on the editorial collective of a short-lived counter-culture magazine called the *Oxford Strumpet*. Ah well, chutzpah and ignorance stepped in to persuade me I had a career plan. Beirut was then a bustling hub of commerce, with numerous banks and businesses working hard to provide services to the massively growing Middle Eastern oil industry.

I launched my career by working as a copywriter in a local high-end advertising agency, racing twice daily from my desk there to attend immersion classes in modern standard Arabic that were held at the Jesuit university in another part of town. Eight months later, Lebanon's civil war broke out, and I was ideally placed to turbo-charge my career in actual journalism.

By the time I was 23, I was regularly getting front-page stories about developments both in Lebanon and further afield published on the front page of the London *Sunday Times* and the *Christian Science Monitor*. The work was exhilarating, exacting, and sometimes fairly dangerous. The work of a good reporter is also, I think, more than a little bit Quakerly. As a reporter, you need to look around you and listen very closely, and scrupulously record the truth as you see it. You need to be able to interact respectfully with people with whom you may (personally) disagree very strongly, both in order to record their sayings and their actions accurately and in order to be fair to them. In doing this, you need to set your own emotions and judgments aside while you are "getting the story," and try to stay pleasant and open. (I worked for a short while for the Reuters bureau there. They had a rule of thumb that, since their product gets used by newspapers in many other countries that have different needs, any story you write should be structured so that an editor using the story in any place could cut the story to the length he/she needed at the end of any paragraph, and be left with a journalistically "balanced" story. There's discipline!)

So my journalism career was advancing very well until one day in 1981, when my then-husband was covering the Iran-Iraq war in Tehran from the Iranian side, I was covering it in Baghdad from the Iraqi side, and our two small children were home with their nanny in Beirut... and she contacted me in a panic to tell me one of the local Lebanese militias had *put a sniper onto our roof*, which of course made the whole building into a valid military target.

I utterly and humiliatingly lost my nerve. I took the first car I could back across the desert to Amman (a 17-hour drive), flew back to Beirut, scooped up the nanny and the children, and took them all out to the safety of London.

So that was the end of my burgeoning career as a Middle East correspondent. I was stranded in London with two small children, no career, and as it happened a broken marriage. I turned to writing books, with the first two being on the PLO and on the history of modern Lebanon. To support myself and my kids while I wrote them, I had to come here to the United States where I got fellowships at well-heeled universities that allowed me to do the writing.

My first summer here, in 1982, the Israeli military invaded Lebanon (again). This time they went all the way up to Beirut where they circled the "progressive-held" part of the city in which my husband, all our friends, and I had been living and bombed the bejeesus out of it. Later, the Israeli military surrounded the Sabra and Shatila refugee camps where I had earlier provided English coaching to a small group of girls.

The Israelis brought in their local Falangist Party allies, who committed terrible mass killings, rapes, and other atrocities in the camps and to this day I don't know what happened to most of the girls whom I had coached. (There was a continuing reign of terror in the camps for many years thereafter.) But within days, as the scale of the massacres became clear, the peace movement that still existed in Israel at that time mobilized very broadly and brought something like 20% of Israel's entire population onto the streets in protest. That "peace movement" would peter out after the 1993 Oslo Accords and finally died a sudden death in 2000...

From the late 1980s through the mid-1990s, I worked in two related ways on Palestinian issues. One was to stand up wherever I could for the rights of Palestinians as being full members of the human race and to refute the many layers of lies that continued to be told about them and their cause here in the United States. Another was to join or lead various projects to bring peace-minded Palestinians and Israelis together to try to jointly brainstorm rights-based solutions to their conflict.

Those latter projects, sadly, came to almost naught. Jewish Israelis increasingly gravitated toward rightwing, ethnonationalist parties that refused to make any concessions to Palestinians but worked only to consolidate Israel's hold over the lands occupied in 1967, especially in the West Bank (including East Jerusalem) and the Israeli-occupied lands of Syria's Golan.

In 2002-2004, I was honored and blessed to work with an international group of 14 Quakers convened by AFSC to undertake a fact-finding mission to Israel, the occupied Palestinian areas, and all their neighboring states. We wrestled at length together over the issues and ended up writing a book-length report under the title *When the Rain Returns: Towards Justice and Reconciliation in Israel and Palestine.*

In our conclusions, we wrote that it was not up to us, but to the direct stakeholders in the issue, to determine whether the outcome should be one democratic state or two states alongside each other between the Mediterranean Sea and the Jordan River — but that any such outcome should be one that ensures that the full human rights of all these stakeholders gets respected, implemented, and guaranteed on a fully equitable basis. We defined "direct stakeholders" as being all citizens of Israel and all Palestinians including the Palestinian refugees whose families were displaced from their homes in Palestine in 1948 and 1967.

In 2005, the churches and other civil-society organizations in Palestine issued a potent call for a rights-based solution in Palestine/Israel, irrespective of whether there would one state or two. (The similarities between our conclusions and theirs was no surprise. We had listened closely to everyone we met on our factfinding mission.)They also called on social-justice activists everywhere and the rest of the international community to use the traditional nonviolent means of Boycott, Divestment, and Sanctions to try bring the Israeli leaders to a rights-based negotiating table, as had earlier proven successful in combating and ending settler colonialism and Apartheid in South Africa. Four years later, the Palestinian churches amplified this call with their release of the Kairos Document. Though I've served as a writer/researcher and an activist on various other social-justice issues along, working on Palestinian rights issues remains a core leading for me.

War and peace: I can't really think about the transformations my thinking has undergone on this issue (or a number of others) without thinking about my father. He played a deeply formative role in my becoming-as-a-person, since my mother died when I was eight and had been essentially AWOL from my life for years prior to that, due to the chronic illness that had led to her death.

My father was an upper-middle-class Englishman of the old school. Literally, indeed, since the private school of which he was headmaster had been "re"-founded in 1563. He had served as an intelligence officer in the British military during World War 2, having volunteered for Officers Training School upon the outbreak of war despite being far too old to be conscripted. In his WW-2 service, he provided intel help for the forces invading Normandy on D-Day, advanced with those forces (though not in the front line,) and ended up in the military administration the British ran in Germany, alongside the three other victorious Allied militaries.

When we were young, he never talked much about his years in the military apart from a few stories; but inside and outside our immediate family his service was always seen as extremely laudable. My mother's only brother had been killed in WW-2 while he was a flyboy in North Africa and her only two uncles had both been killed in World War 1. During WW-2, she and her family had suffered a lot in London under the Blitz until she and her baby (my oldest sister, Mary) were evacuated to rural Devon. Memorializing the dead of the two World Wars every November 11 was a part of the annual round of community observances in all the communities I was part of in my childhood.

My father's duties in Germany and elsewhere during his WW-2 service were dictated by the fact that he knew some German. In the late 1950s and early 1960s he pioneered some people-to-people outreach to counterpart institutions in Germany.

When I went to Lebanon in 1974, I did not intend to become a war correspondent, but that is what I soon became, both there and in the early months of the massive war waged between Iran and Iraq from 1980 through 1988. My position as a Western correspondent in Lebanon was distinctive. The war erupted eight months after I arrived; and shortly after that I married a nice Lebanese man whom I had met there and had two children, born in the late 1970s. He also worked in the media, as a cameraman for international news agencies.

All the other Western correspondents were males. They lived either in swanky hotels or in nice apartments where they and any family they had were cared for either by staff or by their wives. As for me, I was trying to run the household and look after the kids while also doing a job that involved crazy, irregular hours and often, a degree of danger.

Later, I came to see that many of the experiences I had had in Beirut gave me powerful insights into the nature of war. They underlined for me, above all, that *wars inflict the greatest damage on women, children, and the vulnerable, and that most of this harm comes not from actual physical impacts of weapons but from the shattering of basic services.*

I learned early on during the Lebanese civil war to manage when the electricity was cut off. We could gin up paraffin lanterns and cook over little paraffin stoves. But when the water was cut off, life was really, really hard. I would trudge down to the well in the basement of our building and haul jerrycans of water back up to our seventh-floor apartment. Every drop was so precious it would be used multiple times. Finally, after being used, say, to boil pasta and then wash the floor, the last remnants would get re-used to flush the toilet.

Frail neighbors often could not manage and might have to take the dangerous trek back to their ancestral villages. One neighbor was shot by a stray bullet as she stood washing dishes at her sink. I also had the valuable experience that the family of my husband, Sohel, was divided between the two warring halves of Beirut. He belonged to one of the numerous smaller Christian sects that dot Lebanon. We lived (as nearly everyone working for the international media did) in West Beirut, the part of the city that became controlled by the generally more "progressive" and pro-Palestinian parties and militias. But plenty of Sohel's cousins and other family members lived in East Beirut, the area controlled by rabidly anti-Palestinian parties and militias, led by the Falangists.

During the six years of civil war that I lived there, 1975-81, I had to report on numerous massacres. Most of those were committed by the Falangists and their allies, whose militias engaged in ruthless ethnic/sectarian "cleansing" of all the spaces they controlled, of anyone who was not both Lebanese and Christian. The Palestinians and their progressive allies committed a smaller number of less brutal violations. The leaders of many of the leftist Lebanese parties, as of the Palestinian guerrilla groups, were Christians and around a third of the population of the "progressive"-held part of Beirut where we lived were Christians. The rest were Muslims, and there were some specifically Muslim militias that fought alongside the leftist militias and the Palestinian guerrillas.

But fairly often, I would take the blood-chillingly scary trip across the "Green Line," to East Beirut, whether to follow a news story, interview a leader of the Falangist Party or one of their allied parties — or to go with Sohel to pay a family visit to some of his cousins. The atmosphere in East Beirut and its Falangist-controlled hinterland was often terrifying. There was a ravine where, as members of leading "Christian" families would openly recall, their fighters would nightly toss the bodies of Palestinians or leftists whom they'd killed. (The 15-year-old daughter of one leading family, the Chamouns, laughingly told me and her parents that they had stopped their school-bus by the ravine on the way from school that day, "to see what new bodies there were there," as she casually tossed her schoolbooks onto their dining-room table.)

On walls throughout the Falangist-held parts of Beirut there was a stenciled message stating baldly "It is the duty of every Lebanese to kill a Palestinian." It was signed by a small group called "The Guardians of the Cedars." I never saw that any attempt had been made by anyone else to cover or obliterate it. But some of my husband's cousins lived and did the best they could to survive the war there.

Lebanon's civil war dragged on and on, for many years after I had left the country. Numerous outside governments and arms traders had a hand in it, keeping it going for a staggering 14 years. The ideological lines which at first had seemed pretty clear-cut became more and more muddied as the years went on. Sometimes the Syrian Army was fighting on one side, sometimes another. Sometimes this militia was fighting closely with that militia — and then within a moment they would be at loggerheads, their fighters duking it out against each other with all the heavy weapons their outside sponsors had given them... right in the middle of the city's crowded streets.

I left the country in 1981. It was not until 1989 that the war-weary politicians who led what was left of Lebanon's allegedly "democratic" political system dragged themselves to the Saudi city of Ta'if where a finally concerned Saudi leadership distributed enough money among them to buy a new political agreement. The country has suffered many terrible woes since then — including three devastating attacks from Israel's high-tech, US-aided military, in 1993, 1996, and 2006 — but its people have not fallen back into anything even close to an outright civil war.

One thing I learned, up close and at first hand, is that a "civil" war among citizens of the same country is one of the most un-civil kinds of war there is. Another is that once the hate-fueled genies of a civil war are let out of the bottle, it is very, very hard to stuff them back in; and that even if the claimed "ideological" cause espoused by one combatant group or another might change radically or soften, the war itself can still have enough momentum of its own by then that it continues in one form or another, regardless of whatever tattered ideological issue may be at stake. (There are, after all, numerous big interests lined up behind the actors you see on any such battlefield; the arms merchants and financiers will often find a way to keep things going.)

Another is that when the fighting has been going on for a while, there really are no "good" actors. Everyone is sullied by the miasma of war. But over time I also, paradoxically, came to the conclusion that though, during a war, some people may carry out the most atrocious, inhuman acts, that does not mean they are intrinsically bad people.

I came out of my experience of the Lebanese civil war exhausted and with some notable symptoms of PTSD. But I was fascinated by all aspects of the experience — the political, the psychological, and the strategic. I quickly wrote those two books on the politics of the Palestine Question and on Lebanon's history, and then I took up a fellowship to do a program in strategic studies at the University of Maryland. Those studies helped me to put the phenomenon of the "small, third-world civil war" I had lived through in Lebanon into a broader geopolitical perspective.

One of the things I knew, from both my experience and my studies, was that wars are most damaging to people when they drag on. By then, I was writing a regular column on global affairs for the *Christian Science Monitor* (CSM). In 1990, Iraqi leader Saddam Hussein invaded Kuwait and summarily annexed it to Iraq. I saw that as a big challenge to the world order that had existed since WW-2 and a rude re-eruption of "might makes right" in international affairs. In my writings at the time, I supported the numerous efforts that various parties including the United Nations and the Soviet Union made to find a way to negotiate Saddam's exit from Kuwait.

But the U.S. military had a massive military machine all ginned up and ready to go in Europe, and since the US-Soviet Cold War was winding down at that time (after the 1989 fall of the Berlin Wall), it was fairly straightforward for Pres. George H.W. Bush and his military leaders to ship large parts of that military machine over to Saudi Arabia and the Gulf and use it to push the Iraqis out of Kuwait by force.

By the end of 1990, it was clear that Bush was preparing for a war. I had a deadline due for my CSM column, and I wrote something that afterwards I came to regret. I wrote that that if there was no alternative to using force to help Kuwait regain its sovereignty, then the best thing would be if that force would be overwhelming and bring about a speedy and decisive victory. That was what happened. Tens of thousands of Iraqis were killed in the US-led assault, and there were big uprisings against Saddam in both the north and the south of Iraq.

Nobody gave effective help to the rebels in the south, whom Saddam's forces then slaughtered in place. In the north, many of the

Kurds who rebelled were able, when countered by Saddam's forces, to flee to Turkey; and they were then able to return to parts of Northern Iraq under the cover of a US-imposed "no-fly zone." In the push to "contain"/punish Saddam, Bush and then Clinton imposed and then maintained very tough economic sanctions on the whole of Iraq (except the part in the north where Kurdish Iraqis lived in a de-facto US protectorate.) Those sanctions continued until 2003, wrecking Iraq's health and education systems. An estimated 500,000 Iraqis died as a result, as Madeleine Albright infamously admitted.

Throughout the 1990s, feeling guilty from the writings in which I had advocated a "quick and decisive" war to free Kuwait, I wrestled with the whole question of pacifism. In 1996, I started worshiping with Quakers, and within a few years I became more convinced than ever that war can never "be the answer." In 2000, I formally joined Charlottesville Friends Meeting.

In the early 2000s, I undertook a new research project, in which I examined the efforts three countries in sub-Saharan Africa had made a decade earlier to end very destructive inter-group conflicts. The countries were South Africa, Rwanda, and Mozambique, and I got the privilege of doing a small amount of field research in all of them. One of the greatest gifts that work gave me was to introduce me to several ways in which people not from the (very judgmental) Abrahamic faith traditions look at the issue of human violence. I found these lessons presented particularly clearly by many of the people I interviewed and talked with in Mozambique, where there still were — and I hope, still are — strong networks of *curanderos/as* (traditional healers) from across the country's rich patchwork of different ethnic groups.

These healers 'view of the human condition is very different from the individualistic way that "Westerners" look at it. Their view is that *it is the natural condition of humans to be in cooperative, productive relationship with other humans*. That, they say, is the "natural order" — as opposed to the "Western" view that it is the natural human condition to be violent and that the goal of "civilization" is to tame that violence.

The *curanderos/as* (and many other people) I spoke with in Mozambique thought that violence, rather than being "natural" to humans, was a malevolent outside force that could, in essence, capture and take hold of humans and use them for its own ends — as opposed to the Western view that humans can easily "use" violence and then set it aside when they choose. Honestly, the view of the Mozambican *curanderos/as* — which is also shared by many non-Western peoples around the world — made a lot of sense to me. It resonated in particular with what I had learned about the violence I saw "taking hold of" so many of the people who had participated in the civil war in Lebanon, a quarter-century earlier.

Empires, human rights, civilization: I grew up in the bosom of one "Western" empire that was rapidly crumbling and for the past 37 years have been living in the bosom of another, that has been at an earlier stage of the crumbling process.

The decolonization process I lived through in England in the late 1950s and 1960s had been imposed on the government in London by economic necessity. Briefly speaking, by around 1919 the empire that had earlier been a massive economic boon for the Brits was starting to become a burden. Then, WW-2 placed a huge additional burden on Britain's economy. India, Pakistan, and Palestine were the first colonial holdings to be sloughed off, in 1947-48, and the rest followed. When I was growing up, the scratchy black-and-white newsreels shown in our cinemas would regularly include footage of the British "Governor-General" in some distant clime (usually a military man, and often wearing knee-length shorts). He would solemnly bring down the Union Jack from a flagpole in the tropics somewhere and then stand stiffly to attention and salute as the flag of the newly independent nation would be hauled up. He would then exchange a quick handshake with the country's new leader, who very frequently was someone who until just days earlier had been roundly excoriated as a "terrorist;" frequently, this new leader and all of his followers had been held in a British prison until just a week or two prior...

As we grew up, the general culture in Britain did not dwell either on fact that the decolonizations we were seeing had been imposed by economic necessity, or on the numerous terrible legacies of the very lengthy colonial era that Britons were leaving behind. If Indians and "Pakistanis" were fighting brutal wars in what had been British India, or Arabs and Jews were fighting in what had been British Palestine, then that was surely the result of "age-old hatreds" or other forces that, prior to Britain leaving, the always-benign British administration had earlier been able to hold in check.

The long history of the British Empire having deliberately pursued "divide and rule" policy wherever it went was mentioned as seldom as were the origins of the great wealth of so many British institutions that had been built through centuries of imperial plunder. Instead of looking at the harms our colonization had imposed, most Brits were content to pat themselves on the back for the "generosity" and "vision" of the decolonization. In general, decolonization was seen as "a good thing," though there were pockets of nostalgia for the old empire. My father, for example, would sometimes peer over his copy of the *Daily Telegraph* to pronounce that, "Well, really, so often good government is better than self-government" — with the assumption there being that British rule of some distant colony had *ipso facto* been "good" government... And once, he even brought home a little booklet for me and my sisters to read: it was titled, "Why not Apartheid"? The atmosphere in the boarding school I was sent to was similarly conservative.

But I started to get a different perspective on things when I was 14 or 15. This was a single-sex school with very infrequent *exeats* [or breaks] and almost no chance to meet boys. But my friend Lesley and I discovered that one way to meet boys was to attend chapter meetings of the United Nations Association that were organized at a local church.

I don't recall going to more than two or three of the meetings, but they were truly eye-opening. (The boys, less so.) At one of the meetings, we even held a debate on *whether the United Nations should pass a resolution that would allow the bombing of government forces in White-held "Rhodesia,"* where in 1965 the head of the strictly White-controlled local government, Ian Smith, had made a Unilateral Declaration of Independence (UDI), rather than comply with demands from London and the United Nations that the country needed to shift to majority rule before it could gain independence.

Not all the British-origin people in Sub-Saharan Africa had been as happy with the colonial order of things as Ian Smith. We had a (White) next-door neighbor when I was growing up who emigrated to South Africa and returned a few years later because he couldn't stand the colonial order of things there. Later, I started to meet British-origin people (Quakers and others) who had been living in South Africa for some generations and had played strong roles in the country's anti-Apartheid movement there. And later yet, I learned about a British Quaker social worker called Eileen Fletcher who had gone to Kenya in the mid-1950s, during the height of a brutal mass-incarceration campaign the British authorities there were mounting against the country's indigenous Kikuyu people and their Mau Mau independence movement.

Eileen Fletcher had been hired to do "rehabilitation" work in the mass-incarceration camps in 1954 or so; but when she saw the terrible conditions in the camps, she resigned in protest and, after returning to London, penned three articles recounting what she had seen. Her testimony sparked investigations by Labour MPs and provided the backdrop to the campaign that, four years later, led to the closing of the prison camps and paved the way for Kenyan independence. (One of those held and abused in those camps was President Obama's grandfather.)

To be honest, when I left Britain for Lebanon in 1974, and then came to the United States in 1982, I was really glad to escape the suffocatingly classist and racist atmosphere of the British social system... But now, I find myself living in, and a citizen of, another settler-colonial state (the USA) whose settlers, nearly 200 years before Ian Smith, had made their own Unilateral Declaration of Independence against the colonial metropole, in large part because they wanted to have more freedom to grab the lands and resources of those around them while dispossessing, on some occasions genociding, and always oppressing the indigenes who lived here.

And this country, too, has constructed a globe-girdling empire that seeks to control the lives and destinies of peoples in as many other parts of the world as possible. Members of the U.S. political elite are nowhere near as explicit in proclaiming the existence (and civilizing mission) of their "empire" as members of the British elite were, back in the day. Instead, and especially since the end of the U.S.-Soviet Cold War, members of the U.S. political elite have talked and acted as if somehow Washington "represents" the peoples of all the world, even though the U.S. population makes up much less than 5% of the global total of humankind.

For example, U.S. leaders, politicians, and corporate-media pundits frequently claim that "the international community" is behind a policy of X, Y, or Z, when what they are referring to is the U.S. government and whatever makeshift coalition it can cobble together to support this policy. That way, members of this elite and all the U.S. Americans they are able to influence can feel good that whenever Washington takes any actions overseas, it is doing so "on behalf of" all humanity — and this is the case even when the governments representing the vast majority of the world's people clearly oppose Washington's policies.

Thus, a large number of U.S. citizens still feel that their country — and by extension, they themselves—have been "specially anointed" in some way to take a whole range of actions around the world when what has really happened is that they (we) are "specially privileged" to be part of a citizenry that enjoys such power at the global level. And with that privilege comes, in my view, some special responsibilities: to understand the many harms that U.S. policy has inflicted on numerous peoples around the world and to work to end those harms; to understand the institutional roots of U.S. privilege and to seek to dismantle it; and to lift up the voices of everybody around the world who has been treated as "less than" by U.S. policymakers.

And since Quakers who happen to be U.S. citizens share in the special privileges afforded by U.S. citizenhood, these Quakers, I believe, have special responsibilities — not shared by Quakers who happen to have other passports, or none — to work on these issues of dismantling U.S. privilege on the world stage. (Having the passport of a stable, wealthy country is a great, and often unacknowledged boon. Personally, I have the right to two such passports. But I have many Palestinian friends who have no passports at all and have suffered the insecurities and vulnerability of statelessness continuously since 1948. What can we do to end that situation?)

Another special responsibility that those of us who are Quakers or other faith-led pacifists who are citizens of rich stable countries have, I believe, is a responsibility not to "preach" nonviolence or any other doctrine to various oppressed people around the world who are fighting for their rights. I am someone who tries not to use physical violence in any part of my life and to dissociate myself from the structures of institutional violence. Moreover, as just noted, we U.S. citizens all have a massive task to perform, in trying to wean our own government — the one for whose actions we, as citizens of democracy, are directly responsible — from its long held addiction to the use of violence on a massive scale.

But if Vietnamese, or Iraqi, or Algerian, South African, Kenyan, or Palestinian people choose to use violence as a means to end the oppression they have suffered at the hands of rich, exploitative (and always super-violent) "Western" powers, then it is not my place to criticize them for that choice. If asked, I might point out to such people that in my experience, the use of violence may (or may not) win some worthwhile political goal — but it always also leaves troublesome legacies within the community that uses it… If asked, I might point out that there are numerous fundamentally non-violent tasks that need to be carried out if a nation or people is ever to achieve self-determination or self-emancipation…

But why would I expect to be asked? Any expectation that Westerners would have any "special knowledge" about how an oppressed people can best achieve its liberation would be an act of extreme hubris. Being an anti-imperialist in the bosom of the powerful Western empire that is the United States sometimes feels especially hard since this "empire" does not (as the British Empire did) clearly announce itself as such; indeed, it can be hard for many people to see any "empire" at work here, at all.

But we U.S. Quakers are very lucky to have the example of John Woolman to learn from. Woolman, a British-heritage Quaker who lived in a community of mainly-Quaker colonial settlers near Philadelphia, is best known for the strong leading he had, and acted on, to learn at firsthand about and bear witness to the situation of enslaved persons in the U.S. South — in particular, those who were held in bondage by Quakers.

But in his journal, he also told of the work he had done to act on his leading to understand and bear witness to the situation of indigenous, native Americans some ninety years, as he noted, after European settlers who were Quakers started implanting their colonies on those Indians ' native lands and hunting grounds, in "Penn"sylvania and other regions.

(A personal note here: for me, it was reading John Woolman's journal over the course of a few days in January 1996 that finally convinced me I needed to be a Quaker. How powerfully his words spoke to me; and they still do. And how amazing is it that a simple, faithful fruit farmer like John Woolman could 250 years ago have penned a memoir that, bound in a paper volume, can still speak to us today?)

God and such: When I was growing up in England, the Church of England (Anglican) was a key pillar of the English Establishment. The monarchy, of course, had been inextricably bound up with Anglicanism since the days of Henry VIII (1509-1547). The school my father was headmaster of was, like most other "public" (that is, private) schools, an Anglican foundation.

In the world of such schools in which my father moved, we knew there were a couple of schools that were Catholic; one was Jewish; a couple were Quaker... but the vast majority were Anglican. And in British society more broadly, being "C of E" was always regarded as the default option. Unless you were affirmatively Jewish, or Catholic, or Hindu, or Muslim, or a member of a "non-established" protestant church like the Methodists, Congregationalists, Church of Scotland, Quakers, etc, then you were assumed to be C of E. Besides, being C of E never committed you to believing anything in particular. In our town, Abingdon, there were five different C of E churches, ranging from very High-Church (incense! bells and smells!) through very happy-clappy.

In vacation-time, our family might attend any of them. But during the school terms we would always go to the school chapel, presided over by the school chaplain and by our father, both decked out in white surplices and MA hoods from Oxford or Cambridge. But a lot of this was purely tradition-affirming ritual. In the C of E, you were not required to actually believe anything theological or cosmological. Much later, I learned about the role that C of E bishops had played in helping subdue the "native" peoples in Kenya and Uganda — a role they continued to play even through the 1950s.

How important it was to have the questioning Quakerism of someone like Eileen Fletcher to bear witness in London to those horrors. (Earlier, the Quaker-influenced Roger Casement had similarly borne public witness to the many vile atrocities the Belgians committed in

Congo.) When I was twelve or so, and at the C of E boarding-school I was sent to after our mother died, we were confirmed into the church by the local bishop. I recall that during the confirmation-prep sessions we attended in the chapel, I had a strong longing for something special to happen to me at the time the bishop would "lay hands" on me. Something about the apostolic succession of such hand-laying — dating back to Jesus Christ and St Peter themselves! — excited my imagination.

Nothing did happen. And as I became increasingly rebellious at the school, skipping mandatory chapel on Sunday mornings was one of the first (and surprisingly easy) acts of rebellion I undertook. Seven years or so later, when I was in the maelstrom of the war in Lebanon, my alienation from anything churchy became complete. The Falangists and their allies in the other "Christian" militias would go into battle with stickers of the Virgin Mary adorning their rifle butts. In a Maronite Christian monastery north of Beirut I saw the head of the monastery direct a squad of novices as they unloaded boxes of heavy ammunition from a truck and carried them across the courtyard to put them into one of the monastery's storerooms.

In 1976, the head of the Falangist militia, Bashir Gemayyel, organized a tour for members of the media of the ruins of the former Palestinian refugee camp at Tel al-Zaatar (Hill of Thyme), where we saw and on occasion had to step through the crumpled remains of hundreds of Palestinian civilians slaughtered by Gemayyel's fighters when they had finally stormed the camp the day before. Before Gemayyel's men led us into the camp, Gemayyel gave a short press conference at which he said openly, "I am proud of what you will see inside the camp."

If I had had any lingering nostalgia for organized Christianity, my experiences in Lebanon put an end to it. After I came to the United States in 1982 and had moved from Boston to Washington, my father put me in touch with his friend Canon Charlie Martin, who headed Peace Committee at Washington National Cathedral. Martin wanted the Peace Committee to become active on the Palestine Question, so he commissioned me to write a periodic newsletter for them on the issue, which ran for about 15 months, starting in 1987.

But these American canons, unlike their counterparts in the U.K., really wanted me to commit to some profession of their faith. I was unable to. Still, however, I pursued an intermittent search for a moral/spiritual community; and for a few years I hung out with the Unitarians. Then, I discovered John Woolman's *Journal*, and from that day forth I was hooked on Quakerism.

Let me just enumerate what I loved about Woolman. First and foremost, it was his commitment, when seized by some spiritual concern, to go and gain firsthand knowledge of the situation that had aroused that concern — and then, to come back to his Quaker meetings of origin (his Monthly meeting, his Quarter, and his Yearly Meeting, PYM) to bear witness to what he had seen and experienced.

Thus, when he was seized by the issue of slavery and specifically the ways many Quakers were participating and profiting from the practice, he decided to take his pony down to Virginia and North Carolina, to go and see for himself. When he was seized by the issue of the wars the Pennsylvanians were being asked to fund and to support in the west of the colony, against "the French and the Indians," he resolved to travel to Western Pennsylvania to see and learn about the situation of the native Americans there, for himself. When he was seized by a concern about the "triangular trade" across the Atlantic that many English-heritage Quaker shipowners were involved in, and that centered around transporting enslaved persons and rum, he decided to take one such ship across the Atlantic to England to see for himself and to share his concerns with members of London Yearly Meeting. It was on that journey that in 1772 he contracted smallpox and died.

Woolman is best known for his writings, in the *Journal* and elsewhere, against slavery; but I have long found some of his most powerful writings to be his journal entries about the journey he made to Western Pennsylvania ("Wyoming"). And he made that journey, remember, at a time when all indigenous people in America, especially those in Western Pennsylvania or elsewhere who might have taken up arms against the British, were routinely dehumanized for being "savages" or worse.

In his journal, he alluded to some of the physical difficulties of the travel — but he spent more time recounting the self-doubt he experienced along the way, asking whether he was pursuing this enquiry mainly as some form of self-aggrandizement, rather than from humility. He waxed eloquent on the sad state he found the "Indians" to be living in, 90 years after the first arrival onto their shores of the European colonists who had devastated so much of the natural habitat on which the Indians had long depended. He wrote,

> Love was the first motion, and then a concern arose to spend some time with the Indians, that I might feel and understand their life and the spirit they live in, if haply I might receive some instruction from them, or they be in any degree helped forward by my following the leadings of Truth amongst them. (p.127)

A European settler stating that he hoped he might be able to learn something from the American indigenes? Now, that was revolutionary. He wrote a riveting account of how, at one house he was visiting, he felt he had startled an Indian man also arriving there, and the Indian had raised his tomahawk in a gesture that startled Woolman. But Woolman immediately felt that perhaps it had been *his* presence that had startled the Indian, so he held his hand out to him in friendship and the Indian reciprocated in kind... I was bowled over. I found so many rich lessons to learn from those parts of his journal, a volume I have returned to again and again. After first encountering Woolman, I started attending a small Quaker worship group that convened in northwest Washington. Eighteen months later, my spouse and I moved to Charlottesville, VA, where he had a job at the University of Virginia. I became involved with Charlottesville Friends Meeting and rapidly found it to be a powerful and very nourishing spiritual home.

Back in the late 1990s, some of the older generation of Quakers who had established the meeting 50 years later were still alive and very active. There was Chic Moran, who had been a CO in World War-2 and right after that had gone with AFSC to help rebuild damaged parts of Poland. There was Elaine Bell, who with her (earlier deceased) husband Colin had done pathbreaking work with AFSC in Geneva, Philadelphia, New York, and elsewhere. There was Jay Worrall, who had written a detailed account of the Quakers who had had a long (and often morally troubling) history in Virginia since the late 1600s and who had also contributed greatly to Charlottesville, working with African-American allies to dismantle some of the institutionalized racism the city had long suffered from. There was Gladys Swift, who feistily carried her large, yellowing anti-war placard to street-corner vigils long after her fading eyesight and flawed sense of balance made it quite unsafe for her to do so...

All those amazing role models and friends — and others in the Charlottesville meeting — wore their "theology" lightly. But their lives did not just "speak," they rang out with clarity and purposefulness. And now, they are gone. Gone, too, is Bill Anderson, a deeply spirit-led African American in Charlottesville who was part of the nationwide Episcopal Peace Fellowship. From time to time, Bill would tell me, "I always liked the Quakers, because they freed my people," by which he meant his own ancestors, who had lived over near Richmond. "But Bill," I would say, "the Quakers should never have even held your people in slavery, so you can't say that ending it was a good thing."

We never did resolve that argument. So now, what can I say — for my own six amazing grandchildren or anyone else in the coming generations — about the God question?

Not very much, I am afraid. Sometimes, in Quaker meetings, I have pondered this question. Quakers like to say that, "There is that of G-d in everyone," and that is a statement to which I fully subscribe. As noted above, I do not think there is any such thing as a "bad" person. There are people who sometimes do terrible things; but each of those, whether it is Adolf Hitler, or Pol Pot, or Stalin, or George W. Bush, still has some spark of the divine within them. I think it's important to remember this — especially when it seems very hard to so.

So then, what is that "G-d"? My best answer at this point is that it is that thing, that essence, that something ineffable, that is inside every person. And then, there is the tradition — or, as I see it, the many different traditions to which we can have access. Jesus of Nazareth was undoubtedly a fine, fine teacher. So were many of the Hebrew prophets. So are the Dalai Lama and Thich Nath Hanh. So were George Fox, John, Woolman, and Dietrich Bonhoeffer. (Why is this list all male? Let's add in some Quaker sheroes like Mary Fisher or Mary Dyer.) So are the Mozambican *curanderos* and *curanderas* from whom I learned so much in the early 2000s.

When Chuck Fager approached me about contributing to *Passing the Torch*, he said it was for "retired" Friends. I was honored by the invitation and accepted it, relishing the chance to think through and put down on paper some things I have thought about deeply over the years.

However, I rejected the description of being "retired." I am blessed by belonging to a generation of women from relatively wealthy countries who have been able to get a good education, have children, survive childbirth, become grandmothers — and still have plenty of energy to devote to social-justice or professional pursuits. I am definitely not retired from working hard on the concerns for peace and justice that I have long been seized by. Right now (late 2019), I have three main concerns I am exploring:

My continuing concern that the Palestinians should be able fully to exercise their G-d-given human rights, and that US Americans and others around the world should end the systematic dehumanization and marginalization to which the Palestinians have been subjected for the past 100-plus years.

A concern that many of my friends and longtime allies in the human-rights movement in the United States (generally, people who have never spent time living in a war-zone) became so easily enthused by the idea of supporting Washington-led "regime-change" projects in Syria or Libya that relied on the use of anti-regime violence by the US and others and thereby rapidly dragged those countries into extremely destructive civil wars.

A broader concern that many Americans will find it hard to adjust to the crumbling of the globe-girdling US empire that has already started, and to the concomitant shattering of long held illusions about the country's "manifest destiny" in the world. Given that the country still commands a massive, fearsome arsenal, these moments could be extremely dangerous.

I realize I have written little here that is personal, little about the way that my close ties with family and f/Friends have enriched my life and given rich dimensions of meaning to it. Writing about such things would require another whole essay (or five.) But meantime, the years pass and I know that my Torch will one day, like others, have to be passed. I am very grateful to Chuck Fager for having let me take part in this project and much look forward to reading everyone else's contributions.

— Helena Cobban is still a member of Charlottesville Friends Meeting though she and her husband William Quandt recently moved back to Washington DC. She is a Senior Fellow at the Center for International Policy. A fuller biography can be found at her Wikipedia page.

H. Larry Ingle: A Brief History of a Quaker Historian

I am an historian whose work has concentrated primarily on Quakers. Among members of the Religious Society of Friends, historians of that group enjoy a special status flowing from the simple fact that traditionally among Quakers there are no persons — indeed, no bodies — with special oversight or authority over either theology or beliefs. Without creeds as guides, such in-

H. Larry Ingle

sights are left to individual members. The religious experiences and encounters that Friends have with God's leadings during their meetings for worship set, expand, and at once limit the Truths Quakers hold. Because such glimmers of Truth occur during gathered meetings where all those present are able to know them, the experiences unite all those present into a collective in which all are apart.

And when such insights emerge in outward and public actions, as for example in Friendly efforts to end racial slavery, champion women's rights, defend homosexuals, and engage in antiwar activities, they are chronicled and explained by historians, who thus use their key to open the past and guide those in the present into the future.

Historians, in practice, then take on something of the role of a prophet who draws from past experiences to illuminate what may — even should — lead to guiding those now living into a future with still unknown possibilities. No wonder that historians of Quakerism need a dose of humility.

This same humility is likewise needed because even prophetic historians remain human beings, not gods, products of their times and places, and are often captured by the worldviews of the people they grew up and came of age with. One of the most telling comments in this regard comes from one of the prime nemeses of Quakers in the middle of the seventeenth century, the English Lord Protector Oliver Cromwell. He wrote to the Presbyterian Church of Scotland in 1650, "I beseech you, in the bowels of Christ, think it possible you may be mistaken." And Britain Yearly Meeting, perhaps unaware of its genesis, perhaps not, still advises its members to "think it possible that you may be mistaken." Those reminders are particularly valid for serious historians who must constantly grapple with the patchiness and resulting gapes in their sources.

I am also a convinced Friend, not an uncommon state for modern Quakers, most of whom have come to the Society from a variety of religious backgrounds and heritages. I was raised a Southern Presbyterian in Piedmont (central) North Carolina, in a church that theologically echoed the ideas of evangelicals, such as Baptists and Methodists, though the small unincorporated town of Whitsett, had only one church, the one I joined after I learned to recite its catechism about 1946. As I look back on it now, I view it as the church of the tiny local establishment, attended by people who believed they set the moral and religious tone of the community. My parents, each with a year or two of college, were both farmers and textile mill workers. During the economic boom of World War II that pulled the nation out of the Great Depression, my father formed a partnership with another entrepreneur to buy a nylon mill in Gibsonville, three miles from Whitsett; toward the end of the war it went under.

During my childhood we had a "colored woman" (my parents insisted that we all refer to her that way) — her full name was Mattie Bain Whitsett Fox — who lived in our house to keep it clean and prepare our food for us while my parents worked. She also worked occasionally for our neighbors next door. They belonged to the People's Methodist Church in nearby Gibsonville, a Pentecostal-leaning split-off from the mainstream Methodist body and, as far as social status was concerned, an obvious step down from Springwood Presbyterian. What makes this relevant here is that the churches in our area in the 1940s had yearly "revivals" when an outside preacher was invited in to "revive" the congregation and convert new members. The children of the folk next door went with us to Springwood's revivals, and my brother and I went to theirs. Mattie Whitsett never went to ours, but she did go — sitting in the back, of course — to the People's Methodist revival, a fact that I later realized spoke loudly of the differences between the social classes —

and their values — of the two churches and the people who attended them. I've reflected often on the significance inherent in this childhood memory, for it spoke deeply of the ambiguities that have continued to pervade southern American social and religious life and practice.

Equally important was my four years at Wake Forest College from 1954 to 1958, for it was at that North Carolina Baptist school that my journey to Quakerism began. My history professor, native Mississippian and World War II veteran David L. Smiley, captured my imagination and turned me toward history. He also taught a Sunday school class for students in Wake Forest Baptist Church, and, like his college classes, it was packed; in both he stressed the need to express one's religious convictions in one's daily life. He once told a Sunday class that he thought students at the end of every year ought to go out and put into practice what they had learned.

I promptly visited a local black Presbyterian church in Winston-Salem and offered to teach a Sunday school class there myself. By that time, too, I had decided to become a Presbyterian minister, so I was tapped to teach a class of youngish adults. When the minister was going to be out of town one Sunday, he invited me to preach from his pulpit. When I told my parents that I would be preaching, they were horrified that it was at a "colored" church, so they decided they could not attend.

Smiley's experience of the wartime destruction in France and Germany had made him a pacifist, so, as I reflected later, that helped explain the Quaker noises he often uttered in his lectures. It being the mid-1950s, when I turned eighteen, I had to register for the draft, and by the time I graduated, I felt led to declare myself a conscientious objector, even though I enrolled at Union Theological Seminary in Richmond, Virginia, in the fall of 1958. Fortunately, my ministerial student status put my possible induction on hold. Six days after my graduation, my long-time girlfriend and now nurse Becky Heath and I were married at her Methodist Church. Our marriage has lasted a lot longer than the one term it took me to sense that graduate school in history was more to my "calling" than the ministry. Despite its reputation as a "liberal" Presbyterian seminary, its faculty turned out to be rather conservative when it came to the sit-in movement that hit Richmond's department stores about the same time we got to the state's capital. A group of students met with the best-known professor, but he refused to publicly endorse us in protesting Jim Crow segregation with the sometimes-notorious Congress of Racial Equality. So that fall, I matriculated at American University in Washington where I got my master's degree and an extra year of course work toward a doctorate.

While living in Washington without the shield of being a ministerial student, I registered with my Greensboro draft board as a conscientious objector. Despite the relatively large number of Friends in and around Greensboro, the board turned me down, and I appealed. In those days the appeal necessitated an FBI investigation into my background. And that meant that my parents learned of the legal but unseemly peace stand that their, adult son was taking — they were not happy to say the least. But by mid-1959, Becky and I had a daughter and my parenthood assured me of a practical draft exemption.

During the two years we were in Washington, I participated in an Easter vigil for nuclear disarmament at the Pentagon sponsored by the American Friends Service Committee. We also attended our first Quaker meeting, the one on Florida Avenue — the very one that California Quaker and future President Richard Nixon never worshipped at despite his years in the nation's capital. As an ex-ministerial student, I was impressed: there was no pastor, no order of worship, an openness to contributions from all as led by Christ's Spirit, and an obvious egalitarianism. On that latter point, I still remember that sitting side-by-side near us on that wintery First Day was a woman wearing a fur coat and a younger man whose dress suggested he was one that we would soon be describing as a "hippy."

Beginning in the fall of 1961, I was hired to teach at Wilmington College, a locally supported junior college in the North Carolina city of that name. Now it is the University of North Carolina-Wilmington, then it was probably the sorriest junior college in the state, and no place for someone who saw himself as a budding scholar-to-be. The first year I was there I got a glorious twenty-five dollars to purchase books for the woefully inadequate library — and that was when the average price of a book was about $5. I loved the students, most of my colleagues, and hated the environment: the nearest bookstore a hundred miles away, the political climate hopelessly conservative in the first years of President John F. Kennedy.

Two of my colleagues and I got into trouble with the college administrators when we went to our three separate precinct meetings in 1962 to introduce motions urging our local conservative Democratic congressman to support Kennedy's program. If I had not already decided to go to the University of Wisconsin in 1963 to finish my PhD — where Smiley had gotten his — I would have had to struggle with the academic freedom implications of the college's decision not to rehire me for the 1963-64 year.

Instead, on the late August day in 1963 that Martin Luther King was delivering his March on Washington "I have a dream speech," we loaded up our Studebaker Lark station wagon with our two children and our few possessions and headed to Madison. Wilmington, incidentally, did not then have a Friends Meeting.

We spent only one year in Wisconsin, some kind of record, my major professor, David Cronon, later told me. Most youthful historians-to-be customarily took classes, got their spouses a job, and took up to eight years or longer getting their degrees. My instructors were all excellent, but the two who made the greatest impression were diplomatic historian William Appleman Williams, guru of the "New Left," and Harvey Goldberg, historian of modern France. Good friends, they were strikingly different in their approaches to teaching — Williams was laid back and casual in his classes, almost nonchalant, while Goldberg was so diligent that he memorized his lectures that flowed like a smooth syrup as he sweetened his sweeping survey of European social history from 1688 to 1750; the only time he ever brought a piece of paper to class was when he had a quotation to read.

Goldberg took six weeks getting to 1688, but he made every minute worthwhile, so much so that the class was peopled by different folk almost every day, so that Becky came with me to class once, just to watch him perform. We went to Madison's Friends Meeting a few times but often dropped in on a Unitarian Church designed by famed Wisconsin architect Frank Lloyd Wright.

My extra year of course work at American transferred with no problems to Wisconsin. The only problem was that I needed two years in residence to fulfill the requirements for the degree. But I found a provision in the catalogue providing that if a student passed the preliminary examination and paid the annual seminar fee then that year would count for residence credit regardless of where the student was actually living.

That was a lifesaver. I finished my first and only year of residence by June 1964. Then I got a job in the History Department at Presbyterian College in Clinton, South Carolina, beginning in the fall. Before then, I took my prelims at the library at the University of North Carolina after spending the summer going through the papers of Claude Kitchin, my dissertation topic. Kitchin was a Democratic congressman from North Carolina, majority leader of the House during part of Wilson's administration, a fierce opponent of American entry into World War I, but a staunch supporter of disenfranchising black voters. Also, in Chapel Hill, we attended the Friends Meeting nearly weekly. In Clinton that fall, I paid my seminar fee for the requisite two semesters, taught my four classes, and what time I wasn't a husband and a father, plugged away at my dissertation. I was awarded the degree in 1967.

At that time there were no Friends Meetings in South Carolina, so we attended Clinton's First Presbyterian Church, where I also taught a free-ranging adult Sunday school class. First Presbyterian was really an establishment church in a state where status had always been vitally important and in a small town where Presbyterianism was central to nearly everything that went on. If MY class "strayed" into social issues like desegregation — as it did — or matters of political importance like the Vietnam War — as it did — people who were not there heard about it.

And politics also beckoned as likewise explosive. Nineteen sixty-four was a turning point in the Palmetto State's politics, as in the South generally. Barry Goldwater, a conservative senator from Arizona, won the Republican Party's nomination for President, and South Carolina, afire with anger at the national government's support of civil rights, burned from THE COASTAL low country to mountains with the echoing outcries of his ardent supporters. The state's Democratic senior senator, J. Strom Thurmond, dramatically announced that year that he was supporting Goldwater and would leave his father's party to join President Abraham Lincoln's.

About ten of us on the faculty decided, not unaware of the background, to attend the small town's Democratic Party's precinct committee conclave, only to have the two resident attenders discover when they arrived that they were outnumbered ten to two. Fruitlessly fumbling for their key to open the door, they hastily determined to reschedule the meeting. At the later date the ten of us found ourselves facing over twenty irate Democrats who decided that President Lyndon Johnson's supporters could not be tolerated. To them, loyal to their Palmetto heritage and Jim Crow racial separation, this was a Goldwater year. Our appeal to the county Democratic gathering in nearby Laurens got a hearing that proved no better. I now had two marks against me at Presbyterian College.

The third one, probably more decisive, dwelt with things more fundamental to the college and its conservative economic and political practices. In the college chapel, the campus's principal meeting place for assemblies, the administration had ordered a sign with the words "Christian Education Equals Free Enterprise" printed on it in bold letters. Usually hidden over the stage, it was dropped down to reassure potentially wealthy contributors that we were a safe school when donors were expected.

When the college invited senior Senator Thurmond to speak there during his campaign, I refused to stand while practically all the rest of the audience leapt to their feet to applaud the politician, and when the administration scheduled Army General Harold K. Johnson to deliver the 1965 commencement address during the height of the Vietnam War, I wrote a letter to the student newspaper to explain that I was not attending, to protest this back-handed endorsement of the conflict in Southeast

Asia. I was soon summoned to the office of Marc C. Weersing Presbyterian minister-president and was admonished on my responsibilities as a faculty member. But I did not heed his plea to attend the Johnson talk.

That summer, as vice-chairman of something called Speed-Up, an interracial program created in Columbia to tutor African American high school students in preparation for desegregated schools and college, I faced the most trying of my confrontations with authority. Two students from the college, both girls, agreed to live in a black home in Clinton and help local students bone up on English, math, and education generally. Just before the program was to begin I (our chairman of Speed-up had to be out of town, leaving me with the task of overseeing the startup effort) took a press release down to the weekly newspaper office. It was not long before the editor called to invite me in to wait on him. "Get those white girls out of that nigger house," he warned, "or I cannot be responsible for what happens," but he agreed to run the press release once we complied.

Knowing, as both of us did, that Clinton had once been a hotbed of Klan activity, I called an emergency meeting of our committee, and we decided to try to find another place for them to stay. The dean of the college, Joseph Gettys, also a Presbyterian minister, agreed to allow the two young women to stay in the college's dorms. Despite all our efforts Speed-up collapsed within days. The lesson I took away was, don't kowtow to pressure when you are doing something that's right and proper; we should have simply called the bluff of our Clinton *Chronicle* editor. The repercussions then fell on me; the lesson now is for all of us.

Overriding my department head and despite Wisconsin awarding me a PhD in January, the administration informed me in early 1967 that I would not receive a contract the following academic year, meaning that I was fired — not illegal, given that I was still in my probationary period. I wrote the American Association of University Professors, but quickly securing a job as assistant professor in history at the University of Chattanooga in those plush days, I did not appeal the dismissal.

We moved in June 1967 to what was locally known as the "Scenic City" in southeastern Tennessee. To four folk who had just been through hell in small town South Carolina, the place seemed an Eden, with its more than 100,000 people. I began my tenure at UC with a summer school class in Recent American history. Our family promptly joined Pilgrim Congregational-United Church of Christ, the "liberal" Protestant church in town where many university faculty members belonged, as I could find no Friends meeting in Chattanooga.

As it turned out, I simply did not know where to look. In the summer of 1969, just before I was to take up a Danforth Fellowship in black studies at Yale, we were in Pittsburgh for a summer of study in the same field at Carnegie-Mellon University. While there we sought out the local Friends Meeting, where I found a pamphlet published by the Friends World Committee for Consultation listing a meeting that gathered in a private home in Chattanooga, with an address and telephone number. Taking down that much desired information, I called when we got back in late August and began attending this Sunday evening meeting that met once a month, with fewer than five worshippers. But then of course the Ingles had to leave for New Haven in September, where a Friends Meeting was, but we had rented a beach house in nearby Milford.

Back in Chattanooga in the summer of 1970, I attended the local meeting on Sunday nights until our worship group decided to meet weekly at the local YWCA. I dropped Becky and our children off at Pilgrim and then picked them up after our ten o'clock worship ended. This practice divided the family, but, as it turned out, that didn't last long because in 1973 I got a Fulbright grant to teach for the academic year in Cape Coast, Ghana, West Africa.

That was an eye-opening year for all of us. We had never been abroad, much less to exotic and unknown Africa. Our kids loved it, and to this day, they vow that it was the most valuable year of their lives: our eleven year old son Jon had a linguistic ability that allowed him to go to the top of his class in the local language Fante, and our daughter Jaan, three years older, found ready friends among the numerous expatriate teen-agers from the rest of the world on campus; both still delight in chanting song verses in their practiced West African English accents.

There Becky and I met an English couple, Walter and Maisie Birmingham, who also happened to be Friends, both "weighty" as it turned out; Walter, an economist, was also an expatriate member of the University of Cape Coast's faculty. They had helped establish the One-percent Fund — the genesis of our Right Sharing of World Resources Fund — London Yearly Meeting's effort to encourage British Friends to contribute that much annually to aid global development. They had also served as wardens, the British word for directors, of Toynbee Hall, an East London settlement house in one of the poorest areas of the city. While there in the early 1960s, before we knew them, they had befriended and given a job to John Profumo, the wealthy minister of war in the British Conservative government whose sexual dalliances with model Christine Keeler, forced his resignation from the Cabinet, producing one of the major state crises of the time. Profundo was dramatically changed by their Quakerly solicitude for him as another troubled human being, so he worked there until the end of his life, becoming its chief fundraiser.

Every First Day we rode with them in their tiny Morris Minor to the Cape Coast meeting, a preparative meeting under the aegis of Legon meeting in Accra, Ghana's capital, 90 miles away. A Ghanaian student,

Kofi Mensah, accompanied us each week to the small gathering of about a dozen. We enjoyed a proper English tea with the Birminghams almost every day, got to know them quite well, and by the end of the year we saw how Quakerism infused every aspect of their lives. To live by simply, Maisie baked whole-grain bread daily. When Walter gave his inaugural lecture on coming to the University, his title was derived from one of the first queries of Friends, "How does the truth prosper among you?"

They were also vegetarians — the first ones we had ever known up close — until then I had always considered people who eschewed meat as being slightly off, but this couple, about 20 years older than we, could not accurately be described as even a little kooky. In July 1974, we left for Chattanooga changed people, our family determined to be vegetarians and just as impressed with Quakerism. We had found admirable Quaker mentors, something every Friend needs.

To join Chattanooga Friends, I would have had to go through West Knoxville Meeting, our sponsoring meeting. I did not know anyone there, so I wrote Walter and Maisie and asked them if they would consider it to be a violation of Quaker practice for them to recommend me for membership. An answer came back that they knew us well enough for them to accede to my request, so I became a Friend through the London office of Friends World Committee for Consultation. In Chattanooga, we got in touch with West Knoxville, so I could transfer my membership to Chattanooga. I learned a valuable lesson about Quakers in this little affair: a way to bypass a Quaker rule can always be found if a sincere person tries hard enough and can build a convincing case.

Three or four years later, after Chattanooga Meeting had been recognized as an independent monthly meeting and Becky had decided that she was benefitting more from waiting worship than the bustling at Pilgrim Congregational, she joined our meeting via the standard clearness committee. Maisie and Walter are both deceased, but we visited them three or four times before they died, and they served as informal in-country guardians for our son when he finished his high school at Bootham Friends School in York. Never far from our minds even yet, they remain powerful influences on us as Friends.

Despite the fact that the University of Chattanooga, a struggling private college with about 2000 students, was in a conservative part of the state, I found the administration open and willing to tolerate its faculty taking public actions that were frowned on in South Carolina. The first year I taught here, I joined an interracial picket at the City Hall to protest the treatment of blacks at a playground in the Avondale section of the city with no repercussions, despite the fact that the executive assistant to the University President had to cross our line when he came for business. And I encountered no problems when I wrote letters or op-ed columns to the main newspaper, the Chattanooga *Times*, which was owned by the New York *Times* — in fact the two papers, from front page to columnists on the editorial page, typographically looked alike.

An even more earth-shaking event occurred during that first year also, for in the spring of 1968, the President of the University announced that because of declining local private support for the college the next year would witness its merger with the University of Tennessee. So, the private University of Chattanooga would become the University of Tennessee at Chattanooga. Some of my older colleagues feared that probable rising enrollments would mean a decline in student selectivity (and, in their minds, quality), but I noticed no appreciable change after the merger in 1969.

Professionally, the change was good for me. A colleague, James Ward, who became my closest faculty friend after he came in 1969, convinced me that we could produce an American history college book. However wild that idea might have sounded to one who had seen only a couple of journal articles under his name, it immediately appealed to Little, Brown, and Company, which signed us up and gave us a healthy advance on royalties for the two-volume work that came out in 1978. Reading, editing, and rereading each other's prose, we grew closer, talked about lots of things all over the map, and learned how to take (and dole out) the most fundamental criticism. Plus, it was just downright fun — and it sold well enough that another publisher brought out a second edition years later.

After that project was done, Jim, a Roman Catholic by birth and faith whose research involved railroads, pushed me to produce a book on something — perhaps even Quakers, he suggested, without any idea about what might come. I had done lots of reading about the history of Quakers, of course, and knew something of where the gaps were. By the early 1980s I settled on the Great Separation in five yearly meetings in 1827 and 1828, what I called in the words of my book's subtitle, "The Hicksite Reformation." It was the principal event in American Quaker history, and I was amazed that it had never had a scholarly blow-by-blow historical retelling, an unbelievable situation given the presence of three major Quaker colleges in the Philadelphia area, where the division originated. And here I was, residing in a faraway isolated burg (for Quaker sources) called Chattanooga.

A non-Quaker sociologist, Robert Doherty, had studied the division and concluded it was rooted in an urban-rural conflict, the city Quakers too sophisticated, worldly, and integrated into the larger religious community for the farmers, who like rural people generally, had little time for those who considered them "lesser beings without the law." My ultimate findings did not challenge this interpretation head-on, focusing instead on exploring its implications. For the split fueled what might be called the "liberal" forces within the Society of Friends and gave them meetings in which they believed they could maintain themselves free of the often-oppressive discipline that the urban Quakers tried to impose. The insurgents, who accepted the name "Hicksite" after their leader, Elias Hicks, a Long Island teacher and farmer, wanted a "reformation," I argued, to get the Society back to George Fox and the early founders.

Quakers in Conflict: The Hicksite Reformation came out in 1986 from the University of Tennessee Press, with a revised edition in 1998 from Pendle Hill; it has seldom been challenged in the Quaker world. Unfortunately, it is out of print now. When Friendly readers championed its exploration of Quaker liberalism, they overlooked my warning toward the end that the schism demonstrated that someone within the Society of Friends has to exercise discipline lest members splinter off into anarchic individualism.

This caution was then highlighted by the experience of Philadelphia Yearly Meeting (Hicksite) in dealing with one of their own dissidents, Benjamin Webb, from Wilmington, Delaware. Webb surely deserves the label of "free-thinking" Quaker if anyone does. From the pages of his weekly the *Delaware Free Press*, he defended the views of two other free thinkers, the notorious Fanny Wright and the socialist Robert Dale Owen, both British, and so Webb proved himself to be a "ball that has rolled beyond our reach," as the first clerk of the seceded yearly meeting phrased it. Within five years after the division Webb's monthly, quarterly, and yearly meetings disowned him for his "destructive" actions.

Irony of ironies, the Hicksite liberals proved that they could use the discipline against their opponents as adeptly and ruthlessly as their Orthodox counterparts used a heavy hand scarcely lightened by their liberalism. My warning was that somebody has to exercise discipline, but it should be done without passion and bias, something very, very difficult to do. The Hicksite opponents of the Orthodox Evans family rightfully bridled at its members 'haughty tactics but found themselves having to imitate them when it came to dealing with people like Webb. Such historical ironies were sobering indeed, even more so for people tempted to avoid them.

In fact, my observation is that for contemporary Friends, those living now near the start of the 21st century, this temptation is the most alluring of all that confront us. Many members today are refugees from other, more restrictive, religious groups, and they understandably glory in the absence of creeds they find among Friends, as well as the freedom this lacuna gives them. They also rightfully regard any hint of the return to the restrictions they ran away to join Quakers as something to be carefully avoided.

Yet just as rampant individualism threatened to undermine any sign of structure at the beginnings of Quakerism — a few followers of the dissident John Perrot even questioned having stated times to meet to worship — so its modern version can erode united action of any kind involving any situation. Solving this problem is certainly like walking the edge of a knife, but it's one none of us can shy away from. As a group, we much champion individual leadings, even as we affirm that God's spirit does guide our deliberations.

In the 1980s and early '90s, Chattanooga Meeting, with not more than a dozen members, decided to undertake a major project, leading public demonstrations against Chattanooga's commemoration of Armed Forces Day. This annual event, going back to post-World War II days, was a product of local patriotic fervor to honor those who served in the nation's armed forces, larded of course by the city's boosters and politicians; they were egged on by the two local newspapers and television media, who loved that the parade drew large crowds downtown to showcase something beside the industrial smog that attracted unwanted attention from the national media.

In the few other places that still observed the day, it took place on the third Saturday in May, but because Saturday was not a school day, in Chattanooga the Friday was declared a half-day holiday for the schools so high schools bands could be compelled to play the jivey patriotic music that added to the excitement.

The first year, I read a prepared statement at the city Commission and a half-dozen Friends stood among the crowd holding signs that pled "Celebrate Peace, Not War," but in subsequent years we also distributed leaflets that expressed our views and collected signatures for ads opposing the parade in the newspapers. Our lack of influence was hardly enhanced by these ads, because the editorials, especially in the knee-jerk right-wing afternoon *News-Free Press*, continued their broadsides against anyone unpatriotic enough to do what we recommended. When the longtime chairwoman of the event retired from her job as Registrar of Deeds in the 1990s, the sponsoring committee announced that the celebration would be scaled back, though the parade, if not the prayer breakfast, continues. In most years there is no weeks-long buildup, and the day passes without much notice.

My next excursion into Quaker history involved George Fox, the founder of the movement in the 17th Century. Before and immediately after becoming a Friend I had read rather widely in the history of the faith, starting, of course with Fox's own Journal, followed with Hugh

Barbour's *The Quakers in Puritan England*, then the modern standard one-volume account, and then going on to the non-Quaker Christopher Hill's *The World Turned Upside Down*. Hill was a Marxist, and his book did not come out until nearly two decades after Barbour's. Reading historical journals, both Quaker and secular, I realized that Hill was regarded by most mainstream Quaker commentators as an interloping "sociologist."

He was trying to import left-wing notions into their familiar interpretations of the rise of Quakers. And it didn't take me long to realize that Fox, almost 300 years after his death, had no real biography, most of the attempts to produce one doing little more than paraphrasing his Journal or secondary sources. Historians are normally preoccupied by context — events of a political, social, religious, economic, military, even geographic nature — I saw that Barbour concentrated on theological thinking and practice with almost no attention to secular political and — in the 1640s and '50s — military matters, such as two shattering civil wars.

Clearing out some of this underbrush would be a satisfying project of course, but I was overlooking a number of things — my background was primarily in early 20th century American political history, a long way, to be sure from 17th Century English history. Indeed, I had never had a course in English history at any level and knew little more of the Stuarts and their rule beyond their names. Moreover, I knew enough to know that handwriting and spelling had not been standardized in the 1600s and that people certainly did not use typewriters then either. Just making sense of something as elemental and basic as grammar and spelling would be a different, daunting problem.

And there remained the problem of context. That was solved rather fortuitously by our television habits. Becky and I, like many other Americans, loved the British-produced "Masterpiece Theatre" series on PBS. In the mid-1980s we watched "By the Sword Divided," about a 1640s English midlands family forced to confront the divisiveness occasioned by the civil wars. As depicted in the series, the war was carried on in the same midlands area of Leicestershire in which George Fox was a teen-ager. The Round-headed rebels — so-called because they had shorn heads to distinguish themselves from their opponents the royalist aristocrats or cavaliers with their shaggy, shaggy-locks — New Model insurgent soldiers were shown marching into small villages, driving their cavaliere enemies away, and taking over established chapels, and "purifying them from Catholic and pagan" corruption by smashing stained-glass windows, tearing out statures of saints, and using into these formerly sacred precincts for shelter.

Why, I nudged Becky and said to myself, Fox certainly must have heard of such goings-on in his neighborhood and may even have witnessed the uproar or visited a violated church later. I ran to check my copy of Barbour and discovered that, though he said on p. 2 that Quakers lived through the "revolutions" of the time and later offered a paragraph or two on some high points of the war, he was more interested in purely religious or "spiritual" matters, hardly worldly ones. That was not good enough for me as an historian. I decided to try my hand at a scholarly biography of Fox.

So, I had to give myself a seminar on Tudor-Stuart England. I read more broadly into Quaker history, and then prepared to go to England to look at what historians call "primary sources" — in contrast, the last American to publish a biography of Fox never passed through London's Heathrow airport's passport control and contented himself with printed sources. Becky and I landed in England's green and pleasant land at Gatwick Airport on Boxing Day — the day after Christmas — in 1988, with a return ticket for the end of May — that was a bit over five months to devote to research. Luckily advised by Maisie Birmingham, then serving on London Yearly Meeting's Meeting for Sufferings, we stayed at Quaker International Centre. It was only two blocks from Friends House on Euston Road where the Library of the Society of Friends was, two blocks from the Institute of Historical Research, and a block more to the British Museum where the British Library was then housed; some days I visited all three.

Because QIC, as it was known, had a resident intentional committee that welcomed guests like us from all over the world on all sorts of missions, we got to know lots of fascinating people, plus we were in walking distance of London's theater district. When the library was closed for a while, we could go westward on the train to Shaftesbury to visit the Birminghams or once or twice to visit a Public Record Office, where local meeting records were sometimes housed. And we attended London Yearly Meeting because "readers," as we were known in the Library, were asked to vacate to accommodate yearly meeting visitors. Except for having to become accustomed to feeding our gas heaters with 20 pence coins to keep warm in our room at QIC, we found the entire experience to be eye opening and exciting.

Getting back home at the beginning of summer, I started writing on what I knew would be the biggest project of my career, for Fox was a major figure in both Quaker and English history. By 1990, I had written perhaps a third of what I thought was sterling prose, but I realized without some time off teaching, I would not make the progress that I wanted — besides, I was finding so much of importance that I wanted to get the path-breaking news out. So, in the spring, I saw an announcement that

Pendle Hill, the Quaker study center outside Philadelphia had created the Henry Cadbury Scholarship to allow a person like me to live in that community for a year and work on a project.

I applied and word soon came that I had been named the first Cadbury scholar for the following academic year. Even though it meant leaving Becky at home — we agreed that my replacement at the University could rent out an extra room at our house — I would be able to write the last two-thirds of the book. Too, it was in walking distance of Swarthmore College, with one of the best Quaker historical libraries in the country and where there was a free bus connection to Haverford College, with its own fine collection of Quaker sources.

There were lots of distractions at Pendle Hill — something was going on practically all of the time — but I was controlled by the necessity of writing and getting my manuscript finished; unless something was compellingly interesting, I spent the time in my room writing. Plus, early in 1991, I contacted Oxford University Press about my book, and they promptly informed me that they would like to see the finished product. I couldn't have been happier that such a prestigious house that published on both sides of the Atlantic was interested.

The completed manuscript that I sent to Oxford in early 1993 certainly put Fox in his personal worldly and religious context. Its title came to me one evening as I was drifting off to sleep. I remembered that the Patriarch of Constantinople was known in the Eastern Orthodox Church as "First among Equals," and I thought, "why not Fox as 'First Among Friends'" (I didn't want to capitalize the preposition, but Oxford deemed otherwise.) One reviewer later complained that I had bought into the establishment notion that Fox rather than some unnamed or unknown others created the Society of Friends; what he forgot was that the evidence led me to that conclusion. The evidence I found forced me also to seriously modify my preconceptions. Following Christopher Hill, I wanted to depict the early Friends as challenging not only the religious world but also the secular political, social, and economic one as well; the world, as William Penn saw and said, was upside down and needed to be righted.

During the seminal 1650s, Quakers operated in this fashion, but after the Stuart Restoration of 1660 and the so-called "peace testimony" of January 1661, they turned inward and became less revolutionary. Instead the necessity for controlling rowdy, fringe, and anarchic elements among Friends caused Fox to create instruments that would restrain those of his followers who inclined in those directions. In this fashion, contrary to my prior inclinations, he was also "First Among Friends," aided politically of course by his allies, including of course his wife, the wily and capable Margaret Fell Fox.

To the dismay of some, my biography did not contain much exploration of theological matters — something I learned from the Hicksite "Reformation" was often vapid and ultimately useless in contrast to the need to get down what had actually happened. Nevertheless, it has quickly become the standard treatment. It's not the final word, obviously, but it will do until another innocent scholar happens by and decides to give the subject another look. With *Quakers in Conflict*, my Fox biography meant that I had produced volumes to cover two of the most important aspects of long-neglected Quaker history.

At the same time my historical research was going on, I became involved with the principal Quaker organization, the American Friends Service Committee (AFSC). In 1976, I was appointed to the Executive Committee of its Southeastern Regional Office, which met in High Point, North Carolina, at the time near the center of southern Quakerism. As a relatively new Friend, I was happy to be involved with a fabled organization that traced its roots back nearly fifty years to World War I and which, representing the American Society of Friends had received the Nobel Peace Prize nearly two decades before. Its quarterly regional meetings lasted over a Friday and Saturday, and sometimes were something of a grind because business focused on tedious matters.

About two or three years into what was to be a six year term, we took up a major issue, referred to us by the Philadelphia home office, whether to move the regional office to Atlanta, the growing, burgeoning center of the south from a small city tucked away in one corner of Guilford County where there were lots of Quakers but communications were minimal. Being relatively new, I had no hard and fast notions about the wisdom of this matter, but I will never forget that a member from Chapel Hill, a public relations academic from UNC, Bob Gwyn, was adamantly opposed.

He asked simply whether we thought that since New York was the nation's communications center, AFSC would consider uprooting itself from Philadelphia, with its Quaker heritage, to move approximately one hundred miles northward to the Big Apple so as to enhance its public profile. No one answered him, but we approved the move anyway because that's what Philadelphia wanted. With examples like that, I would have had to be a dunce not to realize that it was Philadelphia that called the shots within the southeastern region — and by extension other areas as well.

This truth was underscored when what was called the Women in the Workforce program came up for discussion. Designed by some group in the national office for North Carolina textile workers, the idea was to empower women to demand better working conditions in the Tar Heel state's cotton mills. I knew something about textile mills because both of my parents worked in them nearly all their lives. I suggested that the only way I would approve such an effort was to have a one-year trial to see how it would work out, because I thought it was so theoretical and abstract that it probably would never connect.

We were meeting in Chattanooga that weekend in a camp setting that I had secured, and my one-year trial effort was minuted. But wonders of wonders, at the end of the year the Executive Committee got no evaluation or report on results, in fact, not a word. The outcome was that the much-heralded program died on the vine in North Carolina, was then transferred to West Virginia, where it also dried up. By that time, I had grown weary of regional quarterly meetings that had no real autonomy, and I resigned.

In the summer of 1979, I went to Friends General Conference in Richmond, Indiana, where I met Chuck Fager, a part time journalist, often unpaid, who concentrated on matters Quaker. His interest then was not a surprise — it was AFSC, particularly because the politically liberal *New Republic* opinion journal had just come out with a June cover story about the AFSC called "Shot From Guns," charging that AFSC had gone back on Quaker pacifism not only on the Palestinian-Israeli issue but also in South Africa. That kind of exposé in that kind of periodical promised to cut deeply into AFSC's donors. AFSC supporters and critics, of which I was rapidly becoming one, were appalled.

Chuck mounted three afternoon voluntary sessions that attracted lots of the better than 1500 Friends from all over the country. He kicked off with a series of theses about Quaker service, the first being that Quaker service was "an expression of Quaker worship in the world;" such an approach demonstrated that the criticism was rooted firmly in the religious experiences of those who spoke one way or the other. Couched more as occasions to bare personal experiences, good and bad, with AFSC, the get-togethers demonstrated that concerns with AFSC ran deeply among FGC Friends. From cancelling popular post-World War II work camps for teen-agers — a form of outreach, most Friends valued — to the falling number and percentages of Quakers on its staff, AFSC's foibles got a healthy airing. At the final session, more than 140 Friends signed a listing of these concerns, with Chuck, ever alert to extending the extent of the document's influence, secured the signatures of such illustrious Quakers as the president of Earlham College and the Dean of its School of Religion.

Despite the liberal orientation of Friends General Conference from which most of the signatories came, Chuck wrote an article for *Friends Journal* that stressed its centralist approach and letters to those who signed requesting that they take up the concerns with their monthly, quarterly, and yearly meetings.

Higher-ups within AFSC stood up and took immediate notice of the wide-ranging charges. One official, destined to become Executive Secretary the following April, composed a bit of doggerel destined to highlight the pettiness to which the organization's elitists there could stoop: "There was a Quaker named Fager/ Who was more a faker than a Quaker/ His libel caused [Board Chairman Stephen] Cary/ To tear out his hairy/ And seek to send Chuck to his Maker." It telegraphed the distance that Quaker administrators meant to maintain between themselves and even seriously supportive Friends. In 2016, I published an article detailing this episode and its legacy in the pages of *Quaker History*.

This concern did not fade. A bit over twenty years later, my yearly meeting, Southern Appalachian Yearly Meeting and Association, appointed me to be a member of the AFSC Corporation, a practically useless legal body; its only real job was to legally hold AFSC's property and rubber stamp a pre-arranged slate of members of the Board of Directors. For the rest of its annual weekend meeting it was subjected to dog-and-pony shows to make AFSC true-believers/supporters even more fervent and to reassure or sideline the occasional doubter. In the three years I served, the only thing of substance that we were asked to do was to give our approval to a plan to allow non-Friends to serve on the Board. Despite doubts among the forty or fifty members, I was the only one who raised questions about the value of this recommendation, averring that it was likely to dilute even more the influence of Friends on the AFSC and make it even more like a formerly Quaker school; two of us asked to be recorded standing aside from the decision, which clearly had overwhelming support. After reporting back to SAYMA what I had done, I gladly ended my short tenure on the Corporation.

As an historian and after my Fox book appeared, I undertook some research on AFSC, considering writing its history, but living so far from Philadelphia where most of the sources and its massive archives were, deterred me. I published two popular articles in the ecumenical weekly, the *Christian Century*, one of which drew at least one angry letter from AFSC. The archivist at AFSC was Jack Sutters who had served in that position for years; he suggested that I might look at the period after World War II when AFSC decided to move from Quaker volunteers to using more professionally trained employees.

The result was one of the most important short pieces I ever wrote, "The American Friends Service Committee, 1947-49: The Cold War's Effect," for the journal *Peace & Change* in 1998. I related the story of how the thirtieth anniversary of AFSC in 1947, the beginning of the Cold War, and the receipt of the Nobel Prize combined to give the organization an opportunity to move from volunteer Quaker generalists to one dominated by professionals trained in languages, economics, history, and social work to promote political change. The most important point I found was that the decision was not happenstance, but one made consciously and deliberately by the leadership of AFSC at the time.

The result was the inevitable diminution of AFSC's Quaker influence and the rise of those who dreamed up projects like Women in the Workforce. In fact, that very program originated from the Community Relations Division headed by a long-serving non-Friend, Barbara Moffett, who came across even to the clerk of the Service Committee as "secular, or at least humanistic, in her orientation." With that kind of "diversity," it never dawned on the AFSC's leadership how Quaker service should grow out of Quaker worship. Two starkly clashing worldviews existed here.

[Most of my writings on AFSC over 40 years were collected in the journal *Quaker Theology*, in its issue #32, online at: www.quakertheology.org]

Research for my last major book overlapped with this AFSC work. I spent more than a decade of the research and writing to explore 37th President Richard Milhous Nixon's religion. Despite his lifelong Quakerism, Nixon was not one of my favorites, but I chose a tough, tough project because ferreting out other people's religion is difficult, if not impossible, to chronicle. Added to this was the fact that he was so secretive, private, and often deceptive about the contours of his faith. He devoted three short paragraphs to the topic in his memoir and never saw any relevance it had to the decisions that he made day-by-day, whether they were political or personal or professional ones; he was indeed a strange kind of Friend. Then there was the reality that historians, political scientists, and journalists customarily refuse to explore religion when they write or speak about public figures. For one thing, they recognize that it is subjective, and they don't want to deal with matters that cannot be nailed down firmly. Too, they often know little about religion or how it plays out in the secular world, and so they shy from approaching the subject. In other words, there is a great void when it comes to the faith of public political leaders.

Jim Ward and Chuck Fager, particularly the latter, bugged me about the Nixon study continually, asking me how it was coming along, when I was going to be done, and so on. It came out in 2015 from the University of Missouri Press and was entitled *Nixon's First Cover-up: The Religious Life of a Quaker President*. I debated a long time about denominating him a "ranter," the 17th century word that identified persons who believed the fact that they were saved negated any obligation to obey outward laws, such as not engaging in illicit sex or spousal abuse. I feared that non-Friends who read the book would have no idea about the word's meaning and that any derogatory connotations that lingered on from its previous usage would unfairly damn Nixon or suggest something I didn't want to imply. On the other hand, he was an antinomian, and Quakers used the term to denigrate their opponents in Fox's day — and others turned it around against them. So, I adopted it as a fair description, but I probably, as one review complained, should have gone into its 17th century background a little more.

The book's major contribution to Quaker history may not have been its treatment of Nixon but my account of the background supplied by Evangelical Quakerism, a breed apart from other factions and one practically unknown in the world of historical scholarship. Evangelical Quakers, with the partial exception of deceased George Fox University professor Arthur Roberts, have almost entirely ignored their own history. So much so, that a leading Nixon biographer, the well-known historian Stephen Ambrose, erroneously described East Whittier Friends Church, the pastoral Evangelical Friends group in which Nixon held his membership, as gathering as staidly as a group of silence-center, non-pastoral Philadelphia Quakers. My overall conclusion, that Nixon created his own unique self-serving religion and set of values, would not surprise Friendly readers, but the fact that his local church allowed him to get away with his derelictions and violations of Quaker practices certainly serve to highlight what I see as the problem faced by all Quaker bodies today.

Indeed, in a very fundamental sense, Richard Nixon was every Quaker, regardless of whether the others are "liberal" and unprogrammed, "middle of the road" or programmed, or "Evangelical" or boisterous. This reality reflects our heritage, from the 17th century to the present. The late 1640s and 1650s, the period Christopher Hill and I applauded for its cutting-edge ferment, based its kicking-over-the-traces creativity on the notion that God speaks to each person individually and wishes to see that person acting on the leadings from inside.

This individualism, however, very quickly and easily slips over into the kind of ranterism, if I may use that term again, that emerged earlier within Quakerism. Rhys Jones and his "Proud Quakers" and the better-known dissident James Nayler were the earliest examples of this anarchic tendency. Such individualism had to be contained if the movement was not to splinter off into hostile quarrelling groups.

Fox turned his attention to this matter in the 1660s and 1670s with the establishment of a Presbyterian-like system of ascending meetings with broader and broader authority; its defender — and I tend to group myself with them — say that the scheme saved the essence of Quakerism by subordinating individualism to the scrutiny of wider and wider groups that existed farther from the immediate issues and therefore were more able to be objective.

Yet the shattering division that occurred in the United States in 1827 and 1828 — what I called the "Hicksite Reformation" in *Quakers in Conflict* — occurred a century and a half later because Fox's solution had allowed a relatively wealthy and substantial group of men to pretty much determine the course of Quakerism and who spoke for it.

These reformers, many of them rural folk, chafed at the urban overlords who defined Quakerism and wanted to remove the constraints that Fox's order had imposed on them. They mirrored the earliest Quaker emphasis on individualism and wanted to shake off the same kind of ecclesiastical authority of the established church order that Fox and his earliest followers had stood against. The result was a schism that found Quakers so divided that it required a hundred and thirty-five years and many divisions later to overcome all the bitterness that ensued.

Indeed, this animosity's legacy still feeds an obvious distrust among Friends of different persuasions to this very day. It also makes too many Quakers averse to conflict, lest raising fundamental and basic issues among themselves might lead to other schisms. Speaking truth to power, a phrasing coined by Quakers in the 1950s when the AFSC published the seminal pacifist pamphlet *Speak Truth to Power*, is not something Friends do among themselves even today. They seem fearful of where honesty might lead. They need to get over that assumption.

I write these words on Sunday, September 15, 2019, the day after the Representative Meeting of Southern Appalachian Yearly Meeting and Association, my own yearly meeting, which I served as clerk in 2015 and 2016, met in Knoxville, Tennessee. There it proved unable to rein in a bully who was expending yearly meeting funding for her own purposes. (That noun "bully" was used to describe her in the meeting with no visible dissent, though without universal support.) So upset were some about her leadership of a united effort to face down white supremacy that there was open talk on the floor of schism.

It was shades of 1827-28 all over again. It must be said that others believe the yearly meeting could weather this storm and find a way to muddle through. Simple historians like myself do not like to venture predictions, so I'll leave it by merely saying that it was clear that the assembled Friends did not want to confront conflict and would rather allow the discontent to go on than right the situation by engaging with the problem. They don't want to encourage open confrontation.

The lesson I take away from a lifetime of studying Quaker history is the one I articulated at the end of *Quakers in Conflict*, one often ignored by those who mistakenly thought I was siding with the Hicksites on the question of authority. True, I described and documented the high-handed unsavory tactics of their Orthodox opponents, but I also averred that somebody has to have the authority of make judgments within Quakerdom. Authority need not become authoritarian, but neither can individualism be allowed to splinter the group into its constituent members, for then there will be no group. It is a hard path to walk this fine line between these two options and given Quaker history nearly impossible to make much headway, but treading it is something that is certainly required.

The earliest Friends believed — indeed, they knew because they had experienced its reality — that God's Spirit could unite a collective group of human believers into a unit that had the ability to discern and articulate the divine will for the group. For lots of different reasons this assurance seems to have disappeared. So meeting decisions no longer carry with them the authority that divine power once lent; instead they seem like echoes of the kind of political maneuvering that takes place in the secular world, so we Friends talk about "consensus" as the way to do business rather than finding the "sense of the meeting" or uniting around God's will.

Chuck Fager: Grasping the Ring

I am the oldest of eleven children, from a pre-Vatican Two Catholic family.

A very early memory: St. Francis Hieronymo Church in St. Paul, Kansas; late 1944, or early 1945. I am not yet three and on tiptoe, clinging to and barely able to see over the top of the pew in front of me.

The church seems vast, cavernous and dim. Thick pillars hold up a distant ceiling. What light there is comes from the flickering points of candles clustered around a faraway altar, at which a

Chuck Fager, with ring, 2004

brightly clad priest or two and some altar boys are shuffling around and mumbling Latin. To me their voices are muffled wordless echoes.

A priest turns towards us once, and he is holding a round gold-plated censer on a chain. He swings it two or three times in several directions. White smoke billows from it, rising, then flattening in the air, drifting toward us around the columns. The smell of the incense is sharp and acrid, herbal rather than floral, not unpleasant.

To the left of the altar is a statue of Christ on a white cross, more than life-sized, with a bloody crown of thorns, pierced hands, eyes vacant, and expression unreadable beyond a detached unfocused pain.

Two, or maybe three other statues of similar size stand at some distance from him, on either side of the church, robed but nameless, presumably apostles or saints. They are leaning forward, with arms extended, fingers reaching, whether toward the altar, the Jesus statue, or both is not clear. Do they want to rescue Jesus? Or join him? This tableau of suffering and yearning seems both in motion and frozen.

I have no memory of thoughts about this scene, which must have been a high Mass. I was likely taken to the church several, perhaps many times, before my mother left St. Paul to join my father on one air base after another, and the military became my world.

The church's namesake was a Jesuit revivalist from Naples, not the other, more popular Francis, the one with birds from Assisi, the current pope's namesake. The village of St. Paul grew up around their mission to the long-since removed Osage Indians. The church was built of gray local sandstone and was already more than seventy years old. I was baptized there, as were both my parents, and likely their parents. Today all four of my grandparents, my mother, and various relatives lie in its cemetery just down the road.

My father, who was also from St. Paul, is at Arlington National cemetery, near the Pentagon and across the Potomac from Washington DC. His will specified that he be buried in a basic military-issue coffin. He told me this was what President Eisenhower, a general before he turned politician, had insisted on for his own interment in 1969. As another veteran of that war, my father wanted to follow his example.

It strikes me now that though I was never either a priest or a soldier, these two sites, St. Francis Hieronymo Church and Arlington Cemetery, may well mark the main parameters of my life: the church and war.

****

I don't recall any adult, my parents included, ever asking me to consider becoming a priest, or as they would have put it, to pray to "have a vocation" to "the religious life." (I'm also relieved to say that in all my Catholic years, no priest ever laid evil hands on me. I was spared that plague.) Only many years later did the dynamic surface clearly in my mind: large families were the norm for our kind of Catholicism; and if sizable enough (and eleven surely met the bar), then at least one of us belonged to the Church. As the firstborn son, bookish and seemingly bright, the lot fell on me, without need of fanfare or, it turned out, pressure.

For that matter, this trajectory even survived my apostasy. . . .

. . . That began in 1956, when I was thirteen, at Ramey Air Force Base, on the northwest corner of Puerto Rico. Family quarters there were flat-roofed, cinder block houses, built to survive hurricanes. (A good thing, because while we were there, Ramey was hit by a big one, Betsy; its passage did much damage around the base and the island, but our already large family waited out the big blow with no more than some water on the floor and downed palm trees nearby.)

As part of their weatherproof design, these houses had no glass windows for hurricanes to shatter into razored shards. Instead there were louvered shutters with hand-cranks that opened over screens for ventilation. Even with them wide open, we spent much of our time sweltering in Puerto Rico's tropical climate. Air conditioning was then a luxury, something for generals or for movie theaters.

Unexpectedly, I soon found other blessed relief from the oppressive heat. The Air Force then had plenty of money. And some far-sighted Pentagon bureaucrat decided to spend some of it helping airmen and their families improve themselves intellectually by building base libraries. Just a few months after our arrival at Ramey, a brand-new library opened there.

This library had many of the latest features: bright but indirect lighting; an acoustical tile ceiling for quiet; a high-fidelity record player with classical LP albums to listen to (it was there I found that Beethoven was more than a character in the "Peanuts" comic strip, with life-changing results). Yet above all, it had that crowning new wonder of civilization, the daily miracle, the blessed rescue: air conditioning.

Air conditioning, books, and Beethoven! This had to be the very prototype of heaven. I was amazed it wasn't crowded with classmates from the base high school; but as an introvert, I didn't miss them. It immediately became the center of my life at Ramey for the first two years of high school. I rode my bike there directly from school, stayed til dinner time, returned for all-day stints on Saturdays, begrudged any activity that kept me away, ground my teeth when national holidays closed it.

I was not only there to stay cool. I read books. Devoured them, wallowed in them promiscuously. I brought many home, to fill in the empty hours til the library opened again. Among these were a growing number from the library's "give-a-book/take-a-book" shelf, featuring donated paperbacks. I soon found that this shelf had little staff oversight. So, I took many books from it, always vowing to replace them, but soon fell woefully behind on that score.

Along the way, I began to notice another feature of good libraries, one that others had noted before me with dismay: free access to many books can be hazardous to received, established ideas.

Among the subversive works I uncovered was one called, *Opus 21*, by Philip Wylie. It was a novel, and not about music.

Wylie was a popular writer who churned out "potboilers," books which mixed his breezily written stories with diatribes about the features of American society he despised, which were many. An adult acquaintance had told me about him, and I felt a thrill of illicit pleasure to find some of his titles on the library's shelves.

One of Wylie's abiding targets was organized Christianity. He didn't single out Catholicism, as he had been raised among stiff Presbyterians; but the Vatican was high on his target list. Another was the nuclear arms race with Soviet Russia, which he denounced as suicidally wasteful, though he was no left-wing pacifist. Then there was our church-spawned sexual Puritanism. Yes, his jeremiads covered a broad spectrum of follies, with a carefully trimmed racy paragraph here and there.

Wylie's remedies for all our cultural insanities were less political than therapeutic: he found hope in Freud, and even more in Jung. These names were also new to me. Indeed, almost everything he wrote about was new to me, and at fifteen, almost all of it was over my head. But his writing was exciting, and I knew I wanted to know and understand it better.

So, when a paperback copy of *Opus 21* turned up on the give-and-take shelf, it moved quickly into my pocket, and bounced home in the basket of my bike.

I was still grappling with it when the summer of 1958 waned, and it came time to pack my bags and leave Puerto Rico. I was headed for St. Joseph's Military Academy, a Catholic military boarding school in the western Kansas town of Hays. My parents agreed to send me there to preserve me from teenage temptations at another air base in Maine, to which they expected to be transferred. The Maine base, deep in the northern woods, was notorious as a place where bored, isolated teenagers got into trouble. And I had a Kansas cousin who had been sent to St. Joseph's, with apparently favorable results.

I was eager to go: the school sounded masculine and adventurous, and it was also far away from my crowded, non-idyllic family, which I was likewise eager to be. Packing a suitcase, the day before my departure, along with socks and shirts, I slipped the copy of *Opus 21* into my suitcase.

Which was where my mother found it, as she checked to see what I had forgotten to pack. She looked through it before confronting me with it over the kitchen table.

It was, she said, tight-lipped, shocking, filthy and blasphemous. I had no business reading such garbage, which could easily put my immortal soul in dire peril, undermining all the protective good that sending me to a Catholic boarding school was supposed to achieve.

143

To underline her judgment, she opened the book, then tore it right down the spine, into two pieces. Thus dismembered, she said it was headed for the trash, its proper resting place.

I was shaken by all this but didn't argue. I did quietly resolve to search for another copy after I made my escape the next morning.

But relief came later that night. Lying awake long after my siblings and parents went to bed, eventually nature called, and I padded into the bathroom. Flipping the light on, what did I see in the wastebasket but the two pieces of *Opus 21*!

I still puzzle about its appearance there. Not far from the back door stood a full-sized garbage can. Did my mother think I wouldn't notice it in the bathroom? Or that if I did, I would feel the book was wrecked, or had been desecrated and rendered untouchable? Or – could it be that my father had been shown it and left with the task of disposal?

This last is tantalizing. Raised in the same Catholic atmosphere of St. Paul, he was a silent participant in our churchgoing. Much later we learned of his disenchantment: in his will, he took pains to specify that there be no religious rite or officiant of any kind at his military funeral. Did he perhaps put the book pieces there, as a covert signal of support for my beginning explorations?

In any case, my mother miscalculated by not dumping the book fragments in the big garbage can, which had plenty of rotted food waste to soil it. Once seen, I knew I had to have it. The dismembered volume was now more than a book: it was a memento of what I was leaving behind, and a martyr's icon for what was now about to begin.

Behind the closed door, I carefully fished the two pieces out of the wastebasket and hid them in my pants pocket. The next morning and afternoon, on a northbound airliner, I alternated between gazing out the window at the passing towers of cloud, and puzzling over the mysteries of the book, broken but, like me, unbowed.

****

The next summer, I was impatiently at home again with the family, which had been transferred, not to Maine but to Francis E. Warren Air Force Base in southeastern Wyoming, a onetime cavalry outpost now repurposed as a nuclear missile base.

I had had, I thought, a good year at St. Joseph's: my grades were high, I was on the exhibition drill team, and my head was full of a new atheism distilled from Philip Wylie's books and snippets of text from other skeptics, David Hume, Sigmund Freud, and the mystic psychiatrist/shaman Carl Jung. Hays, Kansas may have been the middle of nowhere, but it had a state college with a small bookstore and had become the seat of my dawning enlightenment. I was eager to get back there, don my ROTC uniform, wear the school ring I had ordered, graduate, and find liberation from all of it somewhere in college.

Then one afternoon my mother called me to the kitchen table, where she put an envelope in front of me.

I almost never got mail in those days. I opened it cautiously. Inside was a letter, from the priest-president of St. Joseph's, Father Augustus. He was terse but plain: because of my frequently vocal unbelief, he wrote, I would not be allowed to return to St. Joseph's the next year. Having me around was too hazardous to the other cadets' spiritual welfare.

"Well?" Mother asked grimly. "What about this?"

I looked at the letter again, then at her, took a deep breath, then another one.

Viscerally I understood this as a watershed moment. She knew that Holy Mother Church was a stern taskmistress: it was a Catholic's wife supreme duty to produce a new generation of Catholics. She had filled the quota numerically; but I was the front-line against the world that sought to divert us onto the road to heresy and hell.

I could lie, evade, filibuster. Or I could define myself. Is this what later came to be called a "coming out" moment?

Finally, I cleared my throat and said, "It's true."

She didn't give up, of course. But that battle was lost; I was done with the Catholic church.

A few weeks later, a small package came in the mail. In it was my St. Joseph's school ring, ordered (and forgotten) months before.

At first, I thought I should send it back. But then the red and gold band set me to wondering about many things connected with the year at St. Joseph's, some of which I still wonder about:

Above all, what ever happened to Leroy and Ken, my best St. Joseph's buddies, who were among the very few tolerated (and normally quiet, except around me), non-Catholic cadets? I never saw them again. The school itself soon went coed and non-military, renaming itself St. Thomas More Prep, after a martyr to intellectual orthodoxy.

Questions with no answers. But a few things I do know.

One is that as it sat lightly on my palm, the ring took on an entirely different, and much more important set of meanings than it had when I ordered it. Above all, it was the marker of my emancipation. I put it on, and have been wearing it ever since, sixty-plus years at this writing. Wedding rings have come and gone; the red and gold is still there.

Another thing — but this came later — is that I'm not an atheist anymore.

****

Let's fast-forward through college, at Colorado State University, 1960-64. And the following year, which found me married and drawn, moth-to-flame, into the civil rights movement and work under Dr. King in Selma, Alabama. This story is told in my memoir, *Eating Dr. King's Dinner*. It culminates in the shedding of my youthful military conditioning under Dr. king's tutelage, and rejection of war just as the bloody shadow of Vietnam spread over our land, as well as Southeast Asia. I applied to be a Conscientious Objector to the military draft (an option I had never even heard of until a few months earlier), and to my surprise, was accepted.

Once certified as a C.O., I needed to find a civilian job, acceptable to the government as alternative service, for two years. By then, the civil rights fever in Selma had peaked and receded, and without it the town was not a very appealing place. My wife Tish was particularly keen to get away from the boondocks. I agreed, though I was pretty lazy about job-seeking.

But it was time. So, near the end of 1965, fate took a hand, and knocked on my door.

****

And that is indeed how it happened: with a knock at the door of a house on Lapsley Street. There my first wife Tish and I rented a room from Selma's legendary movement matriarch, Mrs. Amelia Boynton.

Mrs. Boynton was out, and I was busy. Tish went to the door, but with some trepidation. We were still wary of strangers; and when she opened the door, she gasped and jumped back: there stood a strange young white woman.

The stranger, however, was just as shocked to see Tish. But when she spoke, stammering something apologetic about being in the wrong place, her lack of a southern accent was
reassuring. This was not, it seemed, a local come to terrorize the Yankee invaders.

The stranger, likewise, reassured by Tish's accent, explained that she was canvassing the neighborhood in search of any black citizens who might not yet be registered to vote. She added that she was part of a group of college students visiting Selma on a study trip through the South.

Intrigued now, Tish invited her in. The visitor was revealed as part of the very first class at Friends World College. It was a new experimental college, based on Long Island, not far from New York City, and was connected with Quakers.

Quakers? Now Tish was fascinated. She had heard or read

something about Quakers awhile back and had written off to Philadelphia for some brochures about them. I hadn't paid much attention, except to the fact that they were supposed to be one of the pillars of religious pacifism; I thought there might have been some connection between them and CCCO, since both had Philadelphia addresses.

Once started, the visitor talked animatedly about both Quakers and their Friends World College: her family was Quaker; the school was a radical and exciting experiment. They didn't take courses as such; instead they studied world problems and weighed possible solutions in the field.

And they traveled, to put faces on ideas and test concepts in the real world. This trip was to the South; but later in the spring they'd be leaving for Europe. After that, term by term, they would make their way around the world, ending up back on Long Island to complete their degrees and proceed to change the world.

By now Tish was spellbound, and the two talked on and on until the visitor realized she was late for rejoining her group. Tish invited her to bring the whole bunch back for more talk later.

When I came in, Tish was still bubbling with excitement. Besides the fascinating details about the school, she had mentioned that I was a CO, and the visitor recognized the term—in fact, said they had COs on their faculty, doing alternative service there and was sure they'd want to meet me. Tish smelled the possibility of a job, and Long Island was about as far away from the boondocks as we could hope to get.

Sure enough, that evening the whole group showed up, crammed into a Volkswagen Microbus. They were led by Arthur Meyer, the school's Assistant Director. We all sat around and talked up a storm, hitting it off.

And Tish had guessed right: Meyer was very interested in my CO status, my need for a job, and (though he didn't say so then) the fact that people in my position were accustomed to working cheap. They were leaving town shortly, Meyer said, but he would pass my name on to the Director, one Morris Mitchell, back in Long Island.

Was this Providence? Quakerism is one of the key elements of the future I would have chosen had I been able to. But there were only a handful of Quakers in all of Alabama and Mississippi, and none lived within many miles of Selma or Dallas County. Yet a Quaker knocked at my door and brought a job with her.

After that day had started the process, it seemed to go like clockwork: I wrote to Morris Mitchell, and he responded, inviting me to apply for a junior faculty position there.

Me? A college faculty member? I hadn't quite finished my bachelor's degree at Colorado State, falling short the summer we left after failing a pottery class. But my movement experience fit Mitchell's problem-centered theory of education. Besides, I wouldn't actually be teaching courses – the job was more like being a camp counselor and driver. My CO status was also an asset for a Quaker school; and I was accustomed to the low pay which was all they could afford.

Before Christmas a job offer came, to begin in February 1966, at Friends World College's home campus, preparing for the arrival of the second class. I accepted gladly, and my draft board in Cheyenne, relieved of further paperwork, approved it without a blink.

In early February 1966, we packed up our still meager belongings and climbed onto a train in Montgomery that was to take us from Alabama to New York City.

One of the first and most vivid images of my new home came two days later, heading east from Manhattan. The VW Microbus carrying us came up out of the Midtown Tunnel, headed east across Queens, and then drove abruptly over a rise, into the biggest cemetery I had ever seen. The headstones spread out for what seemed like miles on every side, their irregular ranks covering the hillocks and hollows all the way to the close horizon. Welcome to New York.

Harrow Hill was a large Long Island estate that had been donated to Friends World College as a headquarters, at least until it could be sold, and a proper campus established. After breakfast the next morning, with butterflies in my stomach, I set out to meet my boss, the distinguished scholar and educational philosopher, Dr. Morris Mitchell.

I walked down an ornate hallway and knocked at the door of a parlor that had been turned into an office.

When the door opened, I had to look up to meet the eyes of its occupant. Morris Mitchell was a very tall man, still powerful and towering at the age of seventy-one. White hair, piercing eyes, and a strong, firm grip.

"How do you do, Dr. Mitchell," I began, "I'm–"

"Don't call me Dr. Mitchell," he said, turning back toward his desk, which was strewn with papers. I immediately caught his southern twang, softened by many years in northern exile, but still distinct.

"Call me Morris," he continued, sinking into his chair. "I'm a Quaker, and Quakers don't hold with titles. I don't even want to be called 'Mister.' 'Mister' comes from 'Master' and I acknowledge no man as my master and don't want to be master of anyone else."

I stood there, dumbfounded but captivated, my mouth open.

This next chapter, I knew at once, was going to be something very special.

But that's another story.

****

148

Alas, it's a story which has not yet been written, except in pieces here and there. In early 2016 I attempted to put the first ten years of it into another memoir, *Meetings*. But that only took me to 1975, with forty-plus years to go; and I am of a generation condemned to live under the ancient curse of "Interesting Times."

I had started on a sequel to *Meetings* in Eleventh Month (Quakerese for "November") of 2016, when a combination earthquake, tornado & tsunami struck the United States, the fury of which is still playing itself out. I for one, have yet to recover enough inner balance in the aftermath to return to that personal account. I hope I can before the curtain falls; but life is uncertain.

Nevertheless, I hope to fulfill my own charge to other authors in this collection, to close with some reflective advices based on that experience, for the benefit of any who choose to consider them.

This begins with a mini credo: summing up my view of Quakerism in two short paragraphs. It's included here not for argument but as a point of reference: this, put as concisely as I can, is where I'm coming from:

Credo

About 370 years ago in England, God had an idea. He (She or They) wanted a group of people to come together and do some pieces of God's work, in some particular evolving ways. So, when a man named George Fox climbed up a place called Pendle Hill, God showed him that there was "a great people to be gathered" beginning there, to do that particular work, as individuals and together, in those particular evolving ways.

That "people" or group became the Religious Society of Friends, the Quakers. It appeared because God gathered it, to do some particular work, in the various ways we're supposed to do it. (Figuring out the work is part of it. What Quakers call the Testimonies are part of it; but only part.) We're not done yet, and God's not done with us, and that's why we're still around.

Advices

1. Fight the forgetting. The "memory hole" of George Orwell's parable, *1984*, twisting, concealing and destroying personal and collective memories deemed inconvenient or obsolete by the reigning powers, is now a reality. As deadly for Quakerism as for all else, it works around and upon us continually, and largely invisibly. Exposing and resisting it is an ongoing imperative for both personal and group survival.

"Truth for authority, not authority for truth."
— Lucretia Mott

2. Think. Friends have much to think about, to find and carry out their missions in a complex and rapidly evolving world. To do that meaningfully, overcoming an entrenched culture of anti-intellectualism regarding all things religious is a key priority. This chosen mindlessness chains us to the world's follies and fads as surely as a slave's fetters. Breaking them will not be easy, particularly among Liberal Friends.

> *"I am using the words 'Christian thought' in my title, instead of 'Christian theology,' because, while many Friends shy away from theology, we do not, or at least we do not profess to, shy away from thought. Yet the word "theology" means simply thinking or reasoning about God, and I am sure that most of us can hardly avoid some thinking about man's greatest object of thought."*
> — Howard Brinton, 1959.

3. To Quaker thinkers: scholars and intellectuals: your work is vital. However, the Society has not been set up to support it. Thus, I urge you to prepare for a bivocational future. As you do, be cautious about the academy. In our time, "higher education" has been progressively corrupted and put out of reach as an honorable career arena, except for an ever-shrinking minority. I see no real viable market for fulltime Quaker thinkers/scholars on the horizon. I don't like this anymore than you, but there it is. Seek the like-minded, but don't let a solitary path deter you. And a PS: as you do your work, strive for excellence. There is too much mediocrity in Quaker thought and history; it does not serve you, your vocation, or the Society's work. Excellence lasts: that is all.

> *". . . every Shabbos morning, [our community] wrestles God. Ourselves, and each other, and God. We do not simply accept the tradition, but we do not reject it either. We wrestle it: fighting it and making love to it at the same time. We try to touch it with our lives.''*
> — Arthur Waskow, *Godwrestling*

5. Other paid Quaker jobs are scarce and seem likely to stay so. But there is one secret, nearly guaranteed path to a Quaker career, if that's your desire. Here it is: learn how to raise money. It can be as honorable as any other work; and if you can do it, someone will always want to hire you. Plus, if all else fails, you'll know how to raise funds to start & work for your own Quaker committee.

6. Break the shackles of the Baseball Illusion. That's the notion that attending, watching, cheering, and (especially) chattering about a big game or spectacle makes you part of "the action." Not so, except through buying tickets. The rest is an illusion, hopefully an entertaining one, but often only a waste of time and energy. Beyond sports, many public spectacles and "actions," including much politics and even "activism," examined more closely, are mostly or entirely illusion.

> *"The future ain't what it used to be."*
> — Yogi Berra

7. Particularly in public work, one or more of what are called the Big Four are prerequisites for moving from illusory spectacle toward real impact. They are: big numbers of people; big money; big names; and/or big media. All have risks and temptations; so does doing nothing.

8. Beware the Gospel of the "Tall Poppies." It is a program to reimpose a Neo-Orthodox sort of top-down control upon the Society, by those who are sure they know what's best for Friends, but don't. Quakerism has been down that road before; it leads to a dry garden at a dead end.

> *"Much of what we tend to regard as the achievement of Friends as a whole was, in fact, the work of individual Friends, or small groups of Friends, often in the face of opposition or neglect of their monthly meetings. (One of the most positive – if often tedious – aspects of Quaker culture may be its capacity to produce or attract individuals who are willing to stand up to it.)"*
>
> — Bowen Alpern, *Godless for God's Sake*

9. Quakerism is sometimes buffered from the full brunt of our own internal evildoing, not from virtue but rather by its flat decentralist structure. But make no mistake: bad Quaker things happen, and if you're faithful enough for long enough, some will happen to you. Or maybe you'll join in with them, if only by complicity.

> *"Since the primary motive of the evil is disguise, one of the places evil people are most likely to be found is within the church. What better way to conceal one's evil from oneself as well as from others than to be a deacon or some other highly visible form of Christian within our culture."*
>
> — M. Scott Peck, *People of the Lie*

10. 99% of Americans have nothing or nearly nothing to do with the military, or the vast machinery that upholds it and spends/wastes most of our taxes (and the resources for our better future). But resting in this ignorance does nothing to inhibit war or advance peace. If you're in that 99% (& most Liberal Quakers are), get out: learn something real about it. (Note: Reading, listening to, or chattering about media reports of "policy" disputes in Washington doesn't count.)

> *"Hence the saying: 'If you know the enemy and know yourself, you need not fear the result of a hundred battles. If you know yourself but not the enemy, for every victory gained you will also suffer a defeat. If you know neither the enemy nor yourself, you will succumb in every battle.'"*

— Sun Tzu, *The Art of War*

11. Discernment: You may not know what's best for you; at least, I often haven't. Your meeting may not either. Many times the paraphernalia of "discernment" is often but a hair's breadth away from organized rationalization & preaching to a choir (committee) named to echo and endorse it.

> *"Therefore, dear friends. . .* continue *to work out your salvation with fear and trembling . . ."*

— Philippians 2:12.

Qui vit sans folie, n'est pas si sage qu'il croit —
He that lives without folly is not as wise as he thinks.

– Francois de La Rochefoucauld, Maxim No. 209

Diane Faison McKinzie: A Vessel for Harriet

I'm remembering the very first time I presented my original one woman show, "The Spirit of Harriet Tubman" in February, 1989, in the auditorium of Prince Edward County middle school, in Farmville, Virginia.

I wasn't nervous, nor did I forget my lines. When I finished, I was excited, and shared the excitement of the students cheering the performance.

Diane Faison as Harriet

****

I was born in Winston-Salem North Carolina in 1947. It was a good year. My parents were Samuel Lester Speas and Creola Bridges Speas. My parents got married in their 20s, but they waited to try to have children for almost 10 years afterward. So, when I was born I was a real happy package for them. I was treated very well and had a very happy childhood.

At that time Winston-Salem, which we often just called "Winston" for short, was the cigarette capital of the world. When I was a child Afro-Americans there had their very own just about everything: theaters, bowling alleys, restaurants, clubs, even a bus line, etc. This was during the time of segregation, so we had our own schools as well. I attended those schools up through my high school years.

153

I was an only child and was given all the things that I needed and a lot of the things that I wanted. My father had two jobs, he was a chauffeur in the daytime, and at night a bartender. My mother was the manager of a black movie theater.

We were not allowed to go to the movies with whites, but I didn't really notice that when I was a child.

Our little house was in what they call Reynolds Town, a historically black section near downtown. We were part of an all-black St. Stephen's Episcopal church, that members of my family had helped start.

By the time I was 11 we were talking about segregation and integration and Martin Luther King. I realized that in my happy childhood, I had been totally oblivious to my larger situation. Since my mother managed the black movie theater, as a child I had no difficulty going to see movies.

So, I really didn't become aware until later of the ugly monster of segregation that lived among us, and that was why we had these things, because we weren't able to go to white establishments.

But by the time I entered high school, the civil rights movement came. In 1960 it landed right nearby in Greensboro, with sit-ins at the Woolworth's lunch counters. I saw these sit-ins on television, and my parents explained about them, that we couldn't eat at the lunch counters because of the color of our skin. That sounded crazy to me. Soon our church became one of the centers for training in nonviolent resistance led by Dr. King's staff.

I joined student protests at places in Winston that did not serve black people. I rode a bus to Washington in August 1963 for the big march and heard part of Dr. King's "I have a Dream" speech, but being young and in that big big crowd, I didn't really understand I was part of making history there.

I went to Atkins High School, which is also historically black, there in Winston-Salem. It was the school where my father and his brothers and sisters and mother all went.

I had my first experience of acting there and was chosen the best actress in my class. In my senior year I was also Miss Atkins High School, and a member of the National Honor Society.

When I graduated in 1965, I won a scholarship to North Carolina Central University, a Historically Black University in Durham. I studied art and art education. One year I stayed home for a semester, to help my father care for my mother who was sick. Then that summer to catch up I took every educational course the college had to offer, which was very unusual, so my degree is education from K to 12. I don't even think they give that degree anymore.

I graduated in 1969 and the year before that I met my first husband, Claiborne Austin Faison Jr., in the classroom. Ironically many wanted to call him the black white boy because he had red hair, very Afro frizzy, freckles and a very light complexion. While we were dating in my junior year, I got an opportunity to teach in New York City after I graduated. I let him know that, and he said, if you go to New York, I'll never see you again, will you marry me?

Oh, I thought that was so funny, so I laughed and said, oh yeah, right. I thought it was a big joke. But that whole year before I graduated, he asked me at least three more times. Finally, I said, well OK, and we got married on June 27, 1968.

After that we waited two years before starting a family, and just as I was getting ready to give birth in 1971, Uncle Sam decided to send some correspondence to my husband because of the military draft, and it said, Uncle Sam wants you. So, he was put in the Navy, and of course the Vietnam War took him away. He had a secret security clearance, so he didn't talk much about what happened to him there, and I knew better than to ask. (But does the phrase "Agent Orange" ring a bell?)

I returned to Winston Salem where I was teaching kindergarten. I was nine months pregnant, by myself except for my father, as my mother had already passed away. I gave birth in Winston-Salem to my first child, Dominique Celes Faison. My husband returned seven months later, not seeing his firstborn child til then. Still in the service, and now an officer, he was being sent to take charge of a Naval air base in Maine. We drove an old beat up car all the way from North Carolina to Brunswick, Maine, and you know we were the only black family in the entire area.

This was 1972, and at that time a lot of white people there had never even seen a live black person, and I must say they were very curious. I gave birth to my second child, Craig Austin Faison in June in the hospital there in Brunswick, and I was the first black woman to ever have a baby in this hospital. Craig was born feet first, 11 pounds with no medication, I had not even asked for any, so I really became a case study. After I took him home, of course my daughter could not understand where this fat little person came from.

My husband was still in the Navy and did not at that time show any of the negative effects from experiencing the Vietnam War.

But I did. We were transferred to Norfolk, Virginia, and during that time the Navy wives would gather on a pier when the ships returned, to see who would come back on them. I remember well, one very traumatic day as we stood on the pier, me with my two babies, and watched his ship coming in through Chesapeake Bay.

Then we saw some Marines coming towards us, the wives and the children standing on the pier waiting for their husbands. They told us that president Nixon had decided to turn the ships around, even though they had already been gone seven months. And as we stood there with our children, we watched the ships turn around and go back out to sea for five more long months.

As I waited once again along with my two children my mental and emotional state started crumbling, as I had been away from my husband and their father for so long. Then I was contacted by my lifelong girlfriend who was my children's godmother, and she decided to come to Virginia Beach and stay with me for the summer, because she knew how my mental state was deteriorating every day. She was a lifesaver.

After more waiting, we finally got word that the ship was coming back again, and we were reunited.

Before my husband and I got married, we promised each other that no matter how many children we had we would also adopt one. And one day in 1979, while we were still in Virginia, on North West Naval base, he called me and said I'm sending the MPs around to an apartment on the base. A lady had called to say she can hear a baby crying and she thought the young lady living there was gone. She asked, can you go around and see?

The MPs had a key that opened the apartments, and once the door was open, sure enough there was a baby in the abandoned apartment. The baby was covered in poop and curdled milk and screaming. The MPs called my husband, and I told him I was taking the baby to the house and cleaning him up. He said OK and I'll call social services. They came and took him to be put under emergency foster care.

Then he asked me if I remembered our talk before our wedding about adopting, and I said, yes, I remember. He said I think this is we maybe got our orders from God tonight. We need to investigate more about this baby. Maybe we can adopt.

Several weeks later we got a call that the foster care mother had asked social services to come and get the baby, because she believed the baby was a black baby, and she didn't want it.

This was odd because the baby was the exact color of my husband and had no hair. He looked like any other Caucasian baby. Anyway, they came and got the baby. But then they were having a problem finding someone else to take him temporarily. Of course, I said yes.

Soon enough we had fallen in love with the baby, named him Clay Austin, and started the adoption process. It took several months, but then we had three children and had fulfilled our goal of giving another child a home like we promised.

We moved from there to a base at Great Bridge, Virginia, in the Dismal Swamp, and he took his position as head of the base There had never been a black officer in charge there we were softly attacked. When I say softly, I mean undertones of racial remarks and such. One day my husband went into his office and on his desk was a note to Lieutenant Faison and the note said, I am a member of the Ku Klux Klan, and I refuse to work for a nigger.

Of course, he was upset, and he found out who it was. The incident was handled very professionally, and my husband had him transferred, though I don't know the details of the legal part.

As the wife of the head officer, I was in charge of the officers' wives club. At my first meeting with the group in my home, one woman wanted to know, well, did you did you go to school? And I said very sarcastically, yes, we're free now, you know. She looked at me very disgusted. I said I finished high school, I have several college degrees, how many do you have? She said I didn't quite finish my degree at one of the colleges you named, and I said well I'm so sorry.

Out on our patio we smell smoke in a distant field, in the Dismal Swamp. It was not on the base, and my husband decided to go see what was happening it was a group of Klansmen, celebrating whatever they celebrate and of course my husband was not going to be the brave one and go into their meeting to see what it was all about.

We kept moving from base to base until my husband retired from the Navy in 1984. By then we were in Richmond, Virginia, where my in-laws, his parents also lived. They were teaching and operating a laundromat and store in a low-income area. My children had a morning job there, which was to roll the quarters to put in the washers.

We had some hard times in Richmond. My father-in-law was a working alcoholic, who was able to keep up his teaching work despite his excessive drinking. My mother-in-law discovered he also had a longtime girlfriend. Then one morning in 1983 before dawn, the police knocked at our door, and asked us to come with them to a park near my in-laws' home. There they asked us to identify a body: my husband said it was his mother. She had been raped, strangled and dragged into some bushes. About 100 feet from her there was another body, that of a drug dealer who had also just been killed. Not far away was her car, with her husband, apparently asleep in a drunken stupor, in the back seat. When the police got him awake, he said he had heard nothing.

This case soon became more brutal and tangled. Later that day, when my husband and I were still trying to absorb all this, we went to the in-law's home. There we found the door open and his father and the girlfriend ransacking the house, searching for his mother's will. She had told us that she had directed that in the event of her death, all her property and interest in the business was to go to her son, bypassing her cheating husband. Of course, there was an altercation and I had to stand between, trying to stop them from fighting. Finally, my father-in-law and the girlfriend left.

If there was a will, it was never found. We soon realized that my husband was also a suspect in the killings. But the police had two main theories of the case: one was that the father-in-law had hired someone to kill his wife. The other was that she had been attacked after pulling over and interrupting an ongoing drug deal in the park.

To pursue the drug deal theory, the police assigned a detective to watch the area at night. That detective was soon murdered. A second detective was assigned; he too was murdered.

All those homicide cases are still open and unsolved. Neither my husband nor the father-in law was ever charged. And there was a court struggle over the estate that lasted months.

When it was time for my mother-in-law's funeral, here came the local news media. They were crazy for the story, even followed me to the grocery store. When my husband asked them to leave us alone, they hid in the bushes.

It was awful. The story was on the evening news, and unfortunately my daughter who is the oldest, was sitting in front of the TV when she saw her grandmother's picture pop up.

Of course, I turned the TV off and tried to explain all of those terms she had heard, which they were not ready for. They were very upset when they understood that somebody had killed their grandmother.

After all this, it was no surprise that my husband said he wanted to leave Richmond. I don't want the children living in this atmosphere, he said. I said OK. Now out of the Navy, he said he wanted to find a teaching job somewhere quiet in the country. Before long he took a teaching position in Farmville Virginia, about fifty miles away. I was teaching in Richmond, so soon he was driving from Richmond to Farmville and back every day, 50 miles each way.

I finished up my contract in Richmond and found a position in Brookville, about 5 miles from Farmville, so the next school year we were working close by. And my husband had soon collected the settlement money from the laundromat, and we started talking about buying property and building a house near Farmville.

We did that, bought 70 acres that was mostly wooded. On it we built our dream house, which was finished in 1987. In the house combined features we had liked in different places we had lived, and made a big bedroom suite upstairs, which included a small living room and library, open-ended and overlooking a cathedral style living room, with big windows and a fireplace big enough for my kids to stand in. We also had a deck all the way around, which had a pecan tree growing through it, because we didn't want to cut it down. The tree was our "outdoor umbrella," and in good weather we also cooked there.

We were also both very involved with the schools there in and around Farmville, which was in Prince Edward County.

I guess I need to say something about Prince Edward County. By the time we got there many years had passed since the days of lunch counter sit-ins and Dr. King's big march. But major civil rights history was not far away.

In 1959, when a federal court ordered Prince Edward County to desegregate its schools, the county resisted by closing them all. White students were issued vouchers to pay tuition at a new private "segregation academy." Black students were left to fend for themselves. Their schools stayed closed til 1964.

They reopened just about the time I started teaching after college. So, in one way it was all over. But the memories were still fresh. And one of them was particularly meaningful to me: Late in 1959, the American Friends Service Committee started work in Prince Edward County, with an office in Farmville for what in 1960 became its Emergency Placement Program. Through it families in non-segregated areas volunteered to take in black students from Prince Edward to attend school there. That program lasted til the schools reopened. It enabled many black students to complete their disrupted high school work.

Friends = Quakers. The connection stayed with me. I learned about their tradition of quiet worship, without a church hierarchy. I liked that idea too. I often spent time on our land in silent meditation. My husband, now out of the military, sometimes talked reflectively about all the killing in war. One of his tasks was to check dead soldiers' bodies which were being returned to the states, and then to go with the Marines who went to the families' homes to break the news. About the time our house was finished, a gentleman named Tim who lived nearby decided to start a Quaker worship group, under the auspices of a regional association called Baltimore Yearly Meeting. We began to gather at his barn for meeting, alternating with our house.

****

Those were good years. The children grew, moved on through school, into college and out into adult life. Both my husband and I were honored for our work in the schools. And each February, when Black History Month came along, we joined in eagerly.

It was in 1988, when I started thinking about the coming February, that I got a bit restless. I liked to do things with my students that were different. But in Black History Month, very often the observance

159

came down to students reading something and writing a report. Suddenly that sounded too dry. I wanted something unique.

So, I went to the library. This was still the old days, when libraries had shelves full of books and barely any computers. I had to touch the books, lift them and open them. And when I came to the Black history shelf, my hand brushed a book and it fell to the floor.

I picked it up. The title was, *The Life of Harriet Tubman.* Of course, I knew about her. Or so I thought. But I turned the pages anyway.

As I read about her this time, something came over me. I felt as though, *this is me.* I felt I was being encouraged to be Harriet's vessel to tell her story, to embody it. (Quakers call this a leading; for me, that's what it was.) I felt I had to show the students who this woman was. Such a small person, but with such a huge courage.

The idea began to grow in my mind. I went home, researched old photos of Harriet, and finally found one that I could come to resemble with a carefully selected costume. I had older relatives, who didn't have much schooling, who still talked in something like the old slave dialect; I had heard it all my life. So, I felt that's how Harriet talked. And it came naturally to me as her voice, I didn't even have to study that part.

I never wrote a script. After all these years, I've never had one. I read about her, I felt it, and I spoke it. I was following the tradition of my people, of just telling her story, not reading it. Storytellers of my people don't have scripts. But I keep learning about Harriet. I don't rehearse either, not really. But sometimes in daily life, like washing the dishes, Harriet comes and starts speaking a new line, or working on an older one, or a gesture. Every year I find out something new about her, and I might add it to the performance, and I might not.

After that first performance in 1988, I began to get requests to perform at other schools, in schools in several surrounding counties. This was very fulfilling to me.

Yet in time, big changes came. One morning in 1997, my husband tugged me awake. When I saw him, I screamed: his chest and groin were covered with blood. It was an advanced case of cancer, which he had not told anyone about.

During this time, one of the attenders at our little meeting, became a real (small "f") friend, and helped me with respite care during my husband's illness. Isn't that what Quakers are supposed to do, help each other?

From there I had more than a year of caregiving as he went through surgery and chemo and experimental therapies and got weaker and weaker.

When he died in August of 1999, I was more than devastated; we had been married thirty-one years. He had been my best friend as well as my spouse. Losing both of those, I felt I was completely lost.

Without him the land and the house weren't the same. In 2000 I sold them and moved north to Prince William County, Virginia, and taught school there til 2004, when I retired. From there I was drawn back toward home, Winston-Salem. In each of these places, there were Friends meetings that welcomed me.

After a few years, my children encouraged me to find another partner, and after some consideration I turned to an online dating group. There, in 2010, I met Crawford McKinzie, known as Mack. We liked each other but felt cautious. After dating for five years, we married in 2015, at Winston-Salem Friends Meeting. Then I moved to his home in Gibsonville, near Burlington, North Carolina.

When I moved to Gibsonville, I felt an overwhelming need to find another Friends meeting to be part of, and I started searching for one. I finally found Spring Friends Meeting in Snow Camp, NC, where I do feel like I belong. Spring had an unexplainable spiritual atmosphere that felt like a warm hug. Maybe that was partly due to the fact that the Meeting has been in that spot since the late 1700s; so many Quakers have lived there, and many are buried nearby.

Mack had been career army, twenty-two years, and was a Vietnam veteran too. He had been in field units there, often under fire in combat areas, sleeping on the ground with rats and taking baths mainly in the rain, — and both the rain and the ground were running with toxic Agent Orange. Even now, sometimes he has flashback nightmares, muttering "They're coming, they're coming" in his sleep, and striking out, even at me.

After four good years together, Mack fell ill, and as this is written, he is contending with a number of very serious conditions. I'm again being a caregiver, essentially fulltime, juggling doctors' appointments, tests and procedures, savoring his good days, and weathering the others.

This routine, I confess, wears me out. And I remember that Harriet too was a longtime caregiver. She built a house in Auburn, New York, where she cared for the poor, including Civil War veterans who were afflicted with what we would name PTSD, but then was called "soldier's heart." Later she took care of her second husband and her aged parents there. She did this work for almost as many years as she was active in the Underground, and then the Civil War. Learning this strengthens my identification with her; besides my second husband, I too took care of my aging parents. She did this caregiving until her own health failed; she lived until 1913.

In my situation, I often get tired, and frustrated. Times of relief and release are sparse. I know that in Harriet's years of caregiving, she found support in her religious faith and her church community. And at Spring, with Friends, when I lead the meeting, or sit and listen in the meeting, it gives me the same renewal like I feel also came to Harriet. And I have to add that the most renewing moments are when I'm performing as Harriet.

I hope her face is soon put on the twenty-dollar bill. And one big item on my "bucket list" is to perform at Harriet's house in Auburn. Even after thirty years, and several hundred appearances, speaking Harriet Tubman's words and evoking her spirit refreshes and renews my heart and soul.

Jennifer Elam: Back & Forth

Heading Home on the Hillbilly Highway

Appalachia is a wound, a joy and a poem.
— Silas House from the documentary 'Hillbilly'

Appalachia is a wound deep in my soul, a joy deeper in my soul, and a poem deepest in my soul that brings together the extremes my Appalachian heritage have been for me.

Introduction

I was born in Kentucky. I have spent my whole life leaving and going back to Kentucky. My Mama always said of her heritage, "You can't live with 'em and you can't live without 'em." Dang! She had that right. Then I face the stereotypes of Appalachians by both those in and out of the region, and I say, "You can't live with 'em and you can't live without 'em." So, here I am - still comin' and goin,' my whole life back and forth.

Home has been an elusive concept for me. Appalachian author, Wendell Berry writes extensively about the importance of "place". Although I have

Jennifer Elam

always felt a deep sense of belonging in the universe and a deep faith in my standing and place with God, I have lived in many physical spaces on this earth and traveled the world widely. More than place, "home" has come in moments: as a child in Sunday School, early life with family, in school, times of growing and learning, times with friends and lovers, sitting in Silence among Quakers, but less so in a place. My theme song for my life is more like Trio's song "Wild Flowers Don't Care Where They Grow." Home includes the moments of transcending the ever-present stereotypes that have threatened to rob me of a sense of home and equality on the earth.

I want to introduce you to some of my ancestors. I hope that will help you understand some of the complexity that makes up the joy and the wounds, the coming and going, and now what I call my Appalachian heritage identity crisis that has demanded reckoning as I get older.

My Mama and Daddy were two of the most hard-working people I have ever known as well as two of the most committed to their family. Daddy was incredibly smart (a measured IQ of 150) and Mama was the most faithful follower that Jesus ever had. They fought about religion ever since I can remember but they made it work for just three months shy of 70 years. They had something going for them.

Mama's daddy died when she was 11 so I never knew George Penn and never heard a lot about him. But, Mama's mama, Forrest Penn (Nana), was an amazing woman, loved and respected by all. Daddy called her Mrs. Penn out of respect. She cared for elderly people that she called her patients to make a living and raise her five children after George died. She and her youngest daughter, Nancy left KY for Dayton, Ohio when I was five so Nancy could go to school to be a dietician. So, we visited Ohio often when I was young, and I stayed with my Nana during the summers for much of my young life.

I loved Dayton and Nana was the best. She was very dignified, called her many friends Mrs., was faithful to her Methodist church, loved to travel the world and visit family (it was always closer for her to visit them than them to come see her) faithfully watched the daytime soap opera "As the World Turns" Monday thru Friday at 1:30, and was the president of the WCTU (that's Women's Christian Temperance Union). She wore nice dresses and took her Bible most everywhere she went. Her upstairs was always rented out to her "boys," renters (Bill, Tom, Henry, and Mr. Gesell) that stayed with her for decades and became my friends too. She also sent postcards every week to every family member, including nieces and nephews.

To me, she was the BEST! When I need to feel stability in my life, I can still picture us sitting at her little table with the red and white checked tablecloth, telling each other about how our day went, eating pork chops and Brussel sprouts (vegetables she only ate "for health's sake"). And every night before bedtime, she had her black cow (Pepsi and vanilla ice cream) and prayers.

Daddy's family was more complex. His mother's family, the Beattys were land wealthy, owning land that had been in the family for several generations, since the 1790's. They were also very dignified and (unheard of at that time) moved to town for a period of time so that their daughter Mary Elizabeth (my great grandmother, Mammaw Beatty) could go to college where she became an artist and a "proper lady." Interestingly, I did not hear about her stories until I was an adult.

Daddy's father's family was from Morgan County, eastern KY mountains of Appalachia. My great great grandpa worked the coal fields in PA to save the money to buy their land in KY and that land has also come down through the family. My two nephews just inherited pieces of that farm. Daddy had 48 first cousins on his father's side and one of the strongest values in Appalachia is loyalty to family. There was so much family that we had to celebrate Christmas for four days just to get in the visits.

My paternal grandfather and grandmother (Mammaw and Fifi Elam) met at the University of KY and the marriage (and the family wars) of the rural bluegrass and mountains began. I never visited them once they were not fighting viciously; they even threw dishes at each other across the kitchen. Fifi bought land from Mammaw's father and started the Rosemound Farm (a dairy at that time). Because of the fighting, I really hated going to the farm.

When my mom and dad married, my dad had just gotten out of the service, World War II. He and Fifi did not agree on many things (how to treat women, how to treat people from different cultures and races, and more). They had words and Mama and Daddy struck out on their own.

These early family influences on me were significant and contribute greatly to the complexity in what I am calling my identity crisis. Much of this piece focuses on the farm and Daddy's family but both sides were instrumental in the complexity of my life.

There are writers who portray Appalachian people as depraved (Deliverance), or entertaining and ignorant (Beverly Hillbillies). There are also writers who romanticize Appalachia, focusing on its natural beauty and the incredible music and dance. I have experienced the extremes and as most stereotypes do, they represent pieces of the whole, but they are incomplete portrayals of the Appalachia I have known and do not represent the Truth of the region.

My early years were spent on farms in the Bluegrass region of Kentucky. We left KY when I was 12 and that is when I learned I was a "hillbilly." I spent my whole life dealing with hillbilly stereotypes, especially in trying to get educated and have a career despite them.

My daddy always said, "just be proud of who you are and where you are from, then they have nothing on ya." He held his Appalachian heritage dear and held it for me. He wanted so much for me; he wanted me to have what I wanted: to go to college, travel the world, and realize my deepest heart's desires. So, all my life, when I encountered the bias, the discrimination, the loss of perceived IQ points as soon as I opened my mouth with my Southern/Appalachian accent, I just declared that such a reaction was the other person's problem and it had nothing to do with me.

I spent much of my life outside Appalachia, assimilating into whatever culture I found myself. To do that, though, I unconsciously turned my back on my heritage as well as a piece of my own soul. I took on whatever accent I needed, talked and behaved in ways I needed to in order to fit in (well, as long as it did not go against my values then). I wanted more for my life than was possible as a hillbilly.

My strategy worked for most of my life until it didn't.

Now I feel called to better understand that Appalachian heritage and its meaning for me. It is time to do that work that goes way back, even to exploring the lives of my ancestors in new ways.

Recently, I was having a conversation with Silas House, an Appalachian writer, telling him about my identity crisis. He said, "Jennifer, it sounds like you feel guilty." I felt the truth deeply, and quickly responded, "NO, not guilt, it's LOSS." Even as a respected academic, Silas has refused to give up his Appalachian accent and calls it "Accent as Activism." I SO admire and respect that.

I

I grew up on five different farms in Kentucky. My paternal grandparents (Mammaw and Fifi Elam) had a farm that had been in Mammaw's family since the 1790's, the Rosemound Farm.

Fifi's parents from the mountains had passed before I was born. Fifi was a hard-working farmer but into abuse and incest; "men do these things" was the apathetic response of the culture around me. Luckily, I was never one of the women directly affected, but as an adult when other family members came out about it, I realized, "Oh, that is what made something always feel WRONG or OFF when I spent time on the farm."

On the other side of his family, my father loved his maternal grandparents, the Beattys, dearly. As a young child, his parents got divorced (and later re-married) and during those years he lived with

Grandma and Grandpa Beatty. Everything I ever heard about them was wonderful – not a negative word about them anywhere. One day my father was telling me how great his grandparents were. Then with a sad look on his face, he said, "Grandpa Beatty and I only had one disagreement in our whole lives, but it was a big one. We did not agree on black people."

II

That was all I ever heard about it. So this much is guesswork. Someone recently asked me if there were slaves on the farm. I never heard any stories of slaves on the farm. My impression was that this part of my family took the side of the north in the Civil War, supported the Union. Kentucky was a border state, caught in the middle.

When I was growing up, there was a black family, the Millers, living on the farm. Hugh and Nannie Miller had nine children and Huberta was the oldest in their family and was only a few months younger than me, also the oldest child and grandchild in the family.

Hugh and my dad grew up together. My dad caused a commotion in the family because he asked questions like, "Why does Hugh have to ride a different bus from me to go to school?" My father asked for integration and equality in many ways, even as a foreman later at International Harvester. He had many disagreements with his father, and this was one.

Huberta is still one of my closest friends. She now lives in the house her parents bought in Jimtown, still a "black" neighborhood, when they left the Rosemound Farm. Her family has struggled as has ours, in different ways. Now, when I go to Kentucky, I stay with Huberta and am very happy about that. When my parents needed care, she had just retired and became a caregiver, a faithful caregiver and dear friend. I don't know what we would have done without her.

In recent times, Huberta and I have talked about racism and how it plays out in her life. She said she has been very lucky (I would say Huberta is exceptionally kind to people, white and black). She did tell me about an incident with police; she was stopped and harassed by the Lexington police because they said there is no way she could afford to drive a nice vehicle like she has. They, of course, could not acknowledge that, like me, she has worked two and sometimes three jobs most of her life to make ends meet and to have the things she now has.

I recently asked Huberta is she ever heard of their being slaves on the Rosemound Farm. She said no and that it would be hard for her to believe that there were.

The greatest gift given to me by the Millers and by my father is that I think I am one of the slowest people I know to "other" people for their racial or cultural differences.

III

As I said, when my parents got married, my father was recently out of the service and had many ideas that were different from his father. Their divide was somewhat along the lines of the Republican and Democratic party divides of today (differences about racial issues, women, people who are different, and more).

To clarify though, as extreme as it seemed then for a son to disagree with his father, nothing resembled the hate that divides today's world. Loyalty to family is one of the deepest Appalachian expectations and that was not broken in the disagreements.

Anyway, my dad struck out on his own. He was my model for independence and critical thinking that has been so important in my life. He earned his independence from the limited thinking of his father, relating to those who are different and relating to women in more respectful ways. And he always said, "we are not poor, we just don't have money."

When I was born, babysitters were not common. My parents worked together through long hard days on the farm. While they worked, as a toddler, I stayed in the play pen and my dog, Lady, stayed with me. She was my closest friend and companion.

As a young child, I have many childhood memories of going with my mother to pick up black walnuts and pop bottles on the side of the road for money to buy food. Back then when a person bought a bottle of pop, a deposit was paid on the bottle. So, when we turned the bottles back in, we got some money. Hard work was important as were habits of thrift, spending our money only for priorities.

Other than weekly visits to family and going to Sunday School, my family lived a fairly isolated life on the farm. Socializing was not something we had time for. When I started to Trapp Elementary school, I was in shock to see so many kids. I had no idea there were that many kids in the world. There must have been at least a hundred. I had no idea how to socialize or what to talk about with them. I ended up not talking in school and many people thought I could not talk at all. Today I would be called a "selective mute."

When I was about four, my uncle who was my father's youngest brother was killed in a car accident. We were never to speak of him again.

Then when I was ten, Lady, my best friend and companion, died violently, when a neighbor poisoned her. Those shocks became lessons where I learned to feel grief but also learned that we don't talk about feelings.

But some feelings were spoken, even shouted. My daddy always told the story of me while working in the tobacco field one day at age 8, raising my arms to the heavens, saying, "God, I don't know what it is, but I want to go to college." We moved to Illinois when I was 12.

My prayers were answered, and I did go to college.

IV

College came much later. In between was work. As the first-born child on both sides of the family, I was loved and adored, spoiled even in some ways. I was also given large responsibilities for house cleaning, cooking, caring for the younger siblings, driving the truck or tractor for the men to pick up hay bales, and working in the tobacco patch. In the fifth grade, my family went into crisis. But we could not make a living on the farm, despite the hard, never-ending work. We ended up living in the housing projects in town. There I loved having so many kids around and it was a very different life. But soon, we moved again.

My Daddy, my Mama, my three sisters and two dogs all rode what I later learned was the "Hillbilly Highway" north to a working-class town, Carpentersville, Illinois, northwest of Chicago. My parents got jobs in factories; my Daddy worked at International Harvester and my Mama worked at Revcor and made blower wheels for fans.

In Carpentersville we all learned we were "hillbillies," and it wasn't a compliment. My daddy always said, "Just be proud of being a hillbilly, and they have nothing on you." But that was harder than it sounds, and I acquired a habit of assimilating blindly, and not talking much. I struggled in Illinois and at age 16 went to live with my mother's mother, Nana, in Dayton. I went to college there and got my bachelor's degree in Psychology at Wright State University, then a master's degree in Sociology/Criminology at Miami of Ohio, and later a master's degree in Psychology at Eastern Kentucky University.

My parents worked in the factories until the International Harvester plant closed its doors, twenty plus years after moving to Illinois. Then he and Mom returned to Kentucky, with what they hoped were the resources to make the farm work. In Kentucky dad got a job working for the Small Business Development Center, helping businesses in eastern Kentucky. He had earned his master's degree by then – one or two classes at a time over many years.

169

By then, I had also returned to Kentucky and was teaching in the community college system. I had studied different cultures and systems analysis and loved thinking about big picture institutional issues and how all the pieces work together. This way of thinking was helpful throughout my life.

I loved my job teaching. I coordinated a small program in Human Services and got close to many women who were coming back to school after raising their families. Dad loved his job helping small businesses to survive and thrive under challenging conditions. I will never forget his delight as he told his simple stories of a woman running a little grocery store and making it work or a disabled man starting a small business of his wood carvings. We both considered those years to be highlights of our lives.

That era ended in 1986 when my program was cut and a couple of years later Dad had a heart attack.

Then I did what I had always done – went back to college. At the University of North Carolina, I got a Ph.D. in School Psychology in 1990 with an emphasis in Early Intervention, working with three- and four-year-olds. I have come to deeply believe in the efficacy of solving problems early and preventing problems later. While in Chapel Hill, I had the distinct and unique opportunity to take a traditional family therapy class at the same time that I took a class on working with families of young children using a strength-based model of education.

The essence of that approach is not to ignore problems but not to focus on them either. The focus is on identifying and building strengths for a foundation resilient enough to hold the problems until they can be solved – not a bad way to think about much of life.

V

I studied, researched, practiced and taught psychology from 1969 until 2014, primarily as a school psychologist for very young children. I spent the last 13 years of my career as a School Psychologist with Preschoolers in eastern Pennsylvania. I had worked as a psychologist with all ages and with many disability groups, but the early intervention efforts were my favorite.

Then, in 2005, I got a new boss, a Mainliner (that means a person from what is called the "Main Line" of Philadelphia – it seems to me that many such believe themselves superior to others) and proud of it. She was sure I knew nothing about psychology. Her bias was so evident – and I hear mine in this story too. For the first time in my life, my strategy of considering the bias of others as not my problem did not work. She had no training in working with preschoolers nor in psychology. But she had the power and wanted things done her way. Her way was that the proper role of psychologists was to diagnose and support the use of medication. She had no knowledge of the potential negative impact of that on 3-year-olds nor did she know about a more evidence-based approach for that age group. She just KNEW...

That boss and breast cancer with complications brought an end to my career in 2014.

Even so, my work with young children and schools did not feel finished.

For a month after my retirement, I had to go on You Tube and listen to, *"The wheels on the bus go round and round, round and round..."* If you are around little children, you have heard that song. I heard it every day for years and wanted to hear it a little longer.

VI

Throughout my young life, my Mama took us to Sunday School. There I learned valuable lessons that have served me well, though many lessons had to be fine-tuned later in life:

Honor your parents; but the translation became, *obey authority figures and all adults are authority figures.*

Love your neighbor as yourself and everyone is your neighbor; but they forgot to tell me that I was supposed to love myself too. But I am still so grateful for the early foundations I learned in Sunday School. I was very close to my mother when I was young; we worked together on all aspects of feeding the family and farming. She helped me with my Arithmetic after I helped her strip the tobacco. As a teenager, I began to question aspects of her religion. But, when she was put down by others for her religion, I always supported her right to her religion, even though I could not expect that in return, because her religion was not tolerant of others who believe differently.

When we moved to Illinois, we attended a church in the Latino section of Chicago. Both my mother and my father invited friendships with people of all races and cultures. When I moved to Ohio, I attended Nana's Methodist church for a while. Soon I quit going to church, but my relationship with God remained important to me.

Years later, while a college student in Chapel Hill from 1986-1990, a friend, Dr. Glenn, said to me one day, "Jennifer, YOU are a Quaker."

Well, knowing just about nothing about Quakers, I had no idea what that meant. But, after UNC, I came back to live in Berea, Kentucky and in 1991 my neighbor across the street invited me to Quaker meeting. I remembered what Dr. Glenn had said and accepted the invitation.

Once in the meeting, I felt at home in a way that I had not felt in any faith community in my life. I WAS a Quaker; the silence appealed to me. The social justice appealed to me. The contemplative spirituality fit.

In 1993, Parker Palmer, a well-known author, was a Lilly professor at Berea College and joined Berea Friends/Quaker meeting. I did not know he was famous as a writer in the fields of education, community, leadership, spirituality, and social change, or I would never have had the nerve to approach him, but he "spoke to my condition" as Quakers would say. I asked him many times to help me understand Quakers... and he did. As a psychologist, I had many questions about the overlap in the many fields of his expertise. He suggested more immersion in Quakerism by studying at Pendle Hill in Pennsylvania. I complied.

At Pendle Hill, I jumped in to learn about the early Quakers and how their lessons can be applied today, about the contemplative life, about the Gospels from a perspective different from the one I had grown up with, and much more.

Most surprising of all, arts and spirituality became a focus for me; not as a fun exercise with children but creativity as a core spiritual connection with the Divine – though children often know more about that connection than adults can know.

Many adults, like me, learned at a young age that art was for "talented" people and that is not me/us. At Pendle Hill, with Arts and Spirituality teacher, Sally Palmer, I unlearned and re-learned lessons about the importance of creativity and spirituality. Creation Spirituality remains a foundational piece of my faith and Creativity remains the foundational core of my hope for the world. Creative expression and thinking are needed today in all areas: education, politics, religion, economics, all of it.

VII

In my early 40's, I had many dreams about the play pen of my toddlerhood. I dreamed that a very large Jesus was helping me to step out of that play pen. Then, I dreamed I was on a beautiful beach, after climbing out of the play pen. Each step of growth and independence has seemed like another step in the climb out of that play pen.

These dreams led to a major research and writing project (listening to about a hundred people's direct experiences of God) that became a book I called "*Dancing with God through the Storm: Mysticism and Mental Illness.*" It was an integration of my spirituality and my profession.

In 2012, Daddy got sick, the first of four periods of time during which he needed extended care. I was then on sabbatical and cancer and conflict were pointing me to retirement. In the middle all this, I heard a new calling: to care for my parents. I spent four weeks in the hospital with Daddy. I kept hearing a calling to care for my parents in their aging and also heard that it would be hard.

I said, "Yes" to this call, but had no idea how hard the hard parts would become, what was waiting for me. Being close to my parents my whole life and early on internalizing the rock-solid commitment to family, it seemed quite natural that I would care for them. My daddy needed me to navigate the medical system and run his farm business …a great joy!

I felt that chance to be the greatest blessing of my life. During their last five years, they lived for each other, in their own home. Coming back into my parents' household for extended periods of time, I learned that some major things had changed in my family. In 2009, we had bought a house for my parents next to the farm that had been family-owned since 1794. After his heart attack and leaving his work at the Small Business Development Center in 1987, my dad had spent his last years pursuing his truest passion: farming the family farm and walking through his favorite pastures. In 2012, he continued to farm once out of the hospital.

In 2014, while mowing hay, the steering wheel broke and he was knocked off his vintage tractor. While falling he grabbed the steering wheel; with no safety catches in place, after knocking him into the mower, the tractor circled back around and ran over him. Amazingly, he survived but was back into the hospital for three weeks. Then after five more weeks, he was back to farming, baling hay in his pastures.

In the fall of 2015 and into 2016, Daddy got colon cancer with major complications. This time it was four months in the hospital and rehab. Then he began supervising the farming rather than working it himself. I managed his business. In December of 2017, I got a call that he was unable to swallow. After a month of intensive hospital and hospice care, and a fierce struggle for life, on January 14th of 2018, he died.

My Mama and Daddy had been living for each other for the last five years. Mama died six days later. I was shocked but not surprised. Had they lived three more months, until Daddy's 92nd birthday, they would have been married 70 years. She was his birthday present when they married on his 22nd birthday.

VIII

During the years of parent care, our country became increasingly divided to a violent degree, as did Kentucky. Sadly, my parents' household became a microcosm of that violence. Coming back, I increasingly found myself targeted and labeled as "evil" for my religion, my politics, and my educated ways.

In the background, the radio played pastors calling in impassioned voices to "root out that evil, and to that end any level of aggression is justified." Soon there were many false accusations toward me, even involving the police. I learned close up the personal hell of what is being called the polarization.

I could not believe my ears at first and could not imagine how people I knew and loved had become a part of that kind of Christianity: hateful words and action, in the name of Jesus. This was called evangelical Christianity as had been my mother's religion, but hers focused on loving all people, the other on "othering" and hate. There was no resemblance to the religion of my mother that I grew up with.

By the time of the 2016 presidential election, I was getting a clue. After the election, I was numb for a week. I had thought that what I had been experiencing was just a small group of Christians in that part of Kentucky that had lost their way. Up to the day of the election, I kept saying over and over, "Dear God, there are so many others that will experience the hate and aggression that I have experienced. Please don't let that happen." But it WAS happening, in so many ways!

IX

When my parents died in January of 2018, I was dealing with major trauma. Since then, I have also spent a great deal of time learning to settle two complicated estates. For survival, I have done enormous amounts of writing, art and dancing. I have done two art shows called "Between Trauma and Redemption" and "Hidden Love Emerging/Healing Love Evolving". Mediating trauma through creative expression is now a passion. "Redemption" is a word I heard in church as a youngster, did not like and did not understand as I do now. Now, it is a bedrock piece of my faith. Although I have led a life of unbelievable blessings, I have also lived enormous challenges. Experiencing the dividedness then recognizing that dividedness had spread across the nation has been the greatest tribulation of my life.

I KNOW that in the past when I look back on my life events, consistently, after something has happened that seems horrible at the time, something amazing has then happened that would not have happened if the challenge had not been there. I believe that will be the case now. I KNOW deep within me that I did not experience the Hell of hateful activities close up for nothing. Such HAS to have purpose in training me for something. This is my definition of redemption.

I am now fully out of the play pen. Since January 2018 I have used all of the resources gathered in my life: deep faith, close community, education, creativity, therapeutic strategies, writing, sacred dance, and more to survive these major traumas. I am healing and I am listening. I now believe that civil conversations among people who are different are the best hope we have for our country.

And I just inherited a piece of that farm. The cows still roam the pastures. The barns and fences need to be fixed and painted. All around this shabby beef farm are fancy hobby farms. My daddy loved that farm but in his '80's and '90's, he was not able to keep it up. I must be his daughter, because despite all my years in cities and the degrees and professional work, there is still something about walking across those pastures and seeing a calf has just been born that is unlike any feeling I get anywhere else in the world.

Are those barns and fences just art media waiting to be transformed into what is next? What is the creative/spiritual potential in that land now?

There is an Indian mound on the farm from 2000 years ago. I stand on that Adena mound and pray. I ask the land what its desire is for now. The land served the Native Americans of long ago. My family has served and been served there for over two centuries.

I recently inherited the farm with my three sisters. Two want to sell, one has built a house on it and wants her piece of the farm in her name. The pressure is on. I don't want to sell, but the dilemmas are huge. We used to be able to get farm help fairly easily. But, not anymore. Also, the labor of people from other countries needing work is gone. The people from Mexico have gone to Canada or been deported. These days most people will not do the kind of work needed to keep a farm going. The next generation is not interested and feel no responsibility or connection with their ancestors.

So, will I sell my part? I don't know yet, but the options seem limited and this is a major factor underlying this "identity crisis."

I had a nightmare recently. I woke up with an image of the farm. Everything was gone; no more barns, fences, cows, horses, sheds, tractors, nothing – just rolling hills of green grass. There was no hint that my family had ever occupied that land, even though they had been there for over two centuries. That is exactly what would happen if I sold it to the hobby farmers.

Could I bear that? Would my ancestors stay in their graves; or just rise up in horror? What is God saying? What is the land saying about what is next?

X

In all these living questions, there's a silent echo of one word: hillbilly. My father's desire to honor our heritage was something I have come to highly respect. I have not seen such hard work and loyalty to family anywhere else in the world.

When I asked Daddy, "What is Appalachian culture?" his answer was brilliant. He said, "there is no such thing. In the mountains, the force most likely to affect one's behavior is the family and the groups that the family is a part of; they used to be called clans. There is nothing that anyone could identify that would be the same across Appalachia. Even the geography of what is considered Appalachia incorporates many different backgrounds, many different countries that people came from, different everything."

In the bluegrass, there are rural and urban differences; dissertations have been written about that. And now within the bluegrass, there are huge differences between hobby farmers (those who have beautiful spaces with horses for tax write-off purposes) and real farmers.

"Well, Papa, what is a hillbilly?" I then asked.

"I don't know," he said. The only thing we could come up with was that a hillbilly is what people elsewhere called people with southern accents in order to put them down (and feel better about themselves) – all based on stereotypes and not much we could identify as real. Depictions of poor people as ignorant, lazy and drug-addicted can be found everywhere in America. I call these Soul of America problems. And where those conditions exist in Appalachia, there are deep historical influences that have led to the poverty underlying the dysfunctions.

Some scholars seem to agree with my Papa's lived observations. The Appalachian historian Richard Drake wrote:

> I am reminded of a survey I made of colleagues here at Berea a few years ago when I asked the resident regional experts — about twelve of them, as I remember — how they defined "Appalachia." No two definitions were alike, and the two sociologists in my survey, in fact, came to opposite conclusions about whether or not there was an Appalachian culture.

But just because I can't find a list of agreed identifying characteristics of the culture beyond the beauty of nature and the music, there are things about being from Appalachia that have affected me much of my life. I left Kentucky and came back so many times, as did my father, as did my grandfather, as did my great grandfather – for economic reasons, for college, for the army, for adventures, and more.

And I've had the experience of repeatedly being put down for being from Appalachia, for being a "hillbilly," whatever that exactly is.

My being from Kentucky always gets reactions from others – from talking about the Derby to not talking but assuming a lot about who I am, how smart I am (and am not), what I like to do, and much more. I have repeatedly encountered anti-hillbilly bias even among those who talk about having a great commitment to equality and are meticulous in political correctness about people of color (but it is not a contest). In many otherwise liberal circles I've been in, where bias toward most others is not OK, bias against "hillbillies" is just fine. Sometimes the stereotypes are so accepted that they are not even recognized or talked about.

But Appalachian people like everyone else are doing the best they can with what they have. They go left, right, left, right through the day, through the years, wanting what is best for their families and especially for their children.

America today is having a crisis of faith, a crisis of meaning, a crisis of purpose, a crisis of humanity, a crisis of leadership in the world...

America is in crisis. It is not just Appalachia. The poverty that Appalachian mountain people have endured has been going on since the Civil War.

I asked my Daddy about the economic difficulties in the mountains. He summarized centuries of history in this way: In the Civil War, Kentucky was a border state. The North came through and took the horses. The South came through and took the cows. The people were left with no way to live on the land. Just as they were about to recover from war, the coal companies came in and took the land. Economic troubles have a long history there.

And what is true about Appalachia that is not true of America? I can't find much. I struggle with these realities.

XI

I love old-time Appalachian music with banjos and flat footin' or clog dancin'. That is the best of Appalachia.

I know that in my own experiences of living and traveling many places in the world, I have experienced some of the smartest, most well-read people in the world in Appalachia. I have encountered people who have the most amazing ability to do a wide variety of things, not just their professions but can fix the car, fix the furnace, fix the plumbing, fix anything, kinds of folks. I have not encountered that quality to the same degree anywhere beyond Appalachia.

I have encountered people of the deepest faith and those with the most alive sense of creativity in Appalachia. I have seen women can food and practice habits of thrift in ways I have never seen elsewhere. I heard the phrase "waste not, want not" a lot when I was growing up. Today, in Kentucky and all over I see an American problem with waste: waste of health by eating processed, unhealthy food and smoking cigarettes because these are the cool things to do and youth feel invincible, waste of gasoline because big pick-up trucks are cool, waste of talent needed so badly because skipping school and involvement with drugs and the multitude of "screens" is cool.

This list could go on and on. There are so many incredible gifts among many Appalachian people, habits of thrift, learning and growing, serving self and others, and faith need to be embraced as the new cool.

We need a "new cool." Could we start it here? There is the talent in Appalachia to take this bull by the horns.

XII

The extremes as described in the media are out there but most of Appalachian life is represented by the pictures of families having dinner, a child going to school, a kid on a bicycle, a man chopping wood, a mom cooking, and all the ordinary amazing things that people all over the USA/world are seen doing every day.

I have walked left, right, left, right through the extraordinary dailiness of commitment to family that the media's extremes never speak of. And I left Kentucky to make and claim my own different life too.

Now, the question is, what will be my legacy in this complex heritage. I don't know the answer yet. But I am working hard every day to give the questions the discernment time and energy they deserve as I seek to clarify my own identity in this complex and amazing heritage I have been given. I translate my Daddy's words: "Just be proud of who you are...then anywhere is home." The time has come to heal the wounds, celebrate the joys and write/share the poems that Silas speaks of. I want Quakers everywhere to appreciate the beauty of my Appalachian heritage that I have come to love, through my complex identity crisis and a lifetime of always going back to Kentucky after being elsewhere, a life of traveling that Hillbilly Highway.

It is time for Quakers both inside the region and out to take up the huge social justice work needed to promote equality for Appalachians. It is time for the effects of the Civil War in which people who happen to be from the Northern part of the United States are seen as superior to people from the Southern part of the United States; time for that war to be over and all declared and treated EQUAL. I pray for the day when we can keep our beautiful accents, be acknowledged as equal, and live in the strength of the values promoted in this special place called Appalachia.

May this equality be the roots of blossoming in all other arenas including education, physical and mental health, and economics! I keep getting an image of driving through eastern Kentucky and seeing wind turbines and solar panels, everywhere…along with children playing, and parents chopping wood and hanging the clothes on the clothesline to dry, a deep integration of the best of the old and the best of a new Appalachia.

XIII

That Indian mound on the farm was one of five lookouts that lie in a circle in north Fayette County, Kentucky for the Adena Indians. I named my part of the farm The Native Heritage Farm. I recently walked through the pastures of the farm with my nephew and we both felt the same depth of feeling. We agreed that walking through those fields, we had a feeling of connection in the depths of our bones and DNA that we did not feel anywhere else in the world. And at the same time, we felt a sadness, also like no other.

My family's acreage is now a small rickety old beef cattle farm amidst what has become miles of gorgeous and perfectly groomed horse farms. The regulations in that part of Kentucky are so intense that we can find no way to make a living or even to break even on the farm. There is no money to be made on the cows and there hasn't been at least since I have known about the farm as a business. My father and grandfather worked their whole lives at jobs to support their "farming habit" as we have called it, because of their total love of farming and the family farm. That commitment may not be there in the next generations. I am exploring the possibility that I might be wrong and hoping.

Life Lessons I Learned at a Young Age that have Served Me Well and Can't Be Taken for Granted (Not that I Live Them Perfectly Nor Do You Have to Live them Perfectly to Live Them Well): And all have had to be tweaked along the way for deeper meanings in their application.

Ten Commandments

The ten commandments have their equivalent in all of the major religions and provide a good starting point in the commitment to quality life.

- Sunday School with Tweaks and Nana's Wisdom (with a touch of personal experience thrown in)

  Early Sunday School made the elusive commandments more understandable for daily life.

- Serve God, Self and Others well
- Tell the Truth (knowing the complexities of Truth)
- Honor your parents (and they don't have to know EVERY-THING you do as an adult); honor your heritage and ancestors
- Listen to your teachers (teachers are everywhere)
- Work hard (and don't become a workaholic so that it takes over your life)
- Have big dreams and try new things
- Keep your Promises
- Develop Habits of Thrift (Know the difference between wants and needs; wants come and go)
- Do your best; Know your best is good enough and know better is possible
- Say please and thank you often and mean it
- Remember you are loved; Listen to my Mama who always said, "I love you and don't you forget."

- Laugh a lot; humor is important
- Listen to Nana and eat your veggies and exercise; everything is a lot easier with good health
- Think about (discern) what is good for you while not hurting others; aspire for win/wins
- Accept others who are different from you as equals
- Look for the good in yourself and others (equality for yourself and others)
- Acknowledge and deal with addictions
- Find healthy ways to express all kinds of emotions
- Fall in love with mother nature; fall in love with something or someone every day
- Sing and dance every day whether you think you can or not
- Be aware and careful who and what you declare loyalty to
- Let go of the cynicism that is easy to fall into
- Pay attention to what you are doing and the ramifications of all you do
- Pay attention to what is happening around (don't put your head in the sand when things are wrong; stand up)
- The world is big; explore it; people in far places become more equal and like you when you get to know them
- When you are afraid, say so; be careful who you say it to
- Be a good deep listener in the Silence and with others
- Share your life and connect with others
- Be kind to self and others; learn what that really means beyond politeness
- Honor integration and equality for all (even Hillbillies)
- We all think in stereotypes; be aware of the stereotypes you use to understand the world, who they help and who they hurt
- Say your prayers/meditate (and know that means something different for different people)
- Be intentionally thankful (many times a day)

- Listen and Follow your deepest knowing (in what you do with your life, big and small decisions)
- The mysteries of the Universe are SO big; be careful what you KNOW…and be aware of who you impose your KNOWINGS upon
- Walk your talk
- Find the compassionate place in your heart and live there
- "Anything worth doing is worth doing well" doesn't mean perfectly; desire for excellence is not perfectionism; perfectionism stifles real life
- Live humbly; share vulnerabilities and discern with whom and how
- Support with Accountability can work magic in moving life forward with good discernment
- Know that opposites often meet and come to mean the same thing; that is the place where creation sparks
- Both/ands often work better than either/or's
- God is BIG enough to handle differences of name and beliefs about it all

Quakers

- Guidelines for Simplicity, Peace, Integrity, Community, Equality, Stewardship
- Learn conflict resolution skills and learn to converse civilly with those who are different from yourself.
- Most poignant in my life has been the wisdom of Matthew Fox and MC Richards through Sally Palmer. Creativity in its biggest and broadest sense is our most foundational core connection to our Creator, the best medicine for trauma, and the source for hope in our world. Constant gratitude for all of Life is essential.

Be sure all of these have ever-changing deep meanings and are more than words and clichés in your life.

Emma Lapsansky-Werner:
"Upward and Out of Sight"

"Where do we find ourselves?" American transcendentalism philosopher/poet Ralph Waldo Emerson posed this question as the opener to an essay which he grandly titled "Experience." He began to answer the question this way: "In a series of which we do not know the extremes and believe that it has none."

Meditating on "experience," Emerson was just slightly more than half the age I am now, yet he had the temerity to write about experience as if he might know what

Emma meditating in the Himalayas

that was! But sometimes our poets and philosophers have a better grasp on "reality" than do journalists and social scientists, and Emerson's musings on the subject of "experience" have indeed stood a test of time:

> We wake and find ourselves on a stair; there are stairs below us, which we seem to have ascended; there are stairs above us, many a one, which go upward and out of sight. ---Sleep lingers all our lifetime about our eyes, as night hovers all day in the boughs of the fir-tree. All things swim and glitter. Our life is not so much threatened as our perception. Ghostlike we glide through nature....

Often, Emerson hints, we misperceive "reality:" "We [cannot always] know ... whether we are busy or idle. In times when we thought ourselves indolent, we have afterwards discovered, that much was accomplished, and much was begun in us."[i]

Having "glided ghostlike" through more than seven decades, I'm enjoying the invitation to explore the "stairs below us" and to contemplate the stairs "which might go upward and out of sight."

Heaven and Hell — 1954

I was nine years old when the United States Supreme Court outlawed racial segregation in the nations' schools.[ii] At my family's dinner table, we children listened with interest as the adults talked about the momentous national journey that *Brown* v. *Board of Education of Topeka* might portend. What I couldn't have known then was how a chance conversation with my grandfather, that same year, would lead *me* on a momentous *personal* journey.

My grandfather (Grandpop, we called him) — the pastor of Asbury Methodist Church, Washington DC's oldest and largest African American United Methodist congregation[iii] — was living with us that year, and he was one of my closest friends. He and I shared a taste for butter cookies, cantaloupe, and home-grown tomatoes. And we also shared what I could not name then: a taste for theological curiosity. I remember being mesmerized by his sermons, and I can remember asking him dozens of questions. ("I've never met anyone with so *many questions*," various family members used to say to me.)

I vividly remember asking Grandpop if God would punish us for a sin that we unknowingly committed, or whether punishable sins were only those we *intentionally* perpetrated. (Interestingly, I don't remember his answer!) Grandpop gave me my first Bible (I still have it) and he frequently read to me from it, thereby feeding what would become my deep love of words, cadence, and rhythm. He had a rich baritone voice, and from him I learned dozens of Methodist hymns. He, my mother, and we children filled our home with song — often spontaneously, but sometimes accompanied by my mother at the piano, and occasionally joined by my very busy father, who also had a wonderful voice.

Grandpop was unperturbed by what some of my other family members saw as my "strangeness" — my head full of inchoate questions and ponderings. "She's been here [in this earthly life] before," Grandpop explained to my parents, and that vision of me seemed to free Grandpop to share with me some of his own tentative theological musings. A graduate of Drew University's Theological Seminary (NJ), his religious training had been conservative and straight-laced, but one time — the same year as the *Brown* v. *Board of Education* decision — he said to me *sotto voce*: "you know, heaven and hell are not *places* you go to when you die. Heaven and hell are *states of being* you create for yourself by your choices and behavior in your life on earth."

With that statement, Grandpop — probably unknowingly — pointed me down a path that led me, three decades later — to membership in the Religious Society of Friends. So — a "stair below me, which I seemed to have ascended."

A next step on that staircase came in high school: a Waldorf boarding school called High Mowing, in Wilton New Hampshire.[iv] During my three years there, (1960-63) I usually found that the mandatory weekly vesper services — a mixture of silence and sacred music — "spoke to my condition." These services — along with the school's powerful commitment to educating left-brain and right-brain simultaneously — left me with the same sense of peace that I would later discover in Quaker meetings-for-worship, and later (even more powerfully!) in Quaker business meetings. (More on that later!)

At High Mowing, I encountered Hal Williams — the school physician — and his wife Dorothea, who were active members of Lancaster (PA) meeting. Their children — classmates of mine — became my friends, and from time to time, I would visit their Lancaster home — and join them for Meeting for Worship. Hal Williams' approach to medicine — farther yet down the road to homeopathy than had been my own medication-averse physician father — was shaped and guided by his Quaker faith, and this, too, reinforced my growing conviction that these people who used silence in their worship, and intertwined their religious faith into their secular lives, might just be "my kind of people."

Family 1958

Another step on the staircase: on April 4, 1958, my father died. He was 78, and I was a few days short of my thirteenth birthday. Some two decades before his death, partially retired from his medical career, he had bought a big parcel of partially forested land, several dozen milk cows, some chickens, ducks, and pigs, and had begun his new life as a dairy farmer. Thus, as a very young child, in summers, when our family relocated from our home in downtown Washington DC to the farm in Montgomery County, Maryland, it was my treat to walk the perimeter of the property with him, examining fences for damage, enjoying streams and tadpoles and snakes, learning to milk cows. My mother taught us how to grow and to can vegetables and fruits, how to slaughter chickens and make sausage and scrapple. The farm workers taught me to drive a tractor. My father's gift to me in those years was his reverence for the natural world. Sometimes, on those morning walks, he would sing with me:

"This is my father's world, and to my listening ears, all nature sings and 'round me rings, the music of the spheres. This is my father's world, I rest me in the thought, of rocks and trees, of skies and trees: his hand the wondrous wrought."

V

Those walks with Daddy taught me what it was like to be cherished — and therefore how *to* cherish. In those walks, the few people we encountered were others who celebrated nature's wonders as we did. The helpers who worked my father's farm, as well as the owners and workers of the neighboring farms were of all races, nationalities, ages, and experiences, and able-bodiedness. They treated us, and each other, with respect and consideration, and we returned this in kind. In those walks, I learned to give, and to expect, human civility and kindness, and I sometimes accompanied Daddy as he provided medical care — mostly pro bono — for the variety of residents of our little rural "neighborhood." Though it would be many years before I encountered George Fox's famous directive that we should "walk cheerfully over the earth, answering to that of God" in the people we encounter, those morning farm walks gave me a practical lesson in how "walking cheerfully" might be actualized. In retrospect, I think the foundation of my brief 1960s romance with socialist political theory — "from each according to his abilities, to each according to his needs" — was laid on those morning walks.

For her part, when we were in Washington, my mother (who didn't like to drive) would use buses and streetcars to take us shopping and to the city's wonderful array of free libraries, museums and parks. During these rides, Mama would (discreetly) amuse us by making up stories about the variety of strangers — young and old, male and female, many colors and demeanors — sitting all around us. Only many years later would it dawn on me that those stories were always infused with human triumph over adversity, with human kindness, with human joy and humor.

She loved to read to us, too, and *The Diary of Anne Frank*, with its hopeful-for-humanity ending — "I still believe that people are basically good at heart" — was one of her favorites.[vi] So was Anne Morrow Lindbergh's *Gift from the Sea*, with its provocative lines like "Women need solitude in order to find again the true essence of themselves," and "Don't wish me happiness. I don't expect to be happy all the time...Wish me courage and strength and a sense of humor. I will need them all."[vii]

My brother and sister and I knew that we were lucky — today it would be called "privileged" — and my family, by precept and by example, made clear that we should remain alert and responsive to those who were less so. I remember that Mama would make our Thanksgiving dinner, then make a second meal of "turkey-and-fixings" which she would pile into my brother's "American Flyer" wagon and roll it down the street to a nearby family that included a couple of "shut-ins" (i.e., people too infirm to leave the house.) She kept our family on a tight budget, so that she could pay tuitions for her own children *and* for a young man she'd befriended during her teaching career, and still have money to contribute to whatever was her favorite cause in any given year. Mama was tiny, but from an early age her family and friends used to describe her as "small but powerful," and "little, but loud." Until her death in 2000, at age 92, she was filled with a zest for life: playing the piano for choral singing in the retirement home where she lived, tutoring the children of the retirement home staff, reciting long Victorian poems from memory, and retaining her voice for justice.

Two of Mama's favorite short poems:

1) "I am only one, but still I *am* one. Let me not allow despair that I cannot do everything keep me from doing the things that I *can* do."

2) "True worth is in being, not seeming; in doing each day that goes by, some *little* good, not in dreaming of great things to do "by and by."

Her advice for health and happiness: "always have something you're looking forward to."

I want to *be* Mama when I'm 92.

In 1956, Daddy had entered a hospital — this time as a patient — and suddenly, for the two years until he died, I became a "latchkey kid." Grandpop had remarried and moved away. At the end of her teaching day, Mama went to visit Daddy. My siblings — now high-schoolers — were involved in after-school sports. So, each day, I could look forward to a couple of hours of solitude before the family reassembled for supper. I didn't turn on the TV or radio or record player, and I came to love those luscious hours of quiet: books, writing, piano, and my unfettered imagination were my companions.

Responsibility and Integrity 1966 -

It was Christmas, 1965 when I first heard of the "The Delta Ministry" which described itself as "a Mississippi project of the National Council of Churches ...an interdenominational commitment in mission unprecedented in the nation's history. The [Delta Ministry] project is a long-term effort to end the low economic, health, and social conditions of Mississippi's poor. It has been characterized as "one of the most critical forms of church renewal."[viii]

And in January 1966, I went on the "payroll" of the Delta Ministry, for princely wage of $20/week. The arm of the Delta Ministry that employed me was the Poor Peoples' Corporation,[ix] a network of more than a dozen craft co-ops, scattered through the Mississippi Delta, that crafted needlework and leather goods (handbags, placemats, aprons, napkins, etc.) and distributed these products through a Jackson, Mississippi outlet called "Liberty House." I had traveled to Mississippi, on a mini mission organized by crusading campus minister Richard Fernandez, to help build a community center. But once there, feeling a call of both responsibility and community, I took a leave from college to continue the work. On Monday mornings I would leave the group house I shared with several other civil rights workers near the campus of the historically-black Tougaloo College (founded 1869, a few miles north of Jackson.)[x] I would thread my borrowed VW Beetle through the roads full of pick-up trucks (with their rifle-racks prominently displayed in their rear windows) to make a thousand-mile round-trip into the Mississippi Delta.

Stopping at each co-op, I dropped off supplies, visited with the local craftspeople, and sometimes assisted them with particular needlework techniques, or with organizing economic books and tax records. Then I would load my car with the fruits of their week's labors, returning to Liberty House by Friday or Saturday. Liberty House, in turn, would ship these items off to the North, where Delta Ministry supporters sold them in local churches or sympathetic small shops. Monday mornings I'd head off again to repeat those rounds. For the first few weeks, I rode with Ben Brown, a twenty-year-old local man who knew the route and was known to and trusted by all of the PPC members. After I learned the routines, though, I drove the route alone.

It was on one of those solo drives into the Delta that I learned an important lesson about integrity, which I find that I have needed to relearn — repeatedly — for the rest of my life. Here's the story: I was driving, in the late evening — (ignoring our PPC training: "never drive isolated roads alone after dark") — when I had a flat tire, right in front of a ramshackle country shack. Having heard that unmistakable flat-tire thump-thump-thump, a man emerged from the house and lumbered toward my car. The ruddy face, beer belly, dirty white t-shirt, broken teeth, and the drawled "Hmph, looks lak ya'll got a problem" called to mind everything I'd been taught to fear about "southern rednecks."

When he said, "Lemme see if I kin he'p ya'll fix it," and then proceeded to change my tire and send me on my way, I could not help but wonder if God had sent that man to force me to confront my own prejudices — my own shortsighted knee-jerk notion that I could know all there is to know about people by the way they look. My mother's narratives about the variety of people on the DC busses came back to me as I drove along, and so did the walks with my father through the farms of Maryland. Still, more often than I like to admit, I have been unable to live up to the promise I made to myself that night: that I would offer to every person I encountered the expectation of integrity, the benefit-of-the-doubt before confining them to the "not-to-be-trusted" category. Some years ~~before~~ later I encountered Fox's admonition to "walk cheerfully over the earth, answering to 'that of God.' " in those we encounter. But

I keep trying to master the lesson that Mississippi-Delta farmer had for me.

This doesn't mean, of course, that I am crazy enough to deliberately position myself in harm's way, but my life *is* a lot more pleasant whenever I can discipline myself to have a "wait-and-see" posture *precede* the "fight or flight" posture. And it does help me gain perspective and a little humility to have had such a vivid reminder that even (and maybe *especially*) we "good guys" on a righteous journey to social justice are just as susceptible to uninformed rush-to-judgment as "those bigoted bad guys." But it's a paradox, since even Fox's recommendation that we *answer* to that of God in people one meets presupposes that we are answering to something that we seek and *can perceive* in those we meet. I'm still working on this conundrum: perhaps clarity about all this is on those "stairs that go upward and out of sight."

And sometimes it's not easy to hold onto Anne Frank's optimism about people being good at heart. In the Spring of 1967, after I'd returned to school in Pennsylvania, I got word that Ben Brown had died a tragic and senseless death, murdered by a Mississippi Highway trooper who was never brought to justice. [xi]

Finding Friends 1976

By 1975, I myself was "somebody's mother." How, I wondered, to give my little ones a context in which to learn the community, integrity, responsibility, and compassion that had been modeled for me? Then the mother of one of my kids' friends told me about Lansdowne Friends School and Friends Central School. When she described their curricula that stressed personal integrity, social responsibility, and a strong spiritual core, I thought about my Grandpop, and about experience at High Mowing, and at Lancaster Friends Meeting. My interest was aroused. I composed my daughter's application to Friends Central: "she's bright; she can learn to read anywhere. I'm looking for setting that will support her growth as a responsible and spiritual citizen with a well-developed moral backbone."

Upon reading this application letter, the headmaster asked me to join the Friends' Central board of trustees. I did so, — and remained there for more than two decades. Thus, beginning in the Fall of 1976, there was at least one Lapsansky kid in a Philadelphia Quaker school until "the baby" graduated in 1997. And, beginning that year, I myself became ever-more-led into various parts of the Friends' world, including stints on the board of the American Friends Service Committee, *Friends Journal*, and the little Lansdowne Friends School that is under the care of my home Meeting.

Over time, Quaker-community undertakings came to be a central aspect of my life: some teaching at Pendle Hill, some decades of curatorship of Quaker archives and professor of Quaker history at Haverford College; visiting lectureships at George Fox College, Earlham, and Guilford, Friend-in-Residence at England's Woodbrooke Quaker Study Center, and involvement in myriad other adventures of Quaker community life — including counting myself as a "regular" at Journey's End Camp's annual family sing!

It was at Friends Central board meetings that I learned what I have come to view as the real essence of Quaker spirituality: Friends business practice. In Quaker business meetings, the "rubber meets the road." In Quaker meetings-for-worship, there is often a palpable "gathered" meeting, in which the intensity of individual- and group-worship fairly infuses the meeting house with a rich spiritual energy. But it is in "Meeting for Worship with *Attention to Business*" that Friends faith is truly tested and honed. Business Meeting, with its focus on "sense of meeting" (not "consensus"!) has brought Friends, over three centuries, face to face with our own individual pettiness, self-righteousness, and humanity, as well as with our connection to the angels. It is in Business Meeting where we are truly called to look across the room at that person who is uttering the most ridiculous foolishness, and try to listen for "that of God" in the hogwash.

Sometimes I find Business Meeting to be truly awful, fully mean-spirited, inviting the worst in human behavior. Sometimes it is merely cumbersome, torturously time-wasting, so that small decisions drag on through literally *years* of deliberation. (The decision to prohibit slave holding and slave trading among Meeting members, for example, took more than a century.[xii]) But sometimes the experience of "sense of meeting" in Meeting for Business is transcendent — "a gift" as one wise Friend described it in a pamphlet encouraging Friends to hold onto the remarkable treasure that is "sense of meeting."[xiii] Sometimes "sense of meeting" can result not only in brilliant solutions that no one person could have dreamed up alone, but also in a sensation of connectedness and unity-with-each-other-and-with-the-Divine that can be described only as "pure joy."

When that happens, it can provide a powerful armor against the day-to-day bruises of battling injustice. Indeed, after experiencing a few *transcendent* business meetings at Lansdowne Friends Meeting through the late 1970s, I was hooked! In 1982, I joined Lansdowne Meeting, with its motley mixture of races, classes, Bible-based Christians, and non-Bible-activists-living-out-their-faith-through-political action. I was home and have been at home there ever since.

And then I discovered Friends' summer camps, first at Darkwaters in Medford, NJ[xiv], then at Journey's End Farm Camp in near Sterling, PA.[xv] Through the 1980s, my three young campers gained experience in group decision-making, community responsibility, and a worshipful posture toward what Daddy called "the music of the spheres." They also learned to milk a cow! And to tend a garden, and to make "soda" out of fresh fruit juice and sparkling water. Journey's End reinforced our family's focus on simple nutrition, simple honesty, and simple compassion. Games designed to demonstrate problem-solving where everybody wins helped me to prepare three young people to enter the adult world with a career-focus on local, national, and international peace. When one of my daughters returned to "JE" as a counselor during her college summers, I felt I'd made sound choices for her foundation.

Faith and Practice 1990-

Another stair ascended...In the late 1980s, Fate came calling. While I was contentedly pursuing a career teaching history at Temple University, I was invited to join a state-wide team of historians on a several-day mission to consult with a Pennsylvania liberal arts college as it developed plans to restructure its history curriculum. One member of that visiting team was Susan Stuard, a member of the Haverford College history-department faculty. Susan and I hit it off, and when she returned to the Haverford College, where a search was in process of a new professor and curator of "Quaker things," she threw my hat in the ring. Roger Lane, Haverford history department's guru of "things African-American" was familiar with some of my research on Philadelphia, on African Americans, and on Quakers, and I soon got a call, inviting me to apply for the job. As many of us do when "God comes calling," I turned down the invitation. I was happy at Temple. I would need to think long and hard about making such a big change in my life.

"Just come take a *look*," the Haverford search committee said. So I did, and soon found myself in the role of Curator of the Quaker Collection as well as professor of history.[xvi] Thus began several of the most rewarding decades of my life — decades where I had ample support to pursue the satisfying work of researching and writing, to cherish and be cherished by a number of dedicated and talented students, to learn from and cherish my spectacular colleagues, and to give loving care to the centuries of records of the Quaker communities that I (mostly) admire.

Haverford's luscious Quaker archives — and the steadfast Friends Historical Association that has been publishing Quaker history for more than a century [xvii] — landed me in a rich network of scholars (a list too long to name here) who helped me, and allowed me to support them in telling some of the complex and exciting story of a community of idealists who still hope for peace and justice in a contentious world. From the "old school" who have explored "Quakers and....": nearly everything from Native Americans, to war, peace, womanhood, race, mental health, education, and a host of other topics, I drank deeply and learned a lot.

Kenneth Carroll, Hugh Barbour, and J. William Frost helped to lead us Quaker historians out of hagiography and into analytic history. Now a mid-career cadre is taking us deeply into revisionist social history and moving "Quaker Studies" out of a niche intellectual track into the mainstream of the American Academy of Religion. It has been exciting to work with this expanding version of "Quaker history."

Choosing Joy

In the twenty-first century, another significant turn in the staircase: a bed and breakfast. The story of how this invitation-from-the-Fates came to be is too long to recount here, but it can be summarized in some excerpts from a long interview, which was published digitally in 2018:

> **Interviewer:** "Minerva's by the Sea, named for Emma's mother and the myth, isn't your average Bed & Breakfast. Through it, Emma Lapsansky is on a quest to change her corner of the world–one breakfast at a time."

> **Emma's response:** "It is important to me to help all kinds of people meet and be heard since it is often the case that we only hang out with people who look like ourselves... I'm committed to a dream of creating at Minerva's an environment — if only for a few people, for a few moments–where "community" crosses boundaries of class and race, age, region, able-bodiedness, sexual orientation, religion — and any other "ism" that we think separates us."

I've had nurturing and inspiring ancestors, and Minerva's-by-the-Sea is my version of my great-grandparents' vision that each person should strive to acquire the skills and mindset to help leave the world a little better than they found it.

Eben E. Parker was my great-grandfather — Minerva's grandfather. In the late 19th century, Eben and his wife Patience put 12 children through college, mortgaging their house to pay for the first. The first was then expected to help pay for the second; the first and second helped pay for the third, etc. down the line. Those twelve then went off to be college professors, social workers, nurses, piano teachers, librarians, public-school teachers, world-traveling journalists and educators, and feminist organizers for the early twentieth-century women's suffrage movement. My mother — Minerva — was the daughter of one of those twelve.

After she was widowed, my mother struggled to pay tuitions for my siblings and me. She then helped pay tuitions for a couple of other students she'd met in her teaching career. She modeled for our family a policy of giving to favorite causes first, then being frugal with whatever was leftover. Today, no matter how slim Minerva's by the Sea's profit-margins are, Minerva's regularly donates to Doctors without Borders and to "Clean the World." (https://cleantheworld.org/) which reclaims soap from hotels, sanitizes it, and distributes it to developing countries.

As a scholar and teacher, my work has been informed by a concern for the large and rich American story — include family and community life, Quaker history, and religion and popular culture in nineteenth century America. I've also collaborated on a textbook that aims to broaden and re-contour the African American story.

But then, more than twenty years ago, I added another mission to my life's work: a "literary" bed and breakfast, with a copious library and periodic themed weekends — book discussions, yoga, birdwatching, singing, nutrition, and writers'-workshop retreats.

In 2007, retired from curatorship, and partially retired from teaching, I teamed up with my three children and — with excitement and trepidation — purchased and renovated a handicapped-accessible building in Barnegat Light, New Jersey, to operate Minerva's by the Sea. Because Minerva's by the Sea opened just as the bottom dropped out of the American economy, I have — as a commitment to my "mission" — drawn on my own savings to keep Minerva's running.

You might say that Minerva's-by-the-Sea is what Jewish tradition identifies as a "mitzvah" — a mission or mandate, or what we Quakers often describe as a "calling" or "leading." My kitchen is *in* the dining room, and we visualize mealtimes as gathering and supporting small portions of a compassionate world community — breakfast by breakfast. We welcome guests from across the world to sit around the table in Minerva's kitchen while I cook and encourage them to make friends with their breakfast mates, and to daydream together about how they envision the world they'd like their heirs to inherit, a world where *everyone's* needs and dreams are respected and taken seriously by everyone else, and we work together, as a human community, to accommodate as much as possible of each other's visions.

Around Minerva's breakfast table there have been conversations about how to advocate for school curricula that include compassion lessons as a central part of children's learning. We fantasize about how hard it is to hate someone or be disrespectful to them once you have joined them in song. I sometimes seed the conversation about our future hopes by asking someone to describe what they liked best about the way they grew up, or what they've recently noticed or learned that has brought optimism to their perspective on life.

In the 1960s, I was among the many folks who attempted to use politics to help create a more peaceful, tolerant, compassionate world. That world I thought we could build in a few decades hasn't arrived yet. But now I frequently cling to something my wise mother used to say, long before it became fashionable to talk of "thinking globally, acting locally." She used to quote: "I cannot do everything, but still I can do something. And I must not let my inability to do everything stop me from doing the small thing that I *can* do."

One of a very few bed and breakfasts that welcomes children, Minerva's offers toys and books and games, and an invitation to young people to join in the breakfast-group conversation about the world they envision in their future, and how they hope to contribute to it.

With a living room full of books and lounge-chairs for guests to daydream in solitude or gather for long hours, ideal for workshop gatherings — Minerva's is, in many ways, a memorial to my mother's generosity, expansiveness, optimism, creativity, and sense of appreciation for the human spirit and its infinite possibilities.

For my mother, every person mattered, and every person's contributions, gifts and dreams — no matter how seemingly trivial–also mattered. She refused to be sucked into the fallacy that some people, some professions, some marks of social status were "better" than others. A deeply religious woman, she aimed to have her students grasp the idea that "I know I'm important, and have an important job to do here, because God never makes junk."

Minerva, circa 1971, with her grandson Jordan Lapsansky.

There are a lot of little pieces to this "Mitzvah," or calling, including my "feminist" desire to make a safe and nurturing place for women to renew and refresh their energies in a world where womanhood is often under assault. Hence, my annual Women's Renewal Weekends.

But more than just a "feminist" perspective, I like to think of it as what novelist Alice Walker called "womanist," which I interpret as not just focusing on what we stand "against" in a heavily misogynist and dangerously near-sighted world, but also standing up for what we are *for*.

A Men's Retreat Weekend, which Minerva's has hosted twice a year for many years, offers safe haven for a men's collective that gathers regularly for a respite from daily competitiveness. Minerva's intends to stand for and with such men.

In other words, part of our mission is to open up spaces to embolden visions, to celebrate human dignity, and to honor humanistic dreams.

We hosted workshops on "transitions," where a psychoanalyst led people in exploring an array of transitional endeavors — from planning career changes or retirement; to considering transgender surgery; to gearing up for a cross-country relocation; to emerging from the grief of a tragic loss. And we have had some pleasing results, as lasting friendships and business partnerships have been forged in serendipitous ways around Minerva's kitchen table.

We have also celebrated and encouraged a teenager who had cut her long braids and donated her hair to cancer patients; and several of our repeat-visit families include children who are struggling with chronic health challenges.

With pillow-fluffing and a listening ear, we have said "thank you"(and gotten to hear the perspectives of) a neo-natal nurse arriving after a long and stressful shift; first-responders and military folks who put themselves at risk; special-education teachers; lawyers, physicians, postal workers, trash collectors, over-the-road freight haulers.

The mitzvah of Minerva's-by-the-Sea may be a small thing, but it's *my* small thing: to provide weary workers with pristine cleanliness; inspiring art gracing the walls; attention to restful color in room décor and linens; healthy, attractive food — and all within a stone's throw of Barnegat Light's clean, unspoiled, uncrowded beaches, with their natural grasses and protected bird-nesting areas — a short walk to the healing qualities of the ocean.[xviii]

"Upward and Out of Sight..."

Emerson ends his muse on experience with a challenge: "Never mind the ridicule, never mind the defeat: up again, old heart! ... there is victory yet for all justice; and the true romance which the world exists to realize, will be the transformation of genius into practical power."[xix]

And how will I end *my* muse on "passing the torch" to those who are on "those stairs reaching upward" into a future that I will not see? With a series of "advices" — which, for many of you readers will be nothing more than "reminders" of how you already live your lives anyway.

- Heaven and Hell: stay focused on the reality that Heaven and Hell are not places you go to when you die. Therefore, choose carefully.
- Choose your perspective on life, and whenever possible, choose joy.

One of my favorite parables is of the two men, seated beside each other on a plane as the pilot's voice could be heard issuing news no traveler wants to hear: "We've had engine failure, the plane is going down, and we don't have enough parachutes for all of you. I suggest that your best chance for survival — and it's a slim chance — is to kick out your window and jump." The two passengers looked at each other, then one jumped, covered his eyes, moaned aloud about the terrible fate ahead, and sure-enough, he hit the ground and died. The second passenger — also without a parachute — jumped out of the window. But he decided to hold open his coat, like the wings of a bird, in order to slow his descent. Holding his coat open meant that he couldn't cover his eyes. So, as he descended, he noticed the rich Fall colors on the trees. He also noticed how cute the children looked from above, as they played in the park. "Hmm," he thought, "this must be the view that God gets, *every day!*" But of course, this second passenger also hit the ground, and perished. The moral of this parable is that while we do not always have control over our circumstances or outcomes, we *always* have a choice about our perspective.

- Enjoy sugar cookies, cantaloupe, and home-grown tomatoes.
- Cherish your own zest for theological curiosity.
- Sing as often as you can, alone, with friends and family, or in formal choral settings.

I'd Like to Teach the World to Sing

I'd like to build the world a home
And furnish it with love
Grow apple trees and honeybees
And snow-white turtle doves

I'd like to teach the world to sing
In perfect harmony
I'd like to hold it in my arms
And keep it company

I'd like to see the world for once
All standing hand in hand
And hear them echo through the hills

For peace throughout the land
(That's the song I hear)[xx]

- Organize your life and finances so that you can invest time and other resources in the things you care about. (In addition to Minerva's by the Sea, some of my A-list includes Quaker education, Doctors Without Borders, the American Civil Liberties Union, the American Friends Service Committee, UNICEF, San Diego's San Ysidro family clinic, and Clean the World)[xxi]
- Choose carefully your battles to "endeavor to mend" the world, and as often as you can, choose "battlefields" that include something you enjoy doing.
- Choose some A-list heroes (Bayard Rustin, Steve Cary, Harriet Heath, Douglas Heath, Dorothy Steere, and my parents, grandparents, and great-grandparents are among the big crowd on my A-list) and get a draft off the dust they have left for you to find on the "stairs." Hold your heroes in your heart as you quietly resist those whose behaviors in the world that make you wonder about humans' "humanity." (I keep a copy of "Brother Outsider" –the documentary film about Bayard Rustin — within reach at all times, and am always awed and invigorated by Rustin's response when he was told to get up from his seat on the "white" section of a bus and to move to the "colored" section: "I cannot move from this seat, for if I do, that little white girl sitting there on that seat near me will not know that injustice is being done.")
- Don't confuse "busy-ness" with "making progress toward your important goals." Instead, heed Emerson's provocative notion on our modern-day worries about "wasting" time: "In times when we thought ourselves indolent, we have afterwards discovered, that much was accomplished, and much was begun in us."
- Take time to relax and read a good book, enjoying the words and cadence and fun inside those pages. Two of my favorites are Mary Pipher's *Writing to Change the World*[xxii] and Chuck Fager's novel, *Unfriendly Persuasion*.

And for those of you with the interest and skill, take time to *write* a book (or even a good article) on a few under-understood Quakers and Quaker "things." We have a recent good study of Richard Nixon's Quakerism.[xxiii] It would be nice to have a similarly Quaker-flavored exploration of Herbert Hoover. There is a master's thesis that begins that conversation, but more could be done.[xxiv] And would anyone like to take on the complex question of Quaker women and family finances over time? Does the reputation of "equality" of gender among Quakers actually translate into economic equality? We have several good studies of various aspects of the Hicksite/Orthodox schism, but precious little understanding of the yearly-meeting-by-yearly-meeting mending of that schism between 1920 and 1968. Would someone like to rise to that challenge?

Or how about a sweeping history of the dozens of Quaker-led "intentional communities" that are/have been scattered around the world? I can think of a half-dozen other "important" Quaker topics that I won't have time to tackle in my remaining years. As of 2019, Haverford's Quaker Collection has new housing, and a smart crew of young scholars running it. Earlham and Guilford, Friends House in London and George Fox College, Woodbrooke and the University of Birmingham in England, or Trinity Western University in Canada, among others, also have bright young minds shining new light on old stories. Go pick their brains!

And some of these mid-career scholars have convinced first-rate academic presses to publish luscious anthologies to orient new scholars and invite them into the larger conversation. And some long-time scholars have also shed new light on old issues. Go get some of those volumes and enjoy perusing a freshened up "Quaker studies."[xxv] Then go write your book!!

- Remember Martin Luther King's admonition that if we want peace, we'll need to work for justice, not just justice for the oppressed and the victims, not just justice for those who see the world as you do, but justice for *everyone*. Remember that no one is free until EVERYONE feels safe and remember the Friends' watchword that "there is no *way* to peace; peace *is* the way."
- That said, remember the words of Frederick Douglass words, nineteenth-century African American abolitionist: "Power concedes nothing without a demand. It never did and it never will... Visionaries may not get all they pay for in this world, but they must certainly pay for all they get. If we ever get free from the oppressions and wrongs heaped upon us, we must pay for their removal. We must do this by labor, by suffering, by sacrifice, and if needs be, by our lives and the lives of others."[xxvi]
- Remember the advice of some un-named modern sage: "there must be people who will take on a project for human good, and, knowing it cannot be completed in their lifetimes, take it on anyway."
- When Fate comes calling, listen! But don't answer until you've given yourself time to cogitate about whether it's God calling — or the devil! (remember: heaven and hell are states of being you create by your choices....)

- With gratitude to those of you who are still climbing those stairs of which we cannot know the beginning or end, I offer you two of my mother's favorite poems.

The first poem, from ancient India, invites us all to stop for a moment and relish the moment:

"Listen to the salutation of the dawn:
Look to this day,
For it is life, the very *life* of life.
In its brief course lie all the verities
and realities of your existence:
the bliss of growth,
the glory of action,
the splendor of beauty
For yesterday is only a dream
and tomorrow is only a vision,
but today, well lived makes
every yesterday a dream of happiness.
And every tomorrow a vision of hope.
Look well, therefore, to this day.
Such is the salutation of the dawn."

The second poem was created by Langston Hughes (1902-1967), the first African American to make a living as an author. Though it is titled "Mother to Son" we surely wish this energy of fortitude for our *daughters* too. This poem returns us to the place where I began this musing: likening the mystery or our lives here to the undulating mystery of a staircase:

Well, son, I'll tell you:
Life for me ain't been no crystal stair.
It's had tacks in it,
And splinters,
And boards torn up,
And places with no carpet on the floor —
Bare.
But all the time
I'se been a-climbin' on,
And reachin' landin's,
And turnin' corners,
And sometimes goin' in the dark
Where there ain't been no light.
So, boy, don't you turn back.

Don't you set down on the steps.
'Cause you finds it's kinder hard.
Don't you fall now —
For I'se still goin,' honey,
I'se still climbin,'
And life for me ain't been no crystal stair.

Footnotes

[i] https://archive.vcu.edu/english/engweb/transcendentalism/authors/emerson/essays/experience.html (accessed 10/13/19)

[ii] https://www.landmarkcases.org/cases/brown-v-board-of-education (accessed 10/13/19)

[iii] https://www.asburyumcdc.org/history.html (accessed 10/13/19)

[iv] https://www.highmowing.org/about/mission-vision-values (accessed 10/13/19)

[v] https://www.etsy.com/listing/582961014/this-is-my-fathers-world-hymn-lyrics

[vi] https://www.goodreads.com/quotes/441565-in-spite-of-everything-i-still-believe-that-people-are (accessed 10/13/19)

[vii] https://en.wikipedia.org/wiki/Gift_from_the_Sea (accessed 10/13/19)

[viii] https://www.crmvet.org/docs/6501_dm_report.pdf (accessed 10/21/2019).

[ix] https://snccdigital.org/events/poor-peoples-corporation-organized/ (accessed 10/21/2019).

[x] https://en.wikipedia.org/wiki/Tougaloo_College (accessed 10/21/2019).

[xi] https://www.justice.gov/crt/case-document/benjamin-brown-notice-close-file (accessed 10/21/2019

[xii] See Gary Nash and Jean R. Soderlund, Freedom by Degrees: Emancipation in Pennsylvania and Its Aftermath. 1991; and Chuck Fager, Angels of Progress: A Documentary History of Progressive Friends, 1822-1940. Kimo Press, 2014.

[xiii] Barry Morley, "Beyond Consensus: Salvaging Sense of Meeting," Pendle Hill Pamphlet #307. Wallingford, PA: Pendle Hill Publications, 1993.

[xiv] https://campdarkwaters.com/about-cdw/history/ (accessed 10/22/2019)

[xv] https://www.journeysendfarm.org/camp (accessed 10/22/2019)

[xvi] A short bio: "Emma Jones Lapsansky is Emeritus Professor of History and Curator of the Quaker Collection of Haverford College. She lives near Philadelphia, PA, where she continues to teach, to do research and to publish, to consult with scholars, to work as a professional editor, and to host periodic writers' workshops. After a one-year break in her undergraduate education to work in the Mississippi civil rights movement with the Delta Ministry of the National Council of Churches, she received her BA in History from the University of Pennsylvania, and her doctorate in American Civilization from the same institution. Her research interests include Quaker history, African American history and especially the intersection between the two, as well as Pennsylvania history, the American West, and various aspects of American social, urban, and material-culture history.

Some of her recent publications include Quaker Aesthetics (Univ of Pa Press, 2003, with Anne Verplanck); Back to Africa: Benjamin Coates and the American Colonization Movement (Penn State University Press,2005, with Margaret Hope Bacon. Pb 2007) and contributed essays to Benjamin Franklin: In Search of a Better World

(Yale Univ Press, 2006) and Pennsylvania: A History of the Commonwealth , edited by Randall Miller, William Pencak, et al. (Penn State University Press, 2003). Her articles also include a contribution to The Oxford Handbook of Quaker Studies (Oxford University Press, 2013); to Quakers and Abolition, edited by Brycchan Carey and Geoffrey Plank (University of Illinois Press, 2014) ; and The Quakers, 1656-1723:the Evolution of an Alternative Community, edited by Richard Allen and Rosemary Moore " (Pennsylvania State University Press, 2018); as well as entries in Darlene Clark Hine, Encyclopedia of African American Women, 2005; Billy G. Smith, ed. Encyclopedia of Colonial America (2003); Margery Post Abbott, et al, Historical Dictionary of Quakerism (2002); Encyclopedia of Violence, (2001); Encyclopedia of Contemporary Culture, (2001); and the online Encyclopedia of Philadelphia (2009-), of which she serves on the editorial board.

With Gary Nash and Clayborne Carson, Lapsansky has authored Struggle for Freedom, a college-level African American history text, the third edition of which appeared in 2018. She is also a co-author on the Pearson Education high-school American History text. Beginning her teaching career in 1968, she specializes in the American West; American colonial history; Philadelphia history; the American family; and Quaker history

Lapsansky frequently consults to museums, public schools, and to pre-collegiate curriculum developers on enriching gender, race, culture, and age content to enliven classroom and public history presentations. She also consults with authors seeking editorial and/or research advice. See has been an invited lecturer at Earlham College, Guilford College, and George Fox College, Villanova University, Princeton University, and University of Pennsylvania, among others, as well as at a number of Quaker meetings and study centers. She is currently at work on two projects: a history of a Bryn Mawr Quaker family; and a study of a mid-twentieth-century Philadelphia multi-cultural intentional community, founded by Friends in 1946.

Having been an active member of the Organization of American Historians and of the Friends Historical Association, a Board member of the Library Company of Philadelphia, and a past board member of Friends Central School, she currently (2019) teaches Quaker History and First-Year Writing at Haverford College.

[xvii] https://www.quakerhistory.org/ (accessed 10/26/19)

[xviii] https://www.kimnagy.com/2018/08/minerva/

[xix] American Transcendentalism Web, https://archive.vcu.edu/english/engweb/transcendentalism/authors/emerson/essays/experience.html (accessed 10/21/2019).

[xx] The New Seekers , an English pop group, formed in London in 1969 by Keith Potger have had a spotty performance history. https://www.lynpaulwebsite.org/NS-Albums.htm (accessed October 9, 2019)

[xxi] https://www.friendscouncil.org/about; https://www.doctorswithoutborders.org/; https://www.afsc.org/about-us; https://cleantheworld.org/ (accessed 10/24/2019)

[xxii] Mary Pipher, Writing to Change the World. New York: Penguin Books, 2006; Chuck Fager, Un-Friendly Persuasion. Kimo Press, 1995.

[xxiii] H. Larry Ingle, Nixon's First Coverup: The Religious Life of a Quaker President. Columbia, MO: University of Missouri Press, 2015.

[xxiv] Ryan T. Peters, Quaker of Virtue: Herbert Hoover and his Humane Foreign Policy, Ann Arbor, Mich. : 2013.

[xxv] See, for example, Margery Post Abbott, Historical Dictionary of Friends (Quakers). Scarecrow Press, 2003; Stephen Angell and Pink Dandelion, The Oxford Handbook of Quaker Studies. (Oxford University Press, 2013); The Cambridge Companion to Quakerism (Cambridge University Press, 2018); Richard Allen and Rosemary Moore, The Quakers, 1656-1723: The Evolution of an Alternative Community. (Pennsylvania State University Press, 2018); Gary B. Nash, Warner Mifflin: Unflinching Quaker Abolitionist. (University of Pennsylvania Press, 2017); Marcus Rediker, The Fearless Benjamin Lay: The Quaker Dwarf who became the First Revolutionary Abolitionist. (Beacon Press, 2017); Chuck Fager, Remaking Friends: How Progressive Friends Changed Quakerism and Helped Save America. (Kimo Press, 2014)

[xxvi] Frederick Douglas, "West India Emancipation" twenty-third anniversary speech at Canandaigua, New York, August 3, 1857. https://www.blackpast.org/african-american-history/1857-frederick-douglass-if-there-no-struggle-there-no-progress, (accessed 10/18/19)

Made in the USA
Middletown, DE
26 November 2019